FORTUNE
ADVISER
1997

FORTUNE ADVISER 1997
FIRST PRINTING 1996

FORTUNE ADVISER STAFF

EXECUTIVE EDITOR: THOMAS A. STEWART
EDITOR: THERESE EIBEN
DESIGNER: TONY MIKOLAJCZYK
COPY EDITORS: EDITH FIROOZI FRIED, CHARLES J. ATTARDI, DON YOUNG
EDITORIAL OPERATIONS: DAVID V. RILE

SPECIAL THANKS TO: ROSALIND KLEIN BERLIN, CATHERINE COMES HAIGHT,
CHRISTOPHER GREEN, CAROL GWINN, GOPAL KHAR, EILEEN NAUGHTON,
CAROLYN SAMPSON AND DAVID SLOAN

FORTUNE EDITORIAL STAFF

MANAGING EDITOR JOHN HUEY • EDITORIAL DIRECTOR GEOFFREY COLVIN • DEPUTY MANAGING EDITOR RIK KIRKLAND • EXECUTIVE EDITORS JOHN J. CURRAN, PETER PETRE • ASSISTANT MANAGING EDITOR ROB NORTON • SENIOR EDITORS BRIAN DUMAINE, SUSAN FRAKER, TIMOTHY K. SMITH, BRENTON R. SCHLENDER (SILICON VALLEY) • EDITORS JAMES ALEY, LAURA COLBY, GOPAL KHAR (LIST EDITOR) COLIN LEINSTER, LEE SMITH, RICK TETZELI, SUSAN L. ZESIGER • BOARD OF EDITORS GENE BYLINSKY, CATHERINE COMES HAIGHT (STATISTICS EDITOR), RONALD HENKOFF (CHICAGO), DAVID KIRKPATRICK, LOUIS KRAAR, KENNETH LABICH, CAROL JUNGE LOOMIS, BRIAN O'REILLY, STRATFORD SHERMAN, THOMAS A. STEWART, ALEX TAYLOR III, SHAWN TULLY • SENOIR WRITERS RICHARD BEHAR, ALAN FARNHAM, LINDA GRANT, MARC GUNTHER, KATHRYN HARRIS (LOS ANGELES), JEANIE RUSSELL KASINDORF, ANDREW KUPFER, BETSY MORRIS (ATLANTA), KARL SCHOENBERGER (HONG KONG), PATRICIA SELLERS, ANDREW E. SERWER, DAVID STIPP (BOSTON) • COLUMNISTS STANLEY BING, ANDREW FERGUSON, MARSHALL LOEB, JOHN ROTHCHILD, DANIEL SELIGMAN, DAVID SHRIBMAN • WRITERS SHELLY BRANCH, SUSAN CAMINITI, KIM CLARK, ANNE B. FISHER, SUSAN E. KUHN, JANICE MALONEY, FAYE RICE, RICHARD TEITELBAUM • WRITER-REPORTERS JUSTIN FOX, JUSTIN MARTIN, ERICK SCHONFELD, JOHN WYATT • CHIEF OF REPORTERS ROSALIND KLEIN BERLIN • SENIOR REPORTERS PATTY DE LLOSA (DEPUTY CHIEF OF REPORTERS), ALICIA HILLS MOORE, LENORE SCHIFF, WILTON WOODS • REPORTERS SUZANNE BARLYN, ED BROWN, ERYN BROWN, TIM CARVELL, SHEREE R. CURRY, ERIN M. DAVIES, JOYCE E. DAVIS, ANNE FAIRCLOTH, HENRY GOLDBLATT, EILEEN P. GUNN, ANI HADJIAN, CINDY KANO (TOKYO), AMY R. KOVER, RONALD B. LIEBER, MICHAEL H. MARTIN, JOE McGOWAN, BETHANY McLEAN, ANDREA L. PROCHNIAK, SHAIFALI PURI, RAJIV M. RAO, EDWARD A. ROBINSON, KIMBERLY SEALS McDONALD, LIXANDRA URRESTA, MELANIE WARNER, TRICIA WELSH • EDITORIAL ASSISTANTS CAROLYN SAMPSON (ASSISTANT TO THE MANAGING EDITOR), KELLY CHAMPION, LYNNE FERGUSON, DIANE HENDRIX-COLLEY (FINANCE), KERRY L. HUBERT (ONLINE LETTERS), GITA MEHTA

FORTUNE CONSUMER MARKETING

DIRECTOR: DAVID KIESELSTEIN
DIRECTOR NEW BUSINESS DEVELOPMENT: DAVID NAGOURNEY
MANAGER NEW BUSINESS DEVELOPMENT: DEIRDRE VERNE

TIME INC. NEW BUSINESS DEVELOPMENT

DIRECTOR: DAVID GITOW
ASSOCIATE DIRECTOR: STUART HOTCHKISS
ASSISTANT DIRECTOR: PETE SHAPIRO
FULFILLMENT MANAGER: MICHELE GUDEMA
DEVELOPMENT MANAGERS:, ROBERT FOX, MICHAEL HOLAHAN, JOHN SANDKLEV ALICIA WILCOX
ASSOCIATE MANAGERS: DAN MELORE, KEN KATZMAN, ALLISON WEISS, DAWN WELAND
ASSISTANT MARKETING MANAGER: CHARLOTTE SIDDIQUI
OPERATIONS MANAGER: JOHN CALVANO
PRODUCTION MANAGER: DONNA MIANO-FERRARA
MARKETING ASSISTANT: LYNDSAY JENKS

IF YOU HAVE QUESTIONS ABOUT THIS BOOK OR THE FORTUNE BOOK SERIES, PLEASE CALL (800) 327-6388.
TO ORDER FORTUNE MAGAZINE, PLEASE CALL (800) 621-8000.

FORTUNE ADVISER 1997

BY THE EDITORS OF FORTUNE
and THERESE EIBEN

FORTUNE BOOKS
TIME INC. HOME ENTERTAINMENT
1271 AVENUE OF THE AMERICAS
NEW YORK, N.Y. 10020

CONTENTS

CHAPTER ONE
THE FUTURE IS NOW

THE NEW MASTER OF THE UNIVERSE	8
"LOOK, MA, NO HANDS" (THE CAR IN THE 21ST CENTURY)	12
TABLOID ECONOMICS: A LURID TALE OF HOCUS-FOCUS	16
STOCKS AND THE COURSE OF TRUE LOVE	20

CHAPTER TWO
LESSONS FROM THE KINGS OF COMMERCE
ON HOW TO CHANGE THE WORLD

THE WEALTH BUILDERS: ROBERTO GOIZUETA AND JACK WELCH	24
IN GREENSPAN WE TRUST	39
WHY ANDY GROVE CAN'T STOP	50
DAN TULLY: HOW TO BULL AHEAD	59
ROGER ENRICO: PEPSICO'S NEW GENERATION	69
CITICORP: JOHN REED'S SECOND ACT	78
WALL STREET'S KING QUANT: DAVID SHAW	87

CHAPTER THREE
MANAGEMENT IDEAS WORTH A FORTUNE

THE NINE DILEMMAS LEADERS FACE	98
WHY VALUE STATEMENTS DON'T WORK	104
HOW TO NEGOTIATE WITH REALLY TOUGH GUYS	110
RAMBOS IN PINSTRIPES	114
HOW TO FIRE PEOPLE (AND STILL SLEEP AT NIGHT)	117
JOIN THE HEADHUNTER'S INNER CIRCLE	128
YOU INC: THE ORGANIZATIONAL CHART	132
ARE YOU AFRAID OF SUCCESS?	135

CHAPTER FOUR
INVESTMENT STRATEGIES FOR A SECURE FUTURE

BE A TAX-SAVVY INVESTOR 146

ADVICE FROM THE PROPHETS OF PROFIT

   GLOBAL STOCKS TO BET ON 153

   66 REASONS TO BUY FUNDS 157

   A STRATEGIST TAKES STOCK OF THE MARKET 159

   FORTUNE-TELLING: THREE EXPERTS GAZE INTO THE FUTURE 162

REAL ESTATE: A SMART ALTERNATIVE TO STOCKS 166

HOW TO LEAVE THE TAX MAN NOTHING 169

CHAPTER FIVE
HOW TO RETIRE WELL: A GUIDE TO PROSPERITY

HOW TO PICK YOUR ADVISERS 174

CREATING A HIGH-POWERED 401(K) 180

HOW PREPARED ARE YOUR PARENTS' FINANCES? 185

WHERE TO INVEST YOUR NEST EGG 187

APPENDIX: FORTUNE LISTS

THE FORTUNE 500 198

THE FORTUNE 500 INDEX 239

AMERICA'S MOST ADMIRED COMPANIES 244

CHAPTER ONE
THE FUTURE IS NOW

THE NEW MASTER OF THE UNIVERSE
page 8

"LOOK, MA, NO HANDS"
(THE CAR IN THE 21ST CENTURY)
page 12

TABLOID ECONOMICS:
A LURID TALE OF HOCUS-FOCUS
page 16

STOCKS AND THE COURSE OF TRUE LOVE
page 20

The true rulers of Wall Street are no longer swashbuckling corporate raiders. Today's captains of industry bow their heads to a new master: the Almighty Shareholder.

THE NEW MASTER OF THE UNIVERSE

BY JOHN WYATT

Billy Q., coffee in hand, scans the morning paper. Bulls won. Lots of political coverage. Market up a bit. A big manufacturer announces a layoff, and the stock rises. Japan reports great economic news: "GDP," it reads, "grew sharply this quarter after years of nonexistent growth." Hmmm.

Billy has $3,000 that came in from a recent photo shoot (he's a commercial photographer) sitting in a money market fund. He's been thinking for some time now about buying a Japan fund he's interested in.

He flips on his computer, punches up his portfolio, which he tracks on the Internet, and takes a look at what his mutual funds and stocks did yesterday. Mostly up, though that health-care company is still a real dog. And yes, he thinks to himself, with the U.S. stock market so high, a little more invested overseas couldn't hurt.

The speed dial connects Billy to a customer service rep at his discount broker. In five minutes, Billy rebalances his portfolio, moving gains out of an aggressive growth fund into a more conservative growth and income fund. He sells Coca-Cola, which had a nice run. And he buys that Japan fund.

THOUGH SUCH transactions are a routine part of Billy's life today, it wasn't always like this. Billy never had visions of being a Wall Street high roller or the next Peter Lynch. Far from it. In college he skipped the boring business pages. He thought a mutual fund was some kind of insurance product. He figured that maybe if he made enough money, he'd hire a broker as his dad did, and pay someone else to understand that financial mum-

8

bo jumbo. Even though, of course, Dad always moaned and complained about that broker.

But Billy had little choice in the matter. The stock market came to him.

It started shortly after he left his first job, where he had accrued money in a savings plan. His employee benefits gave him the option to roll those savings into an IRA. With the help of an account rep at the bank, Billy looked at his options and plunked the money into a mutual fund. For the first time Billy's future—or a tiny strand of it, anyway—was entwined with the stock market. He was now, officially, an individual investor.

The strand became a lifeline when Billy started to work for a big media conglomerate. He made more investing decisions because of the company 401(k) plan. At first he didn't give it much thought. But the 401(k) account's ever-growing sums—sped along by the company's policy of matching contributions—sharpened his interest fast. Though retirement seemed impossibly remote, his 401(k), which he could check on every day, was real enough. So too were the water-cooler stories of colleagues who not only invested with their 401(k), but who also bought and sold mutual funds and stocks, and even invested in seemingly exotic foreign issues like Teléfonos de México, the bellwether ADR (American depositary receipt, which trades on the NYSE) of the Mexican market. The storming bull market of the Nineties put an end once and for all to Billy's financial indifference.

SOCIETY'S TRENDS ALONE have not pushed people like Billy into what's been called the money culture. He is also driven, like millions of others who are uncertain about their future, by a much more powerful factor—fear. When Billy reads about gaping budget deficits, declining wages, and the quickly eroding Social Security trust, he perceives a direct link to his own well-being. He worries about the huge sums the financial planners say he and his wife, Mary, a media planner, will need down the line to fund retirement. He worries, too, about having the money to pay for the ballooning costs of education for his kids and health care for his parents.

Billy's conversion from reluctant investor to bona fide personal finance do-it-yourselfer is complete. He studies his 401(k) plan, his IRA, and his bank accounts and gives considered thought to the wide array of mutual funds and to the multitude of other products (from interest-bearing accounts to variable annuities) available to him. He and Mary work hard to monitor their income and spending patterns. They often talk about how best to manage their financial life together.

Always interested in technology, Billy finds a natural convergence in the worlds of personal computers and personal finance. He buys software to help keep track of the couple's finances. He reconciles bank accounts by dialing in by modem and downloading information directly from his bank. He opens a discount brokerage account to invest more savings in mutual funds and stocks, which he buys online with minimal commissions. He makes good use of investment forums and information services that give him market insights. Best of all, he doesn't feel he needs to turn his money over to a broker, or a planner, or an expert, whom he would have to pay while worrying that he isn't getting his money's worth.

Billy, who'd always felt himself an outsider in the jargon-ridden world of high finance, not only feels empowered by his new-found financial acumen but also actually finds managing his portfolio to be fun. He scans the tables and listings in the business pages that track his investments around the globe with the same avid interest he follows the box scores in his beloved sports pages. He learns about the different characteristics of growth stocks and value stocks, and of big stocks and small stocks. He wields more power than he knows.

Billy Q., part-time investor, has become the most unlikely of Wall Street movers and shakers. His presence is felt in corporate suites across the nation. The true rulers of Wall Street are no longer the swashbuckling corporate raiders of the Eighties, or the mysterious traders who reap millions from tiny pricing differences. Today's captains of industry bow their heads to a new master of their universe: the Almighty Shareholder.

THANKS TO THE POWER and pressure of the mutual fund companies who invest the nation's rising tide of 401(k) money (estimated by Access Research to total $675 billion), together with the money managers who control the nation's $2 trillion pension assets, America's corporate managements have had a new mandate for some time now: Get stock prices up and return value to the Almighty Shareholder, or get out. Fail at that, and Billy Q., or any number of the 22.5 million active 401(k) participants, reviewing their portfolios tomorrow, might get fed up and speed-dial in sell orders, a pressure with which the fund managers who compete for Billy's dollars are intimately familiar. They in turn pass on that anxiety to managements that implement vast plans like restructurings, or stock buyback programs, designed to keep fund managers, and more particularly, Billy, happy.

His investing origins may have been humble, but Billy Q., a.k.a. individual investor, has truly arrived. And with fund managers directing the ever larger pools of money that come from people like him, it looks as if he, and the countless others behind him, are here to stay.

By the end of the decade, radar detection devices will warn drivers trying to pass when another vehicle is in their blind spot. Who says the auto industry is outmoded?

"LOOK, MA, NO HANDS!" (THE CAR IN THE 21ST CENTURY)

BY ALEX TAYLOR III

A S IT MARKS its 101st birthday in 1997, the U.S. automobile industry would hardly appear to be a candidate for dramatic change. It is big, capital-intensive, and slow-growing. When dealers and suppliers are included, autos contribute 4.5% of the U.S.'s gross domestic product. Hundreds of billions of dollars are tied up in existing factories and tools, and return on assets is slim. Profit margins seldom exceed 3% or 4%, and volume increases average less than 1% a year. Autos are an industry for which the words "heavy" and "mature" are virtually synonymous.

Yet the auto industry is about to embark on the biggest transformation of its history. Everything will change: how cars are designed, made, sold, distributed, and driven. General Motors, Ford, and Chrysler will have to stop thinking of themselves as auto manufacturers and start becoming transportation providers.

What's driving this change is electronics: computers and software, sensors and connectors, microchips and satellites. It isn't as if Detroit just discovered this technology. Already the auto industry consumes more integrated circuits than the computer industry. But automakers move slowly with technological advances. Developing new products takes three years or more, and there are billions of dollars already invested in existing facilities that can't be made obsolete overnight.

Now events are moving more swiftly, however, driven by the pressures of cost, competition, and globalization. GM and Ford are revamping their product development processes and reorganizing them on a global basis; Chrysler is trying to lengthen its lead in the speed with which it brings new products to market. All that would be impossible without computers. For instance, automakers can shave design time by creating new models—and approving them for production—entirely on a cathode ray tube. That eliminates the necessity of building full-size clay mockups, a labor-intensive process that can take several months.

Computers have already made their way onto the factory floor, where they schedule production, manipulate robots, and regulate the flow of parts. Soon they will do something far more important: enable manufacturers to farm out less critical sections of the car to outside suppliers who can assemble them more cheaply and with greater expertise. That will allow the automakers to concentrate on areas where they make their most significant impact: design, engine and transmission manufacture, and paint. The trend is being led by the prestige German manufacturers who have set up non-union operations in the Southeastern U.S. At the new BMW plant in Spartanburg, South Carolina, where the zippy Z3 roadster is built, outside suppliers produce all the body stampings, including sheet metal. BMW merely welds the pieces together and paints them when they come into the shop.

GETTING A NEWLY BUILT CAR to the customer will also become more efficient and, just as important, relieve the manufacturer of dependence on the erratic behavior of the independent franchise dealer. Today 30% of the retail price of a new automobile is consumed with the cost of marketing, advertising, and distribution. Despite years of effort by manufacturers, many dealers still use abusive and demeaning sales tactics that prospective customers find distinctly unpleasant.

Technology is making it easier to bypass the dealer. It is currently possible to shop for a car over the Internet, determine its wholesale price, arrange financing, and place an order without leaving the house. Today that order is still executed by a dealer affiliated with the buying service, who usually agrees to sell the car at a fixed amount over the wholesale price. But online car-buying services are attracting some big corporate names like Microsoft and ADP. How long will it be before one of them, in effect, becomes a dealer and begins to conduct business electronically? Then buyers will be able to do all their shopping by computer and have their new car delivered to their door. The service will be especially attractive to lease customers, who trade their cars every two or three years. No longer will cars have to be stockpiled for 60 days on dealers' lots, running up holding costs and deteriorating in the weather.

Computers have also started revolutionizing the used-car business—30 million used cars and trucks are sold every year—by making possible the growth of used-car superstores. These megalots offer a wide variety of nearly new cars organized by model and brand and sold at a fixed price. Consumers navigate their way around these giant facilities by searching databases that provide a picture of each car, describe its condition, and identify its location. Managers track their inventory by recording the number of "hits" each car gets, and then counting the number of times it gets test driven.

B ESIDES MAKING IT SIMPLER to buy a car, computers are making it easier and safer to drive one. Today, technology makes cars run smoother (by monitoring engine conditions), drive straighter (through devices like yaw control), and stop faster (with antilock braking systems). Navigation aids that use global positioning satellites help lost drivers find their way or, in the event of an emergency, direct road service to their exact locations. By the end of the decade, several radar detection devices will be available to warn drivers trying to pass when another vehicle is in their blind spot or give the cruise control instructions when to speed up or slow down.

Once these electronics are installed in a car, they can start interacting with similar systems alongside highways to make a trip smoother and safer. Information about road and traffic conditions can be monitored automatically and beamed into on-board navigation systems to advise drivers about congestion and possible detours. It will be like having your own traffic reporter in the passenger seat. The next step is hands-off driving, in which all the directions a car needs to get to its destination are broadcast to it by a "smart" highway. A test is scheduled later this year on a 7.6-mile stretch of highway near San Diego, where ten specially equipped Buicks will speed down the road no more than six feet behind the car ahead, while their drivers look on.

By the time such highways become operational, many cars won't be powered by an internal combustion engine like the one invented by Gottlieb Daimler more than 110 years ago. Mandates in California dictate that 10% of the new cars sold there by 2003 produce zero emissions, which means they must be propelled by batteries. But the limited energy storage of batteries means that they, in turn, are likely to be replaced by fast, fuel-efficient hybrid systems. Hybrids use two motors linked by electronic controllers, one for accelerating and one for cruising. The first ones should be up and running in 1997. If hybrids catch on, they will make obsolete tens of billions of dollars invested in the development and manufacture of V-6s and V-8s. But then that's what progress is all about.

For manufacturers—and there are no clear leaders yet—there will be massive opportunities for improvements. Investment will shrink and so will costs; things will get done faster and customers will be happier.

Investors should see a dramatic increase in returns on capital, as profits increase and the money tied up in fixed assets decreases. The overall economy will get a lift as resources are freed up and efficiency improves. Electronics may prove to be the elixir of youth for this once stodgy old industry.

A lot of media-promoted whining is showering attention on an economic pseudo-crisis, but maybe some good will come out of it after all.

TABLOID ECONOMICS: A LURID TALE OF HOCUS-FOCUS

BY JUSTIN FOX

BY THE NUMBERS, the mid-1990s have been a pretty good time for the U.S. economy. This is not to say it has been the greatest, but it hasn't been too bad either. But numbers, well, numbers are dry, dull, and lacking in narrative force. This helps explain why, from the perspective of a media junkie, the state of the economy must have looked pretty dire in the early months of 1996. Those were the sad days when the downsizing of America was in full swing. Or, more accurately, "The Downsizing of America."

The seven-part New York *Times* series by that name was the longest thing the paper had published since the 1971 Pentagon Papers. With numbers (carefully selected for their ability to fit into the larger narrative), analysis, and tale after tale of workers set adrift by corporate cutbacks, it attempted to document a supposed sea change in American economic life, a shift from stability to insecurity. This shift, the paper of record wrote, "has produced an unrelenting angst that is shattering people's notions of work and self and the very promise of tomorrow."

This sounded very grim, especially the story of that poor executive in Dayton who had lost his job, gotten a new one in Florida, and now had to commute southward every week *in his own plane.*

Drama aside, there remained that little problem with the actual economic numbers. For one thing, the early-1990s barrage of high-profile, high-volume layoffs peaked in 1994. By March 1996, when the

Times published its downsizing stories, the economy was gearing up for a strong spring and unemployment was down. More important, the series and most of the other journalistic alarms sounded about downsizing were constructed around a premise—that today's American workers can't expect to stay with an employer as long as their parents did—that simply isn't supported by the data. Instead, Labor Department statistics show that median job tenure for men has stayed pretty much the same since the 1950s, while for women it has risen steadily. That's not to say everyone can count on a lifetime job. On the contrary, in the dynamic, ever-changing U.S. economy, job switches are the norm, not the exception. More than 20% of mining, manufacturing, retail, and service jobs change hands every quarter. In construction the figure is nearly 40%; in agriculture, nearly 50%.

Not a lot of farmworkers read the New York *Times*. Construction workers usually don't travel in the same circles as magazine writers and TV newscasters. White-collar employees of big corporations do, and something is in fact up with them. Desk jockeys were much harder hit by layoffs in the 1990s than during the recession of the early 1980s, when blue-collar manufacturing ranks were decimated. Today's job losses are also more likely to be permanent than the slowdown-induced layoffs of yesteryear. IBM, once legendary for its promise of lifetime job security, shrank from 407,000 employees in 1986 to 228,000 a decade later, with the biggest layoffs coming in 1994. Downsizing became a Wall Street–driven fad, with share prices usually jumping in the immediate wake of a big layoff announcement. Some companies—IBM and Sears spring to mind—surely had to shrink to survive. Others overdid it, and more than a few CEOs were rewarded with stock-option bonanzas for ill-conceived downsizings that probably hurt their companies' long-term prospects. Oh, well, nobody ever said capitalism's perfect. It's just a lot better than the alternatives.

FOR COLLEGE-EDUCATED workers who never expected to be confronted with layoffs, this has certainly been alarming. In the 1950s and the 1960s, it really did look as though modern management techniques might enable the GMs and AT&Ts of the world to grow smoothly and shocklessly forever and ever. It also looked as though modern macro-economic techniques might enable Washington wise men to fine-tune the economy. These impressions were, of course, false. It's a good thing they were. One secret of the American economy's glorious success over the past couple of centuries is that it has seldom followed the whims of planners and managers, instead repeatedly heading off in directions they never imagined. That's why for virtually every shrinking AT&T, there's a fast-growing MCI. For every decaying Northeastern milltown hankering for long-gone glory days, there's a swank Sunbelt suburb full of people whose parents never dreamed of living in such luxury. And for every job that disappears, more than one new one is created.

What's more, new jobs these days tend to pay better than the old ones. One study found that 68% of the jobs created between February 1994 and February 1996 came with above-median wages. Those new jobs did not all go to the recently downsized, of course; in general, only about one-third of displaced workers end up in jobs that pay more than their old ones. Sizzling job growth among California computer programmers is of little solace to a fired Connecticut banker. But the continued vitality of our economy depends on the creative destruction that lays some companies and sectors low to make room for new ones. It's always been that way, although at some points the destruction is more visible than at others. All of which means Americans shouldn't count on a layoff-free work life. But most *can* count on continued prosperity.

SO WHY the national obsession with downsizing, job insecurity, and general economic angst? The most obvious reason is that for journalists and the people they hang out with, job security *has* dropped in the 1990s. Another explanation holds that the incredible progress and prosperity of the postwar years that gave many of our parents a worry-free retirement also set up generations that followed to expect the same thing. A third theory is that the first of the baby-boomers, the massive generation that has long bent the national discussion to its will, are turning 50. And 50 just happens to be the age at which average earnings start to drop.

Fine. Let us all whine. The yammering is a bit distasteful, since showering attention on an economic pseudo-crisis tends to pull it away from real ones, such as the steady decline in income since the early 1970s of the poorest 20% of Americans. There's also the risk that Congress could heed the whining and do something really stupid, like pass a law punishing companies that lay off workers or rewarding those that don't. Requiring corporations to be good citizens is fine; we don't want them to improve the bottom line by, say, dumping toxic sludge in our back yards. It's important to remember downsizing is not in itself antisocial behavior. If job cuts are what it takes to keep a company from careening into oblivion or even mediocrity, then the CEO who holds back is being a downright bad citizen. Also, an executive who fears being zapped for firing workers is going to keep hiring to a minimum.

There are some positive results that could come out of all this worrying, however. Federal Reserve officials credit fear of downsizing with holding wage demands low enough to keep inflation in check even as unemployment has dropped. The fixation with job insecurity appears to be bringing on a change in attitudes (being laid off no longer carries much stigma) and a restructuring of employee benefits (health insurance and retirement cash are becoming more portable) that together are making it easier to switch jobs. Finally, people who are aware that their jobs aren't permanent may be more likely to sock away some of their income for a rainy day, thereby hiking the country's minuscule savings rate. Who knows, maybe a little "unrelenting angst" will do us all good.

It is worth asking if you could stand to make just 2% a year
for the next ten years.

STOCKS AND THE COURSE
OF TRUE LOVE

BY SUSAN E. KUHN

IT IS A LOVE AFFAIR. The dance of the investor and the stock market—look at how one twirls in the other's arms. See how he with the money leads her, and she, responding, follows. In the movies neither tires; no one sweats or stumbles. They both smile, in sync, beaming to a world that is eating this up as one of the biggest business affairs of the decade. Both are oblivious—to the future, to their fates.

Fred Astaire and Ginger Rogers are alive today in spirit, only this isn't celluloid, and there's no guarantee of a happy ending. In fact, the odds are increasing that the long-running romance between individuals and stocks may soon be breaking up. Since 1982 the Dow Jones industrial average has been spiraling skyward. Dour advice, like the old what-goes-up-must-come-down, isn't being heeded, even though it has history on its side. In fact, there's not much bearish talk out there at all, and even less understanding of how devastating the stock market's down cycles can be.

In 1996 the Dow Jones industrial average entered its 14th year of wooing investors, and once again, millions of investors were wowed, opening their bank accounts and pumping money into stock funds at a rate that seems to increase as the bull ages. In the first five months of 1996, before the onset of a brief summer slump, individuals poured an astounding $25 billion per month into stock funds on average, according to the Investment Co. Institute, the mutual fund trade organization that tracks mutual fund flows. That compares with a monthly average of $11 billion for all of 1995.

Our cash leads the market higher, and we in turn trust in the Dow to be the fulfiller of all our dreams. We need stocks, the story goes, to fund our retirements so that we won't be forced to work during our "golden years." In addition there are college costs to pay, huge health care expenditures to anticipate.

And oh, how we're courted. Banks, brokers, mutual fund companies— in short, financial services firms of every stripe—are blitzing the airwaves and print pages with ads. If anything, they say we should be investing more. As our companies and our government cut back on benefits, the burden of securing a sound financial future falls more heavily on each of us. This we know. But we forget how rich we are making all these "advisers." Every time we put another dollar in the 401(k) plan, Fidelity or Merrill Lynch grows a little plumper. What interest does this industry have in telling us a bear market is approaching? For that matter, would we listen?

SINCE 1926, according to Ibbotson Associates, the widely cited investment research firm in Chicago, stocks in Standard & Poor's 500-stock index have returned an average of 10% per year to investors, through a combination of capital gains and dividend income. Compared with long-term Treasury bonds, which have returned 5% on average, and cash (3% per year), this is mighty appealing. It leads us to believe that we should ignore stock market fluctuations and, if anything, buy on dips. Recent history reinforces that belief. In 1990, anticipating recession, the stock market fell 20% in three summer months but five months later retraced the lost ground. Bear markets, you say? Why worry?

Wise up: Seventy years or so is an awfully long time, and one instance— 1990—is simply too few. For individuals, it is more realistic to consider investing in stocks over ten-year periods. Looking at the Ibbotson data this way, clear bullish and bearish patterns emerge. In two long blocks of time, from 1926 to 1940 and from 1960 to 1973, investors who bought and held stocks for a decade achieved single-digit rates of return. In the worst decade of recent history, from 1965 to 1975, individuals in stocks didn't even make 2% per year. For that decade it would have been far better, history suggests, to have invested your savings in the bank.

Today is a good time to remember 1965. Looking to 1997 and beyond, it is worth asking if you could stand to make 2% a year for the next ten years. In 1965, investors pondering the future could have protected themselves by remembering past performance never guarantees future returns. The cautious among them may have looked at the previous 15 years of 15% per year returns on average and surmised that maybe, just maybe, the party wasn't going to last. Guess what. Today, investors can look back and see the same thing. They've ridden an equally vigorous bull.

Ten years is a prudent time frame for stock market investors. But in fact, most of us can't sit still that long; we chart our portfolio's progress annually. Remember 1987? We may shudder at memories of the one-day 508-point drop, but in truth it didn't wreck the year: Aided by dividend income, stocks eked out a 5.2% annual return. To find anything approaching a double-digit yearly loss, we have to reach all the way back to 1973 and 1974, when the market lost 14.7% and 26.5% successively. To all the news reports that say individuals are prepared to stand pat in the face of a market fall, ask this question: How many of today's investors were around in '73 and '74? Not many.

THERE'S NO REASON to give up on stocks. But it is wise to stop staring at them with dreamy eyes, and start asking hard questions. You don't have to chart the future of the market in precise detail. No one can do that. The questions all of us must ask concern ourselves. When do you need cash? If you are planning a trip in six months, keep your money in the bank, or buy a CD. A sometimes-dreams-come-true 50th birthday present for yourself in five years? Then buy a five-year Treasury bond. If it truly is the long term that you are saving for, say a distant retirement, give yourself ten years in stocks or more. Own a diversified basket of equities, in foreign countries like India or Mexico, which are risky but have a better chance of explosive economic growth, as well as in the U.S. Consider investing in real estate, which many regard as undervalued. Think broadly, ask questions, find a financial planner you can trust who will work in your best interest. Don't buy into a tale you don't understand.

Hey, it's your money. This thing going on between you and the stock market? It's just a dance. You can quit anytime, when you want to, but don't plan on getting out just before the music stops. Though there's something to be said for fidelity (with a small "f"), the truth is you can fall out of love as easily as you fall into it. We hate to think about heartache, we ever optimistic Americans, but it's staring us in the face. All we can do is be prepared.

CHAPTER TWO

LESSONS FROM THE KINGS OF COMMERCE ON HOW TO CHANGE THE WORLD

**THE WEALTH BUILDERS:
ROBERTO GOIZUETA AND JACK WELCH**
page 24

IN GREENSPAN WE TRUST
page 39

WHY ANDY GROVE CAN'T STOP
page 50

DAN TULLY: HOW TO BULL AHEAD
page 59

**ROGER ENRICO:
PEPSICO'S NEW GENERATION**
page 69

CITICORP: JOHN REED'S SECOND ACT
page 78

WALL STREET'S KING QUANT: DAVID SHAW
page 87

How a patrician Cuban émigré and a train conductor's son unlocked the secrets of creating shareholder value.

THE WEALTH BUILDERS: ROBERTO GOIZUETA AND JACK WELCH

BY BETSY MORRIS

THERE ARE ALL SORTS OF WAYS to grade a chief executive. Look at his return on equity. Calculate his return on investment. Take quarterly note of his earnings growth. Rank him against his peers. Rank him against his industry. Or judge him by the most fundamental measure of all—how much wealth he has created for his shareholders.

If it's the last point that you're really interested in, then the yardstick to use is market value added, or MVA, a calculation devised by the New York City consulting firm Stern Stewart. The calculation zeroes in on shareholder wealth by asking a very basic question: What is the difference between the cash that investors have put into a business over its lifetime and the amount they could get out of it today by selling their shares?

When big American companies are evaluated this way, the field is not crowded at the top. Two men—Roberto C. Goizueta, chairman and chief executive of Coca-Cola, and John F. Welch Jr., chairman and chief executive of General Electric—stand head and shoulders above the rest. No others come close.

What MVA really measures is how efficiently the chief executive has been able to use the capital entrusted to him—how well he's been able to keep his eye on the ball. By that standard, Goizueta and Welch are genuine champions. Goizueta created nearly all of Coca-Cola's MVA—$88 billion—during his own tenure. Welch created all of GE's $81 billion MVA on his own watch.

What are the qualities that set them apart? "Both men have an ability to sort out the noise from the signal and then to drive just for the essence of what's important," says George M.C. Fisher, chairman and chief executive officer of Eastman Kodak, who knows both of them well. "A lot of executives can intellectualize the process, but these two can follow through."

Though they share a unique set of wealth-building skills, the two men couldn't be more different. One, the son of a wealthy Cuban sugar magnate, became an impoverished immigrant when, as a young adult, he left Cuba for Miami to escape Castro's orbit. He and his wife had $40 between them and 100 shares of Coca-Cola stock. The other, the son of a railroad conductor, was a hotheaded young ruffian who wanted to go to Dartmouth but couldn't.

Goizueta is aristocratic, formal, ever polite, always measured— a gentleman CEO who likes a nice predictable schedule and a certain sense of decorum, and never seems to take off his suit jacket. Welch is impulsive, captivatingly charming, still proud of his *Animal House* fraternity, most comfortable in his shirtsleeves. Goizueta has a deep and abiding respect for tradition; Welch has little use for it. Goizueta doesn't like open confrontation; Welch thrives on it. One is a technician; the other, a charismatic. One runs essentially a one-product company; the other, a conglomerate with a dozen businesses, nine of them big enough to be on the FORTUNE 500.

For Goizueta, the concept of shareholder wealth is almost an ideology. A video monitor at the entrance of the main building at Coca-Cola headquarters shows the stock price, updated several times a day. It is the first thing employees see each morning and the last thing they see when they go home at night.

For Welch, an avid athlete, business is the most absorbing game of all. The creation of wealth is how you keep score: It is the result of winning, which is what business is all about in the locker-room GE culture.

Yet there are uncanny similarities too. Both men are chemical engineers. Both were raised as Roman Catholics. They became chairman and chief executive officer of their companies exactly a month apart in the spring of 1981. Their birthdays are a day apart in November. Both inherited blue-chip corporations, then proceeded to navigate them through one of the most troubled times for blue chips. Both were plucked from relative obscurity to take the top jobs.

In some very fundamental ways, Goizueta and Welch did business similarly. They weren't distracted by outside events. They figured out what they needed to do. They told their employees. And then they did it—relentlessly—over the past 15 years. Their stories say something about ego, something about succession in a big bureaucracy; something about strategies. For Welch, getting the top job meant that the big game was beginning. For Goizueta, it was a chance to rebuild all that he'd lost. For both men, it was a chance to settle up with the past.

"MY GRANDFATHER HAD A SAYING FOR EVERYTHING."

WEALTH IS A THEME that has run through the lives of Goizueta and Welch in very different ways. Goizueta was born to it on November 18, 1931. His maternal grandfather, Marcelo Cantera, had emigrated to Cuba from Spain with little more than a high school education. But he was a hardworking and thrifty man, who would impress on his grandson the importance of cash. When the Depression hit Cuba, he had saved enough to acquire a sugar-refining business and some real estate, and then to build a mansion in Havana large enough for his extended family, Roberto's parents and their children. It was a tight community and a nurturing one. Roberto's paternal grandmother lived next door, and numerous cousins lived nearby.

And it was a childhood rich in culture, for the clan had its share of Renaissance men. Roberto's father, Crispulo Goizueta, attended the University of Pennsylvania and worked as an architect before returning to take over and add to the family holdings. After he retired, Marcelo wrote verses (he wouldn't permit them to be called poetry) in elegant handwriting, and "held court" in an office off the living room, with his young grandson at his knee. "My grandfather had a saying for everything," recalls Roberto, who would grow up to run his company by many of the Spanish proverbs his grandfather had taught him.

For Roberto, it was an easy road to adulthood. He took a school bus to the Belen School, a nearby Jesuit institution. Then for a year he attended Cheshire Academy, a private secondary school in Connecticut, to learn English. He moved on to Yale University, his way smoothed both by outstanding performance and by connections at Cheshire. He majored in chemical engineering, a discipline he thought would be helpful when, someday, he would take over the family business.

In some ways it was too easy. When Goizueta returned home to work for his father, he was restless. "I had no compass. Everything was perfect. It was very difficult to do anything wrong," he recalls. He wanted to strike out on his own. Although he could easily have used his family connections, he answered a blind ad in the newspaper, landing a job as an entry-level chemist at the Coca-Cola Co. in Havana. He reported for duty on July 4, 1954. "It was going to be a temporary thing for me, $500 a month," he recalls. "My friends thought I was absolutely crazy."

It turned out to be perhaps the smartest move he ever made. After Fidel Castro took over in 1959, it became clear that Castro intended to take over both the Goizueta family enterprise and Coca-Cola's Cuban operations. So in 1960 the Goizueta family scattered, some to Mexico and others to Miami. Roberto, his wife, Olga Casteleiro, their three children, and a nursemaid shared a motel room for a month on Miami's Venetian Causeway. He counts himself lucky; Coca-Cola gave him a job in a new Miami office, and he had his 100 shares, kept in a bank in New York. "You cannot explain that experience to any person," he says. "That was ten times more important than anything else in my life. It was a shocker. All of a sudden you don't own anything, except the stock. One hundred shares. That's the only thing I had. It brings a sense of humility. It builds a feeling of not much regard for material things."

"DON'T GET ME STARTED ON MY MOTHER. SHE'S MY WHOLE GAME."

JACK WELCH came from the other side of the tracks in the small, gritty city of Salem, Massachusetts. He was born on November 19, 1935, four years and one day after Goizueta, into much different circumstances. His father, John Sr., was a conductor for the Boston & Maine Railroad and away much of the time; it was his mother, Grace, who played the most powerful role in his life. She raised him, doted on him, pushed him. "Don't get me started on my mother; she's my whole game," he says.

It was a simple life, in a little gray stucco house on Lovett Street. Jack was an only child; his extended family was his neighborhood. And it was filled with "kids that didn't have anything. You were lucky if you had food on the table," recalls Lawrence McIntire, a childhood friend who is now the superintendent of parks and recreation in Salem. Welch and another pal, Sam Zoll, would caddy at the Kernwood Country Club, picking up $1.25 for 18 holes, which they would then turn over to their parents, who usually allowed them to keep a quarter.

The kids did have one thing that many of them now point to as being a major factor in shaping their success: an excavated gravel pit turned into a makeshift park, called the "Pit," a Darwinian laboratory of sorts in which Welch and his buddies learned how to win, lose, fight, compromise, and charm. There was no recreation department funding, certainly no Little League. So the kids of north Salem built their own basketball court and made a hockey rink from the snow-packed swath left by a snowplow. The older, bigger kids played first; only when they got tired did the younger, smaller ones get a turn. Fistfights were common. "We were all jocks of sorts. I mean, we played ball countless hours, played street hockey all night. That was everything. Sports were everything," Welch recalls.

"We didn't have parental development and supervision, uniforms and all that," says Zoll, who is now the chief justice of the district court of Massachusetts. "Inter-city and playing teams from other cities was left to your own creativity." In that milieu,

Welch made a name for himself. He put the games together and figured out how the kids would get there and home. He became known as a fearless negotiator who, through aggressiveness and charisma, could talk the bigger kids into sharing the basketball court. He was a ferocious and judgmental competitor. His teammates "always knew where they stood," recalls one.

McIntire says that among the kids from that neighborhood, "there is a group of about 15 guys who made out pretty well. A lot of us didn't go to college. We just worked hard and ended up with positions. Jack and all of us grew up in that very competitive atmosphere, so when we went out into the world, we said, 'Hey, we can do anything. Nothing can be as tough as going to the Pit.' "

Welch went to Pickering Elementary and then on to Salem High School, where he was involved in practically everything but was perhaps best known for sports. He was captain of the hockey team and golf team. His class voted him the "most talkative and noisiest boy." In his high school literary magazine, he listed his "repressed desire: to make a million."

If, as a young adult, Goizueta was stifled by his family connections, Welch had the opposite problem. He and two of his close friends from Salem High were nominated to receive Navy ROTC scholarships that would provide full room, board, and tuition to college. Welch's friends won them, and got to go to Tufts and Columbia. Welch didn't. It was a disappointment. "I don't know what my problem was. I didn't know enough people. I can remember my father calling our Congressman and things like that. He didn't really know how to do it very well," he recalls. Welch ended up at the University of Massachusetts, "which at the time didn't have a unique reputation by any means. It was a state school and used to be called Mass Aggie," he says.

His mother wanted him to be a priest or a doctor. He wanted to be a "great hockey player," but he wasn't fast enough. He settled on engineering "because we only had one person in our whole family that was at all educated beyond high school," he recalls. "He was called an engineer, and he worked at a power plant. So I went to engineering school."

29

At college he had a ball, the only engineer in a wild jock fraternity, and still he managed to graduate with honors. "We were on scholastic ban all the time. We drank more beer and had more fights than anybody there. And we'd play cards all night," he says. "And I had great grades." He went on to graduate school at the University of Illinois, got a Ph.D. in chemical engineering, and then, out of three job offers, chose to go to work for General Electric in Pittsfield, Massachusetts. "It was in Massachusetts, where I came from, so it was like going home in a way. That may sound ridiculous, but in those days that was kind of important."

THE ROAD TO THE TOP

FOR BOTH Goizueta and Welch, the road to the top was anything but conventional. After emigrating to Miami, Goizueta spent most of his corporate life in the technical side of the business. His accomplishments there were impressive, and his integrity was respected. But in a company where people talk about having Coca-Cola in their veins, he never ran a soft drink operating division. Although he became executive vice president in May 1975, and was later given responsibility for the company's administrative, external affairs, legal, and technical divisions, in the horse race set up by his predecessor, J. Paul Austin, he was still considered the darkest horse.

What the outside world couldn't see was the strong bond Goizueta had forged with Robert W. Woodruff, who had run the company for decades and was still referred to as "the Boss." Woodruff frequently invited him to lunch, and Goizueta respectfully attended what he calls those "command performances." On his way home after work, he would visit Woodruff to chat, much the way he had sat with his grandfather many years before. He had the kind of modesty and humility that the courtly Woodruff surely respected. "I never set a goal to be this or that. I always believed that if you could do the best job you can, somebody will notice it sooner or later. You hope it will be sooner,"

Goizueta says. Donald R. Keough, Coca-Cola's former president and chief operating officer, says, "Mr. Woodruff trusted him and admired his integrity and saw in him a fundamental toughness." Woodruff also must have appreciated Goizueta's fundamental respect for tradition and decorum; for if Coca-Cola was to be changed, it would have to be changed very carefully.

There was nothing especially subtle or careful about Jack Welch, on the other hand. When General Electric's famous management-succession machine first cranked up and delivered to Reginald H. Jones a list of some 30-odd candidates in 1975, Welch's name wasn't on it. He was young. He was, Jones says, "the least typical GE guy. Definitely a maverick in his style." At GE, you weren't anybody unless you were part of the "electrical ring"—the businesses that were part of Thomas Edison's direct legacy. Welch had been hired in a little bastard outpost of the company called the Chemical Development Organization, charged with developing new chemical businesses. "We had a Green Beret, almost SWAT team mentality," recalls Reuben Gutoff, who was Welch's boss at GE for 12 years. The enemies were not just outside competitors but the GE bureaucracy too. "We talked a lot about that—the bureaucracy-speak, the bureaucracy babble. We had met the enemy, and it was us."

If Goizueta was a good corporate soldier, Welch was a rebel. Rather than entertain GE customers at Palm Beach, Florida, he would take them to Lake Placid, New York, organizing ice hockey games and ski races, most of which he won. He argued against the bonus system, which included a high percentage of deferred stock; with four children, he needed income. At one point he told Jones: "It's golden handcuffs. It's imprisonment." He resisted moving to the corporate headquarters in Fairfield, Connecticut, because he wanted no part of the bureaucracy, and he got away with it because he delivered. But Jones finally prevailed: "I told him he had to get out of being a hick up in Massachusetts, running his own little bailiwick, with everybody genuflecting to him; that if he wanted to amount to something, he had better get down here where the real competition was going on."

THE SPANISH INQUISITION

GOIZUETA BECAME chairman and chief executive of Coke on March 1, 1981. Welch assumed the same posts at GE exactly one month later. The coincidence was a kind of high-water mark in succession planning. As Gutoff puts it, "I think people who come up from the nonmainstream route are not so captured by the folklore, the mystique, the baggage. They are more likely to be able to tell that the emperor has no clothes. It's one thing to have a Lou Gerstner come in to fix an IBM. But if you can get an insider with an outsider's point of view, you get the best of both worlds."

Then as now, Coca-Cola and General Electric were two vastly different worlds. Coca-Cola was a Southern soft drink company with an identity crisis. For nearly 100 years, it had sold essentially two things: the fountain drink made with the syrup that Atlanta pharmacist John Styth Pemberton had concocted, and that soft drink's image. But with soft drinks flagging, Coca-Cola had become paralyzed and self-conscious.

General Electric, northern and industrial, had become smug. Born in 1892 as the offspring of a merger of two electric companies—one of them Thomas Edison's—it had tried to be all things electrical, from toasters and hair dryers to jet engines, many of them tough, cyclical, low-margin businesses. It had gotten so big, bureaucratic, and diversified that it was blissfully insulated from the threats of global competition and changing technology.

Despite the differences, Welch and Goizueta perceived their jobs in surprisingly similar fashion: to come up with some formula that would get them into the right businesses and to spur their tradition-bound bureaucracies to accept change. In Atlanta, Goizueta began to gather data. In September 1980, as president and chief operating officer, he had met with his executives for business planning sessions, and what had traditionally been a series of presentations became a fact-finding mission for Goizueta. Just the fact that he was asking questions was such a shock to the culture that it became known as the Spanish Inquisition.

But it was clear to Goizueta that things had to change. His immediate predecessor, J. Paul Austin, had been ill. Coke management, along with the rest of the world, it seemed, had lost faith in the soft drink business. *Business Week* magazine ran a cover story on "The Graying of the Soft Drink Industry," warning that shifting demographics spelled doom for soda pop. Wall Street analysts were bearish. M. Douglas Ivester, now Coke's president and chief operating officer, recalls one of them insisting, "I don't care what you say, your company can only grow at 3% a year."

The business was a mess. The domestic bottlers had a stranglehold; many had contracts that had assured them not only fixed prices but ownership in perpetuity too. Worse yet, Coca-Cola had been losing market share, bit by bit, for nearly two decades. But the company, afraid of doing anything that might hurt the trademark, was paralyzed. "Coke had been a single thing in a single package, like an egg. That's Coke," recalls Keough, the former COO. "When it came to the trademark, there was always a tentativeness. What are people going to think?" So besides trying to fix soft drinks, Austin's management had acquired what had come to be known as "the supporting cast": wine, coffee, tea, plastics businesses—even a division that made steam generators and industrial boilers.

Goizueta set to work looking for a way to impose order. Even before he got the job, he came up with a two-page, double-spaced document, simple as an egg and dry as dust, titled "The Job of the Chief Executive Officer." It outlined, among other things, what he could delegate and what he couldn't. He also developed a mission statement that laid out his vision for the company, which he would update every few years.

And early on in his tenure, he developed what has come to be known as gospel to almost everybody who works at Coca-Cola: that the name of the game is creating wealth for what he calls "shareowners," and that the key is efficient allocation of capital. The way to accomplish this, Goizueta says, is to employ one simple little formula that has now been all gussied up and given a fancy name that consultants sell for lots of money. As Goizueta puts it, "You borrow money at a certain rate and invest it at a higher rate and pocket the difference. It is simple. It is the essence of banking." The theory, which essentially amounts to economic value added, or EVA, is one he didn't learn from the consultants. He learned it from his grandfather, who used to say: "I am a great believer in cash flow. Earnings is a man-made convention, but cash is cash. The larger the company is, the less it understands cash flow. The smaller the business, the better it understands cash flow ..." and so on.

As Keough puts it, "Roberto is a person who thought like an owner. He wasn't a hired hand. His family were owners. He had tremendous pride in ownership. That was very important to him."

After developing the formula, Goizueta followed through. He got rid of the companies that didn't meet his returns. He resisted the temptation to get into the cable and pharmaceuticals businesses. He renewed the company's commitment to soft drinks—the introduction of Diet Coke rejuvenated the business. He did buy Columbia Pictures, not to hedge his bets, he says, but to shore up earnings until he could get the soft drink problems straightened out. And he introduced New Coke.

The latter two moves only served to reinforce his commitment to soft drinks. "I don't like surprises. Even good. He who can surprise me with good news can surprise me with bad," Goizueta is fond of saying. And the movie business was filled with surprises. When Goizueta and Keough previewed *Ghostbusters,* they thought it was silly. "That's how much we know about picking hits," says Keough.

New Coke also pointed Goizueta back to Coca-Cola's roots. For a man who doesn't like surprises, for a company scared to death to monkey with its trademark, it was the crucible. Ronald L. Kuehn, chairman and chief executive officer of Sonat Inc., spent time with Goizueta during the backlash. "He was more serious than usual. He was obviously very intense. He didn't like it at all that Coke might have made a faux pas," Kuehn recalls. But nobody involved ever saw him lose his temper. Goizueta recalls walking on a beach at Sea Island, Georgia, with his father, Crispulo, in May 1985. "Dad was upset. I said 'Dad, you have to have faith.'"

The experience had huge significance for him. "I realized what I should have before," he says. "That this was a most unique company with a most unique product. We have a product that people have an unusual attachment to. I had never felt so bullish about it." From that point on, says Anthony Adams, a professor and consultant who has observed Coca-Cola from both inside and outside the company, "it was as if a light bulb went on. Aha! This is the essence of what we own," says Adams. "From that point on, Roberto has reduced the company basically to its trademark, and the returns are so astronomical as to be off the boards. It just absolutely added a jet engine to their performance."

"YOU GO IN PUMPED UP. YOU GO IN READY FOR COMBAT."

IF GOIZUETA'S approach to the creation of wealth was cerebral, Welch's was primal. He had worked in businesses that were good and businesses that were bad, and he knew which he preferred. While the old darlings of GE had included businesses (like housewares) that supposedly endeared the company to consumers, Welch's darlings were the winners: what would come to be known as the "invest and grow" businesses like plastics, medical supplies, NBC.

To him, the whole notion of wealth creation was not an ideology but the game itself. It was pure rules of the Pit. The strong survive; the big, the fast, get to play. The more you win, the more wealth you create. And the first and most obvious rule: "Don't play with businesses that can't win," he says. "Businesses that are No. 3, No. 5 in their market—Christ couldn't fix those businesses. They're going to lose anyway."

So a year after Goizueta's Spanish Inquisition, Welch gathered his executives together to lay out his formula. Businesses had to be No. 1 or No. 2 in their global marketplace. If they weren't, he told them, we will fix you, sell you, or close you.

If Goizueta, ever respectful of the past, worked to effect change without causing too many ripples at Coke, Welch created a tidal wave. Just like a coach trading his players, he began bailing out of the businesses he didn't think were going to strengthen his hand. Tradition didn't matter; winning did. In one 12-month period, he unloaded both housewares and Utah International, a mining subsidiary Jones had acquired just eight years earlier in what had been celebrated as the biggest U.S. merger ever. Within another 12-month period, he bought RCA and Kidder Peabody. Although GE's strategic planning process, complete with 400 strategic planners at headquarters, had become the darling of the B-school set, he dismantled it. By 1988 he had bought and sold scores of companies and reduced his work force by 100,000.

There is in almost every aspect of GE management a heavy element of competition. John Opie, vice chairman of GE, prepares for every meeting the same way he'd psych up to run the 440 or to play football. "You go in pumped up. You go in ready for combat," he says. And prepared to take a certain amount of heat. If Welch doesn't like an acquisition proposal, "he might say, 'You're crazy, that's too much money; not even close. Go get it for half.' You'd better have a thick skin, or when you come out, you will be a hurting person."

Welch has organized his management much the same way he used to organize ball games. Each quarter he gathers his top executives at the leadership development center in Crotonville, New York. Everybody knows the company initiatives: to increase such things as productivity, inventory turns, quality, working capital, customer satisfaction, and other goals Welch has set. And by the end of the sessions, everybody knows where each division stands. "Everybody wants to be at the top," says Robert L. Nardelli, president and chief executive officer of GE Transportation Systems. Being at the bottom is a humbling experience. "When somebody is floundering, there is a little bit of a Quaker shunning; the guy's not so popular at the coffee breaks," says Paul Van Orden, executive in residence at the Columbia business school and a former GE executive. "Jack has an awful lot of very talented people running those businesses. By rubbing them together, it can be very effective."

The GE approach clearly has its hazards. Welch admits that it is impossible to know everything about each of his businesses. "I don't know what color the refrigerator is or how it all works, but generally speaking, we know what the higher issues are ... it's sort of a smell, a scent, a trust in the people." That may have contributed to the Kidder Peabody fiasco in which GE was forced to take a $210 million charge against earnings after Kidder trader Joseph Jett allegedly created $350 million in phantom profits. If Goizueta kept his cool through New Coke, Welch lost it over Kidder. "He yelled, and I yelled, and people yelled back," recalls Dennis D. Dammerman, senior vice president for

THE TOP WEALTH CREATORS

Having created more than $55 billion combined in investor wealth in 1995, Coca-Cola and GE top the annual market value added (MVA) list once again in 1996. Devised by Stern Stewart, a financial consulting firm based in New York City, MVA is the difference between a company's current debt and stock market value, and all its invested capital throughout its life span. A positive MVA shows the amount of wealth created; negative means wealth destruction. This year's list brought Exxon into the top ten, while Wal-Mart "is losing some of its gloss and is in danger of falling out altogether," says Stern Stewart executive Bennett Stewart.

'96	'95		Total MVA Millions	Total investor return 1986-95 annual rate
1	1	Coca-Cola	$87,818	26.6%
2	2	General Electric	$80,792	14.8%
3	4	Merck	$63,440	24.0%
4	7	Philip Morris	$51,627	23.4%
5	5	Microsoft	$44,850	49.9%
6	8	Johnson & Johnson	$42,541	20.6%
7	9	AT&T	$40,152	10.0%
8	6	Procter & Gamble	$40,000	16.9%
9	13	Exxon	$39,041	11.3%
10	3	Wal-Mart Stores	$35,974	18.8%
		Average	$52,624	21.6%

finance. "Were any of us calm for the whole weekend? No, you would've thought we were weird if we had been."

BOTH WELCH AND GOIZUETA are spending the home stretches of their tenures focused less on external adventures than on consolidating their gains. Opposites in so many other respects, they are once again singing off the same page when it comes to trying to break down bureaucracy, speed up decision-making, and keep their respective corporate revolutions going. If there is a lesson in all this, sum it up this way: For management—unlike, say, for Coca-Cola—there is no secret formula. But as these extraordinary opposites reveal, there are definitely essential ingredients.

The powerful Fed chairman is on board for four more years,
to the relief of corporate America.
What does it mean?
Simply this: no recession. No inflation. No voodoo.

IN GREENSPAN WE TRUST

BY ROB NORTON

THE WEIRDNESS BEGAN EARLY this election year. Presidential candidates barnstormed from one state to the next preying on the nation's deep-rooted feelings of economic uncertainty, preaching their unlikely plans for economic nirvana—from the pure flat tax to the gold standard to 19th-century-style trade protectionism—each one warning all the while that his opponents' policies will ruin the country. Back in Washington, Congress and the Clinton Administration were clueless—nine months late with a budget for this year, let alone the next seven. Meanwhile, the markets jumped around like hungry puppies.

Thank God for Alan Greenspan. Arguably as important as who sits in the White House—maybe even more important—is the fact that Greenspan is still running the Federal Reserve—the closest thing the U.S. economy has to an economic pacemaker. How good is this news? Well, the markets roared their approval over Greenspan's renomination. And in a poll we commissioned of FORTUNE 1,000 chief executives, 96% backed the chairman's reappointment (how's that for an approval rating?). More than half give Greenspan an A for his performance at the Fed; almost all the others give him a B.

Greenspan's peers think just as highly of him. "He's the best chairman the Fed has ever had," says Allan Meltzer, a professor at

Carnegie Mellon University and longtime critic of Fed policy. Meltzer isn't just shooting the breeze—he's in the midst of writing a history of the Federal Reserve System. Says Lawrence Lindsey, one of Greenspan's fellow Fed governors: "If the curve you're grading on is 'What's attainable by mortals,' he certainly deserves an A."

Greenspan's highest marks are for the gentle landing of the economy this year after the hot and potentially inflationary growth of 1994. "What he did was very unusual," says Meltzer. "He acted against inflation before it got started—the first time the Fed has done that in at least 30 years." Here's an inside observation, from Rick Mishkin, chief economist at the New York Federal Reserve Bank: "In hindsight, it was as good as we could have hoped. We just nailed it." Says Alan Blinder, who recently departed as vice chairman of the Fed: "This is perhaps the most successful episode of monetary policy in the history of the Fed."

Not everyone loves Greenspan, of course, and he doesn't walk on water. He presided over one of America's worst recessions as chairman of Gerald Ford's Council of Economic Advisers. Lots of people—including business people—remember that well and think he was and is too worried about inflation and not enough about growth. There are even some who positively hate him, and concoct dark conspiracy theories about how he's subverting the will of the people to benefit Wall Street.

So who is this guy? And why should we bet that he can continue to keep the economy on track? If you think you know, wait a second. Sure, you know his public persona: the professorial bureaucrat who speaks before Congress about boring subjects in intentionally ambiguous cadences. But the real man is more interesting. His is a story of intellect and street smarts—of how he learned to examine the clockwork of the U.S. economy and how he built a hugely successful business by explaining its workings to executives. How he turned himself into the ultimate Washington operator and how he became chairman—as if by destiny—of the Federal Reserve just when it most needed him. There's even a lighter side somewhere behind his opaque mask: He's a wry observer of the political folkways of Washington, and though he has a monastic streak—sometimes spending entire weekends lost in the data, preparing for congressional testimony—he's also a bit of a bon vivant, making the Washington party scene and playing tennis at mountain resorts with his longtime companion, NBC news correspondent Andrea Mitchell.

Not that Greenspan seeks the limelight. He's happiest when his profile is low. Fed chairmen are in the news in only two situations: when inflation is rising or when recessions happen. The economy under Greenspan has pretty much stayed out of trouble and has performed fairly well recently. GDP growth has averaged 2.6% since the 1990 recession, compared with 2.9% in the 1980s, and inflation was below 3% in 1995 for the fifth year in a row—the first long stretch of low inflation since the Kennedy Administration. Greenspan himself seems far more relaxed these days than he did a few years back. He even told a visitor to his hushed office not too long ago (the loudest noise is the hum of the well-used PC) that he was managing to catch up on his leisure reading—of early econometric theory.

Happily, there is good reason to believe—as Greenspan and many of the Fed's other senior policymakers do—that we will see even lower inflation over the next two years and that the economy will continue to grow, recession-free, through the near future. But you'll never hear Greenspan promising more than he can deliver. He's a cautious person, and pragmatism, for him, is a way of life.

THE EARLY YEARS

GREENSPAN WAS BORN and raised in New York City, went to public school, and attended New York University—eventually winding up with a Ph.D. in economics. Always interested in public policy, he hung out with libertarian novelist Ayn Rand's band of free-market intellectuals in the early Fifties, about the time he got started in economic forecasting. That was also a golden age in econometric research, and chances are that he spent as much time with *Measuring Business Cycles*, by Arthur Burns and Wesley Mitchell, as he did with *The Fountainhead*. David Mullins, vice chairman of the Fed from 1991 to 1994, credits Greenspan with inventing a business back in the 1950s: economic analysis for senior business executives. "He was the first to adapt forecasting specifically for CEOs," says Mullins, now a partner at Long Term Capital Management, the quant trading firm. Greenspan was soon in demand as a forecaster and adviser, and eventually wound up on the boards of companies like Alcoa, Capital Cities/ABC, J.P. Morgan & Co., and Mobil.

Greenspan began visiting Washington in the late Sixties, first as an adviser to then presidential candidate Richard Nixon. He served in the Ford Administration during the tumultuous middle 1970s. Along the way, he developed the perfect Washington personality: rock solid in his own beliefs and impervious to the ritual abuse that comes with the territory. He became a master at suffering fools—patiently if not gladly—and he learned when not to take things too seriously.

A story about Greenspan in the Ford years goes like this: Once he was waiting to testify before a Senate committee chaired by the late Hubert Humphrey. Greenspan had back trouble at the time, and Humphrey knew it. As another Administration official's testimony dragged on, Humphrey sent Greenspan a note saying, "Alan, I can see you're having trouble with your back. Why don't you leave, and we'll say you were called by the President." Greenspan replied by note that he was okay. Later, as the questioning of the other official droned on, Humphrey motioned Greenspan to the dais and whispered, "Go. We've got enough testimony. I don't want you to be in pain." Again, Greenspan declined.

Finally it was time for Greenspan's testimony, and the red light came on, signifying Humphrey's turn to ask questions. "Dr. Greenspan," he intoned balefully, "are you ashamed, as you should be, about how destructive your policies have been to this country?" Greenspan gritted his teeth and answered without smiling.

Such training was invaluable for a future Fed chairman. Think of the ranks of nitwit Congresspeople who take shots at the Fed chairman today during his appearances on Capitol Hill, sometimes as often as once a week and for several hours at a time.

FEDSPEAK 101

What do they talk about at the FOMC? Here are Robert Black and Richard Syron (then presidents of the Richmond and Boston Fed banks) discussing monetary policy in 1989.

Mr. Syron: Excuse me, a point of information: Are you suggesting "slightly" and "might" on the second part or "somewhat/would" and "slightly/might" in terms of symmetry?

Mr. Black: I was suggesting "slightly/might" on both of them.

Mr. Syron: "Slightly/might" on both?

Mr. Black: Yes. That predisposes us not to move unless we have some evidence that we don't now have. It's a stronger vote to remain where we are than "somewhat" and "would," I think. We may be getting into minutiae here, but ... If I were voting, I would [accept] "somewhat" and "would"; I even toyed with the idea of "somewhat" and "might" and other permutations and combinations of that.

Mr. Syron: "Slightly/would," I suppose.

"GREENSPAN'S FED FROM TOP TO BOTTOM"

TODAY GREENSPAN'S POWER as the undisputed leader of the Federal Reserve system is downright awesome—but he had to earn it. The Fed is a strange governmental creature. It's made up of the 12 regional Federal Reserve banks, each with a president, board of directors, officers, and research staff, plus the Washington-based board of governors, with the largest phalanxes of research economists. The Fed is secretive by nature, suspicious of outsiders, and possessed of an esprit de corps that borders on fanaticism.

INFLATION IN THE GREENSPAN ERA

Consumer price index
Percent change from previous December

4.42%	4.41%	4.64%	6.25%	2.98%	2.96%	2.74%	2.60%	2.60%
1987	1988	1989	1990	1991	1992	1993	1994	1995

When Greenspan was appointed chairman in 1987 by Ronald Reagan, he was greeted with some suspicion. "You get a new chairman who hasn't had a career at the Fed, and there's a period of intense observation," says one Fed official. "Greenspan was different; he was a political guy, a bit of a celebrity." And remember, he succeeded Fed insider Paul Volcker, the towering, glowering legend who had slain the demon dragon of the 1970s: double-digit inflation.

Two things helped right away. First was his manner. Greenspan is libertarian in person as well as in theory—a believer in individual liberty and rights. He treats everyone from hotel waiters to heads of state with respect, and there's not a hint about him of the snobbery that's typical of academic economists. The other things that helped were his mastery of the theory and details of the economy, and his obvious love of data. That impresses people at the Fed, and it can't be faked.

Greenspan's first big test was the stock market crash of 1987. It came just two months after he showed up at the Fed. His cool and decisive reaction to the crash—guaranteeing enough liquidity to preclude the cycle of asset deflation and monetary contraction that drove the economy down after the 1929 crash—has been widely praised. Inside the Fed, though, his ability to see that the stock market problem was transitory and his willingness to reverse policy and raise interest rates in mid-1988 were equally important. It sent the signal that the Fed was determined to keep its foot on the throat of inflation and was willing to take risks to do it. A case can be made that this attitude helped produce the 1990 recession—or at least prevented Greenspan from fighting it more aggressively once it began.

Greenspan bonded, early on, with the Fed's research staff. Fed economists at the time were studying a way of predicting inflation called P* (don't ask). Greenspan supported the project and got involved personally. When the research paper was published, buried in a list of acknowledgments, in alphabetical order, was the name Alan Greenspan. It was a classy, egalitarian touch, and Fed economists beam even today when they tell the story.

Leading by example and winning over the staff is especially important at the Fed because of its idiosyncratic management structure. The chairman's power derives almost exclusively from his position as presiding officer of two committees. One is the board of governors—made up of himself and the six other presidential appointees who serve in Washington (it is mostly concerned with regulatory and administrative matters). The other, which holds the real statutory power over monetary policy, is the federal open market committee (FOMC), made up of the seven governors and the presidents of five of the 12 regional Federal Reserve banks (they take turns voting).

Running the Fed, then, depends crucially on the chairman's ability to run a meeting. Greenspan, by all accounts, is very good at it. Newly released transcripts of FOMC meetings (they are published with a five-year lag) show him at work, letting all members have their say, softening the edges of disputes, and suggesting areas of compromise when there is disagreement. "He shows a lot of respect for other people," says former vice chairman Mullins, "and he has the confidence to defer to their expertise." Greenspan, they say, has only been on the losing side of one vote during his entire time at the Fed, and that was a bank regulatory matter so arcane that no one seems to remember what it was about. "By the time I arrived on the scene, in the middle of 1994, this was Alan Greenspan's Fed from top to the bottom," recalls Alan Blinder. "It was like the Fed was an orchestra being played by an expert conductor."

Blinder, who left the Fed in February to return to teaching, never did figure the place out. He's a brilliant man, widely respected in academia and the pride of Princeton University's economics department. And he has a rare ability to communicate complex ideas, both in print (he co-authored a best-selling introductory economics textbook) and in person. Blinder even had some previous Washington experience, having spent the first part of the Clinton Administration as a member of the Council of Economic Advisers.

But he evidently alienated the Fed staff in a hurry. Fed governors don't have independent power bases. The staff reports to the board of governors, and a governor typically has a single personal secretary—a career Fed employee, no less. Blinder insisted on having a personal assistant, over the objections of senior staff members (only one other governor, Lawrence Lindsey, has such an assistant). Blinder announced that he did not wish to serve another term at the Fed in a letter to President Clinton. He has expressed dissatisfaction about his treatment by the staff and said that he felt isolated and excluded during his 19 months at the Fed.

Blinder also has a substantive complaint about the way the Fed is run. He considers the institution's penchant for secrecy excessive, and he tried to get the Fed to be more open and communicative. He mostly failed. "I can't go into details," he says, "because everything at the FOMC is confidential. I have to respect that, even though I don't agree with it." By lobbying for glasnost, Blinder was setting himself up in opposition to a sacred tradition at the Fed— its insistence on discretion and silence. Fed staffers rarely talk to the press on the record. Interviews with governors are subject to elaborate ground rules, such as how close to the FOMC meetings they can take place. One can speculate that Blinder's agitation for openness was one of the reasons for his isolation. After all, if you feel the place ought to keep its secrets, would you share them with someone who feels it should not?

But Blinder never disagreed fundamentally with Greenspan about monetary policy. While the two differed about such details as the timing of interest-rates changes, he voted with Greenspan through the long series of rate increases in 1994. That lack of dissension is highly significant, since it undercuts the most serious charge against monetary policy in the Greenspan era: that the Fed is needlessly holding back the growth rate of the economy because of unfounded fears of inflation.

Critics have said this for years, and they're a varied bunch, ranging from Naderite consumer activists to supply-side Republicans to trade associations such as the Chamber of Commerce and the National Association of Manufacturers. The business lobby has disagreed vociferously with Greenspan in recent years, especially when the Fed began tightening monetary policy in 1994. "We scream loudly whenever we think he's doing a wrong thing," says one trade association economist, adding wistfully, "If only he'd let the economy grow half a percent more." These "growth critics" argue that changes in economic conditions, especially increasing productivity, and also in such things as global competition have transformed the economy so that it can grow much faster than it has recently.

A PRACTICAL MAN VS. HIS CRITICS

THE IDEA THAT there is a limit, at any given point, on how fast the economy can grow without causing inflation is not controversial among economists. Real GDP growth is a function of how much labor and capital are available and how productive those "inputs" are. If the economy consistently grows faster than its potential, industries and regions will run out of either workers or materials, or both—resulting in rising wage demands, rising prices, and other imbalances. No one knows exactly what that noninflationary growth rate is, but most estimates cluster around 2.5%.

Greenspan has said often that the Fed would welcome faster growth, as long as it's sustainable. But he and other analysts at the Fed are suspicious of the "growth school" arguments. If productivity improvements really are increasing the potential rate of noninflationary growth, for instance, the gains have yet to show up clearly in the national data. Of course, it may be that the data are bad, and Greenspan has delivered thoughtful, technical (and widely ignored) speeches on the issue. But there are also reasons to believe the growth school is all wrong. Roger Brinner, chief economist at DRI/McGraw-Hill, for example, notes that growth of the labor force has been much weaker in the 1990s than in other recent decades, which would drive the potential growth rate down.

Greenspan, above all, is a practical and cautious person. He's not about to fool with monetary policy and risk an outbreak of inflation based on nothing more than speculation. Besides, while the true potential growth rate is unknowable, Greenspan believes there are good indicators that show when the economy is running up against its limits, such as a stretching out of lead times in deliveries of goods and increases in overtime hours.

Most of the other criticisms of Greenspan are less consequential. Some "monetarist" economists quibble about the details of monetary policy. There are the gold bugs, who argue that either the nation should return to a gold standard or the Fed's monetary policy should be determined by gold prices. Then there are the conspiracy theorists. Most of their critiques revolve around simple anticapitalism or populism. Some of them move in even stranger orbits. A profile in *Worth* magazine last year spent 11 pages trying to prove that Greenspan was carrying out a secret agenda of free-market fanaticism—unbeknownst to anyone in the U.S. government—based on his youthful acquaintance with Ayn Rand. (That story also dwelt bizarrely on Greenspan's very ordinary physical appearance, making him sound like some sort of cross between Shecky Greene and the Elephant Man.) What these wide-eyed critics have in common is their ignorance of the vast literature on monetary economics and central banking. Granted, it's pretty dry stuff, full of math and pragmatism. But if you read it, you will be convinced that there's nothing all that mysterious, much less *outré,* about the Fed.

Greenspan has grown an amazingly thick skin and pays little attention to the more personal attacks on him. According to people who know him well, if he hears about some piece of journalism that's likely to be upsetting, he just doesn't read it. The only criticism that does bug him is what he sees as hypocrisy, when self-serving people pretend to be disinterested. Example? When Mort Zuckerman, the owner of *U.S. News & World Report* (and other media properties), lambastes the Fed in his personal column for raising interest rates, without reminding readers that his primary business—real estate development—is one of the industries that gain most from inflation.

Alan Greenspan likes to talk in sports metaphors when he's feeling relaxed, so let's hazard one about him: In his ninth year as quarterback of the Federal Reserve, Greenspan is at the height of his powers and the unquestioned leader of the team. He has a near perfect record (though he fumbles once in a while), and he usually does better than the oddsmakers expect him to. He has the look of a winner, and if he were on his way to the playoffs—and you can argue that that's exactly where the Fed is in its own economic season—you would bet on him.

WHAT REMAINS for him to do? One smart move would to be to institutionalize the changes he has wrought by adopting a formal inflation target for monetary policy. Several other nations have done this in recent years, including Canada and Britain, and the Young Turk monetary economists at the Fed like the idea. He could also lobby for a new law sponsored by Senator Connie Mack (R-Florida) that would do much the same thing.

But the real answer to the question, prosaic though it may be, is that Greenspan simply needs to keep doing what he has been doing. Monetary policy may be hard to do and hard to describe, but the basic idea is pretty simple. His first job is to keep the economy growing. A serious 20th-century recession would ruin Greenspan's reputation—though one milder than the last one might be forgiven. The other thing he needs to do is to keep inflation moving down toward 2%—or at the very least, keep it from rising.

Should he be able to do all that, it will be Greenspan's shadow that future historians see when they look back on the *fin-de-siècle* American economy. He will be remembered not only as the best Fed chairman ever, but perhaps as the preeminent central banker of the age.

Only the paranoid survive in an industry where the Cannibal Principle rules. Here's how the CEO of Intel does it.

WHY ANDY GROVE CAN'T STOP

BY BRENT SCHLENDER

EVEN THOUGH it's a glorious Saturday morning and he's coasting downhill astride his jet-black bicycle, Intel Corp. CEO Andy Grove is hard at work. As usual, he's lagging far behind his more athletic wife on one of their weekend treks through the tawny hills above Silicon Valley, and now, for the first time in days, he can really think. His mind, a Brownian motion of ideas, memories, and, of course, worries, floats freely.

Periodically he dwells on what he calls a "concern du jour"— mulling the promotion of a subordinate, or perhaps playing out an imaginary conversation (more likely an argument) with a prominent customer or business partner. Says he: "On my bike rides I can be very eloquent, and since there's nobody to talk back to me, I always come back victorious."

More often, however, he's contemplating the future—not so much what might happen to Intel's sales and stock price, or whether to build yet another billion-dollar chip-fabrication plant, but wider-ranging issues: Why do people watch TV so much? Does it really make sense for phone companies and cable TV companies to invade each other's turf? If personal computers are so damned frustrating, why are people enthralled by them? How come he and Microsoft's Bill Gates and other industry luminaries were blindsided by the sudden popularity of the Internet? Will Hollywood ever come up with something better to offer the digital world than movies, soaps, and sitcoms? Is electronic commerce right around the corner?

You'd think the man in the scarlet crash helmet could use the weekends to just chill. Since Grove became CEO in 1987, Intel's revenues have grown nearly eightfold, to $ 16.2 billion last year, and the chipmaker has leaped from tenth place in its industry to a Herculean No. 1. As builder of the microprocessors that power more than 80% of all personal computers, Intel is on track to ship more than 60 million Pentium chips this year. Wall Street analysts predict that in 1996 Grove's company will continue to grow like a startup, logging about $19.3 billion in sales and reaping $4.1 billion in profits. So promising is Intel's future that Dan Klesken, an analyst at Robertson Stephens & Co., predicts that the chipmaker will hit annual sales of $45 billion by decade's end.

Still, if you think Andy Grove sleeps easy at night, think again. The excitable CEO is just too wired. Not content to exercise a virtual monopoly on the key component of the Digital Age, Grove wants to set the hardware agenda for the entire PC industry and, while he's at it, perhaps the consumer electronics and telecommunications industries as well.

"The PC is it," he says. "We can make it so superb as an entertainment machine, and so vital as a communications medium for both the home and the workplace, that it will battle with TV for people's disposable time." It's a power play Bill Gates might admire— if he were only a bystander. And it could lead Intel to an explosion of growth that could make it one of the most profitable and influential businesses on the planet.

What makes Grove believe in this grandiose scenario is both the steep upward trajectory of semiconductor technology and the fact that the new power users of computerdom aren't techies at all. They're U.S. consumers, who, according to the Electronic Industries Association, last year spent more on PC's than on TVs. These eager newcomers are shelling out big bucks for multimedia bells and whistles to make their machines more entertaining—and multimedia means high-powered chips. Unlike most businesses, which have already invested vast sums in software for older, feebler machines, consumers are free to buy the hottest new boxes. That spells irresistible market opportunity for Grove, who five years ago helped launch the splashy "Intel inside" advertising campaign that made

Intel a household word.

Grove now aims for Intel to define a global standard for consumer computers. He envisions machines that will incorporate, as standard equipment and at much lower cost, all the features of today's best multimedia PCs: crystalline stereo sound, crisp digital video, gymnastic 3-D graphics, rich fax, voice, and data communications. How? The key is to use supercharged Pentium or P6 processors to handle chores that now require additional hardware. As many consumers have learned the hard way, add-ins can cost hundreds of dollars and introduce show-stopping software incompatibilities.

If the plan succeeds, Intel would lord over much more than the multi-billion-dollar PC hardware business; it would also have the upper hand in devising derivatives of the PC that might subsume today's game players, set-top boxes, and even TVs and VCRs.

Already Intel has technologies and products jumping off the drawing board that will accomplish some of these goals: a cable modem that will let PC users tap the Internet or online services via their cable TV lines and download data 1,000 times as fast as via the telephone; another type of modem that lets people simultaneously talk and swap data over a single phone line; PCs disguised as set-top boxes for playing interactive games and controlling cable TV.

Cool stuff, no doubt. But if Grove weren't innately paranoid, he'd still have reason to be wary. While playing to consumers, his grand strategy risks alienating some of Intel's best customers and strategic partners. Its standard designs would turn the PC into even more of a commodity product than it already is, leaving computer makers with fewer ways to eke out a profit.

Though Grove denies it, his strategy also challenges Microsoft's primacy. Grove charges that the Seattle software power doesn't "share the same sense of urgency" to come up with an improved consumer PC. He believes that despite Intel's lucrative 15-year relationship with Microsoft and their fundamental "commonality of purpose," there's room in the business—indeed, a crying need—for a forceful hardware advocate. "The typical PC doesn't push the limits of our microprocessors," he complains. "It's simply not as good as it should be, and that's not good for our customers." Grove maintains that Intel is simply trying to light a fire under Gates to make sure future versions of Windows keep pace with Intel's designs.

A notoriously hands-on manager who for more than 20 years ruled Intel's product-development and manufacturing operations, Grove has dropped just about everything to pursue his dream. These days chief operating officer Craig Barrett, 56, pretty much runs Intel.

Meanwhile, Grove picks the brains of people like DreamWorks SKG's Steven Spielberg and Tele-Communications Inc.'s John Malone, trying to divine how to make PCs more entertaining and better at communicating. He consorts with the young propellerheads who run Intel Architecture Labs, an Oregon skunkworks that he hopes will become the de facto R&D lab for the entire PC industry. Occasionally, he hits the lecture circuit as a demo-toting technology visionary.

One reason Grove is so aggressive is that he believes he has the laws of nature—or at least of the semiconductor industry—on his side. Anyone familiar with the computer business has probably heard of Moore's Law. Coined way back in 1965 by Gordon Moore, an Intel co-founder and still its chairman, this axiom posits that the performance of chip technology, as measured against its price, doubles every 18 months or so. Moore's Law is the main reason computer hardware often seems outdated within months of hitting your desk.

Equally important is a corollary of Moore's Law that explains why the business of building computers is so fierce. Call it the Cannibal Principle. Explains Moore: "The whole point of integrated circuits is to absorb the functions of what previously were discrete electronic components, to incorporate them in a single new chip, and then to give them back for free, or at least for a lot less money than what they cost as individual parts. Thus, semiconductor technology eats everything, and people who oppose it get trampled. I can't think of another technology or industry quite like it."

To Moore, his law and the Cannibal Principle guarantee a wide-open future for the industry he helped create. The 69-year-old chairman, whose 5.6% stake in Intel is worth about $2.6 billion, finds that prospect reassuring. But Grove, whose Intel stake is worth $102 million, remains a worrier. Hence, a powerful third dynamic at Intel—the rule of thumb company wags call Grove's Law. It explains a lot about Intel's notoriously aggressive culture and why the feisty, 59-year-old Hungarian émigré is forever restless. Unlike Moore's elegant theorem, Grove's Law, which the CEO has espoused for decades, is a terse warning: "Only the paranoid survive."

THE EARLY YEARS

L IFE HAS LED Andy Grove to one crossroads after another, and at each instance he has invariably veered onto a riskier, less familiar path. Grove won't divulge much about what must have been the hellish years of his youth in Hungary, other than that he was named András Gróf at his birth in 1936. He lived through the anti-Semitic atrocities of the Nazis and the most oppressive years of Josef Stalin's Soviet domination of Eastern Europe.

He escaped to the West in 1957, arriving later that year at the Brooklyn Navy Yard aboard a musty, recommissioned World War II troopship filled with refugees. "We didn't see the Statue of Liberty or anything," Grove recalls. "They immediately took us by bus to Camp Kilmer, New Jersey, which had been a POW camp during the war. We thought that all the Communist propaganda was true, that America was just another drab, totalitarian state."

Grove moved in with an uncle in the Bronx and enrolled in City College of New York, studying for a degree in chemical engineering. During the summers he worked as a busboy at a resort in the Catskills. A star student whose professors urged him to pursue a Ph.D., Grove applied to the University of California at Berkeley for graduate school, less because of its renown than because he hated the harsh winters in the Northeast.

After earning a doctorate in 1963, Grove probably could have gone on to make a name for himself in academia. But again at a professor's urging, he interviewed for jobs at Bell Laboratories and an intriguing California startup called Fairchild Semiconductor. Recalls Grove: "The choice was very easy: Bell Labs was the place to work back then. So I picked Fairchild."

Among Grove's new bosses were Moore and Robert Noyce, one of two men who independently invented the integrated circuit. Four years later, when Moore and Noyce announced plans to start what would become Intel, Grove was the first to volunteer to join them. "I was supposed to be director of engineering, but there were so few of us that they made me director of operations," he recalls. "My first assignment was to get a post office box so we could get literature describing the equipment we couldn't afford to buy."

The founders quickly learned that Grove was a natural whip cracker. Recalls Moore: "Andy always made it hard for me. I would be all excited that we were under budget or ahead of schedule on a product—and he'd ask why we couldn't do it faster and cheaper. He got very interested in the art of management, and that served us very well." In 1987, Grove was named president and CEO.

"INTEL INSIDE"

FOR YEARS Andy Grove had no use for personal computers, even though Intel owed its livelihood to them. Visitors to his office in the late Eighties would be treated to a salty harangue about how counterintuitive PCs were, how they required users to become experts just to operate them, and how fooling with them was a monumental waste of his time.

That all changed in 1989 when Intel began using electronic mail companywide. Grove had no choice but to deal with his PC every day if he wanted to keep up with what was going on in the company. After Microsoft introduced Windows 3.0 in 1990, using a PC became less of an ordeal. It dawned on Grove that the PC was most useful as a communications medium.

Grove's attitude toward PCs also was mightily influenced by events in the marketplace, particularly by the phenomenal success of the "Intel inside" campaign. By establishing the Intel name in the minds of consumers, the company hoped to dampen sales of "clones" of Intel microprocessors made by Advanced Micro Devices and others. As part of the campaign, Intel asked PC makers to label their machines with a distinctive "Intel inside" logo that echoed the advertising slogan. Not only was Intel able to hold the high ground against its rivals, but customer feedback revealed as well that regular consumers, not just the techies, really did care what made their PCs tick.

Grove, who was becoming a typical PC user himself, also had a disquieting insight. He realized it didn't matter how zippy Intel's microprocessors were because PCs didn't make full use of their capabilities. To his frustration, this seemed beyond Intel's power to fix: The chips and other components of the PCs relied completely on Microsoft's operating-system software to tell them what to do. And even though multimedia was beginning to attract consumers' interest, Microsoft, loath to maroon business customers who owned older, dumber machines, had been slow to add the code necessary to make the newer PCs better at handling sound, video, and graphics.

Savvy computer users could add these features themselves, of course, by installing multimedia circuits, software, and peripheral devices. But the market for those extras quickly became fragmented. That, in turn, has caused software developers to get bogged down designing their games and other flashy programs to anticipate all the possible competing hardware variations, many of which are incompatible. Fumes Grove: "With no common platform to target, applications developers haven't been able to be as creative as they could be. That deprives PC users of what their machines are capable of."

Grove thinks hot new applications will come from two quarters—communications and digital entertainment—and that some of the best applications will combine the two. Intel is hard at work trying to create trendsetting offerings of its own.

"My personal obsession is the popularization of computer communications," says Grove. For nearly a decade, he has championed the idea of digital video for the PC. Grove is also a big promoter of cable modems in the home. Hooked to a cable system and supplemented with a standard telephone line that the consumer uses to send requests and messages back to the cable provider, a cable modem makes possible what techies call rich interactivity. Translation: the ability to instantly receive photographs, illustrated documents, CD-quality sound, and ultimately digital video clips.

Says Grove: "The cable modem is our answer to the bandwidth problem. Right now, using the Internet is like reading a magazine where you can turn the page only once every 30 seconds. With higher bandwidth it can be more like every three seconds. We know it could be big, because when we tried to reposition the trial from one set of customers to another, people started freaking. They didn't want to have it taken away." Commercial versions of the technology probably won't appear for a couple of years.

Grove also is intrigued by the prospect of more sophisticated computer entertainment, but he's less sure what form it will take. "It's like a soapy elephant—slippery and big. The problem is that neither we nor the people in Hollywood seem to know what to do with digital media. Whoever figures it out will have the key to pulling people away from their television sets."

Having spent days each month hobnobbing with Hollywood types, though, Grove concludes that Hollywood and Silicon Valley are worlds apart: "Oh, boy, we don't even have a common language. We don't have common shared experiences. It's not a matter of trust or interest. We can talk for hours, but at the end of it we don't understand each other or the possibilities any better than before. It really bothers me."

The thread running through all these strategies is that Grove and Intel are focusing on the needs and desires of PC users rather than on Intel's more direct customers, the PC makers. Not even the scorching experience of the Pentium fiasco has deterred Grove from courting consumers directly. In that episode, Grove at first denied that a generation of flawed Pentiums could go haywire on typical users. But after a hailstorm of criticism, he backed down and offered to replace the arithmetically challenged chips free. Intel reserved $475 million to cover potential costs, but few customers have asked for new chips. Today the Pentium brand seems stronger than ever, especially among buyers of home PCs.

A S HARD-BOILED as he seems, Grove has an idealistic streak. Just ask him what businessman influences him the most. While Bill Gates names management genius Alfred P. Sloan, the longtime General Motors CEO, as his inspiration, Grove points to—get ready—Steve Jobs: "Look at his history. He was the first to see what the PC was about. The first to recognize the value of the laser printer, the graphical user interface, and object-oriented software, which will become very important sooner or later. With Pixar, his computer-animated movie and game company, he's pioneering real digital entertainment. Not bad for 41 years old. True, he made a few mistakes along the way, but he continues to believe in his own technological vision."

Grove seems to enjoy being in the limelight after laboring so long in the wings while Noyce and Moore held center stage. He enjoys his role as an industry advocate and spokesman too. He's visited Washington to put in his two cents about how to deregulate the telecommunications industry. (The more diverse an industry, the better, he opines.) With all this on his plate, plus his duties at Intel, he still finds time to work on his third book, about managing change.

But Gordon Moore, the business associate who knows him best, says that while Grove seems to have mellowed a bit, he doubts that the CEO has it in him to relax. Says Moore: "In the end, thank God, it doesn't really matter how well things are going at Intel. Grove's Law will always keep Andy awake nights."

*In this market, Fidelity and Schwab get the headlines,
but unheralded Merrill is thriving. Dan Tully intends for the profits
to keep rolling in, whatever the market does.*

DAN TULLY: HOW TO BULL AHEAD

BY SHAWN TULLY

O N WALL STREET'S sloppy playing field, no team has made a more surprising comeback in blocking, in tackling, and most important, in scoring than Merrill Lynch. What was once a fumbling squad of beefy, slow-footed dullards has become a lean powerhouse consistently running up big-point totals against hapless opponents.

So it's not surprising that at the head of this team stands Daniel Tully, a great admirer of Penn State football legend Joe Paterno. Tully, a street kid from Queens now transformed into a burly, snow-topped CEO, likes to praise pal Paterno for exalting dogged team-work over individuality. He loves that Paterno doesn't let his Lions wear nametags on their jerseys or stars on their helmets, and would strangle any smart-ass who pranced to celebrate a touchdown. For Tully, who downs lasagna at Paterno's regular postgame party, business is like a Penn State charge, a mighty human wedge that—play after play—grinds out three yards and a cloud of dust.

Tully is the Paterno of Wall Street. In a field full of hot dogs, he's developed a winning formula based on Marine-like discipline and no-frills cooperation. And it works. Merrill's total client assets grew 24% in 1995, to $703 billion, dwarfing not just Charles Schwab ($182 billion) but even much vaunted Fidelity ($548 billion).

It has a galaxy of 160 in-house mutual funds covering everything from Asian stocks to junk bonds. It perpetually combats Goldman Sachs for first place in equity underwriting, and it trades an astounding 11% of the shares on the big board and Amex.

All that's the domain of Dan Tully, who's so far from being a silk-stocking manager that he once warned his traders that if they broke his rules, he'd break their legs.

Tully's not just set on being the biggest. He's intent on revolutionizing what a brokerage firm can do for you. Dan Tully wants to reorder the sloppy financial lives of the Great Disorganized Elite. America's yuppies, now approaching both age 50 and success, will pay a premium price for sage financial guidance they can't easily get from a Schwab, he reckons. In place of the old "have I got a stock for you" brokers, Tully is training a new generation of soft-sell advisers to restructure your portfolio, plan your estate, and whip up minor miracles, like an interest-only mortgage for your new ski chalet.

Along the way, he makes solid profits in good times and bad. Credit Tully for tackling bloated pay and banishing excessive risk taking, two problems the slick investment banker types either don't acknowledge or can't seem to solve.

In a world of Gordon Gekko look-alikes, it's hard to imagine a more unlikely crew of reformers. A homespun extrovert, Tully wears corny neckties and likes to hand out tiny lapel pins depicting the Merrill bull to everyone from clerks to finance ministers. He didn't leave Merrill's sales office in Stamford, Connecticut, till age 44. Like Tully and David Komansky, his president, many of Merrill's top people are ex-stockbrokers who began knocking on doors in the suburbs. The brass boast few MBAs and no trophy wives. They'd cheer for the Knicks, Budweiser in hand, as soon as serve on the boards of opera or ballet companies. It's their ball field camaraderie that impresses Paterno: "They're just regular street guys. Tully does what I do in coaching: He's great at getting a lot of people to share the same values."

Tully inherited a one-of-a-kind franchise. Most firms specialize, either in institutional business, catering to corporations, governments, and big investors like pension funds—Morgan Stanley, for example—or in selling stocks, bonds, and mutual funds to the broad public, a Schwab, say, or a Fidelity. Merrill Lynch not only straddles the two worlds but dominates them both. Taking stocks and bonds together, Merrill is the world's largest underwriter, and it boasts the largest sales force in the business, blanketing America with 13,000 brokers serving 4.5 million households.

But for Tully, bigness isn't an end in itself; generating a strong, stable stream of profits is—whatever the market conditions. That's a radical change from Merrill's boom-to-bust tradition. High in animal spirits, Merrill Lynch always excelled at growing. But wayward expenses waxed as fast as revenues. Those heavy costs made Merrill's bottom line vulnerable to the wrenching ups and downs in the securities markets.

"GOOD MANAGEMENT IS DISCIPLINE, PROCEDURES, AND CONTROLS."

TULLY'S GAME PLAN is twofold. First, he's taming Merrill's once-wanton fixed costs. A case in point is rent, a huge expense item for brokerage firms. By consolidating a dozen computer centers into two and moving back-office staff from expensive places like New York City to Jersey City, Denver, and Jacksonville, Tully has actually cut real estate costs by $25 million since 1991. In the same period, he's added only about 7% more brokers, squeezing the new recruits into existing offices and demanding that each broker handle far more business.

Second, Tully is rapidly raising revenues, but he's pushing for a business mix that's stable, not volatile.

That's no easy task. By its very nature the securities business is highly cyclical, driven by unpredictables like interest rates, stock prices, and the economic outlook. That's the reason investors penalize the stocks of Wall Street firms with low P/E multiples. The jolts are especially severe in the institutional business. At Merrill, investment banking revenues soared in 1993 as companies floated stock to expand their businesses and refinanced expensive debt from the 1980s; they slipped 32% in 1994, then rose slightly last year. Result: a shifting plank under earnings.

For Tully the solution is to balance the profitable but erratic institutional wing with steady revenues from retail. Then, even in a down year for investment banking, Merrill can post solid profits. When the institutional side prospers, earnings explode. To provide the ballast, Tully is building an ever-rising mountain of assets in brokerage accounts and mutual funds. Those assets generate two types of revenue. The first is Merrill's staple: up-front, one-time commissions from selling stocks, bonds, and mutual funds. The second is the fabric for its future: fees—chiefly from managing clients' money—that pour in year after year. Customers pay Merrill annual or monthly charges for money market funds, 401(k) plans, and trust accounts. The richest source of fees is Merrill's panoply of proprietary mutual funds, into which its clients have funneled $181 billion. Merrill and its brokers divide a 4% or 5% commission for selling a fund; then the firm charges an average annual fee of 0.5% or so for managing it.

Unlike the tumult in investment banking, the flow of fees and commissions is fairly predictable. Typically, Merrill can count on collecting almost 1% on its total client assets, or about $6 billion last year. And Merrill is great at growing that hoard.

The big growth for Merrill is an ever-increasing annuity of $3 billion in fees. That came to 30% of its last year's net revenues, enough to cover about two-thirds of its fixed costs. "There's great comfort in that," sighs Tully. As a result Merrill's earnings are not only bigger but also less wobbly. In 1995, for example, strong growth in fees helped compensate for a rocky start in investment banking. Consequently Merrill earned $1.1 billion on net revenues of $10.3 billion, posting pretax margins of 17.5% and a strong 20% return on equity.

To Tully's chagrin, the market hasn't taken much note. Since Tully took charge in 1992, the stock has jumped more than 120%, to around $60 a share, but Merrill still sells at a lackluster ten times earnings, about the same as its more erratic competitors like Salomon. Even when Merrill announced a fourth-quarter profit surge, its stock actually dropped half a point. Tully has a lot at stake; he himself owns nearly $30 million in Merrill stock and options on 1.7 million shares. (He has never sold as much as one share of Merrill stock.)

So he sees a matchless opportunity to hoist its price by further fattening his pet cushion, fee income. By the year 2000, Tully wants $1 trillion in client assets, up over 42% from the current $703 billion, and enough to generate fees that would cover every dime in fixed costs, like salaries, rent, telephones, and computers.

If that comes to pass, on the day that Merrill opens for business in the next century, every dollar from commissions or investment banking, after bonuses, will drop straight to pretax income.

"THE KEY WAS DEVELOPING 12 DAN TULLYS, THEN 48."

THERE'S NO BETTER WAY to grasp the new Merrill than to understand Dan Tully's blend of smooth blarney and fiery will, flamboyant salesmanship and accounting rigor. Son of a steamfitter, Tully grew up in the tough neighborhood of Woodside, in Queens, New York, a working-class mosaic of Irish and Jews, blacks and Italians. In his teens he spent evenings as a copy boy for the *Daily News*, riding the subways to deliver ads from stores in Brooklyn, say, to the offices in midtown Manhattan, reading his schoolbooks between stops. The system worked so well that the E train became his study-hall-on-wheels. The family's cramped, noisy apartment made it impossible to do homework there. So on weekends Dan studied underground all day, shuttling from Queens to the Bronx and back again.

On the streets of Queens, his temper and tenacity earned him the sobriquet "Donkey Dan." Tully parlayed his fast fists and tart tongue into a powerful role: the picker who chose a stickball team from kids on the street. Usually there was such a throng of candidates that only half could play. It was then that Tully discovered the rewards of doing favors. "I'd often choose a kid who couldn't hit but hadn't played in a few days," says Tully. "Later on you might need that guy to help you with your math or take your place as an altar boy. But I also loved to win."

Tully retains that hunger. His intensity comes wrapped in flamboyant Irish American. His ancestors, he proudly announces, hail from a hamlet appropriately named Moneygall. His idea of a great vacation is squiring his wife and 16 children, in-laws, and grandchildren around Ireland in a special van. Tully greets friends and customers with a broad comic brogue and has been known to croon "Danny Boy" to a roomful of brokers. Seated in his Wall Street office adorned with a giant emerald rug, he dashes off memos with a trademark green felt-tip pen. Tully, who lives in a rambling, converted monastery on the Connecticut waterfront, loves nothing more than taking the dinghy out for fishing on weekends, accompanied by his sons and, on special occasions, a bottle of champagne.

Heading up a Merrill branch office, the equivalent of running a small business, helped forge Tully's approach to management. Significantly, he started in 1955 not as a salesman but a numbers man. An accounting major at St. John's University, Tully soon became the operations manager of the Stamford office, monitoring budgets and margin accounts. There he absorbed the importance of watching expenses. "Even in a branch, you couldn't grow your way out of a cost problem," he says. Eyeing the big money in sales, Tully switched to broker, then rose to office manager. Each month he prominently displayed the firmwide ranking of brokers by revenues. He'd get rid of anyone who consistently finished in the bottom quartile.

"How would your kids feel if I sent their father home with a bad report card?" he chided his brokers.

Tully prodded brokers to cast themselves in his image: a combination of workhorse who arrived at his desk at 7 A.M. and a pillar of the community who served on everything from the Chamber of Commerce to hospital boards. "The key," he says, "was developing 12 Dan Tullys, then 48 Dan Tullys."

In Stamford, Tully learned the Paterno lesson: It's solid, consistent practices—in controlling costs and generating sales—that win. "More and more companies think good management is being mean-spirited," he says. "That's wrong. It's really being tough-minded. Good management is discipline, procedures, and controls."

"BREAK MY RULES, I'LL BREAK YOUR LEGS."

RECOGNIZING TULLY'S TALENTS, CEO Donald Regan practically dynamited the 44-year-old out of Stamford in 1976 to head retail marketing. "I finally decided I had to compete, or end up reporting to people who should have reported to me," says Tully, who helped roll out Regan's wildly successful Cash Management Account. In 1985, CEO William Schreyer appointed Tully president. They formed a classic team: Schreyer was the visionary, Tully the operating man. But it took the wrenching year of 1987 to galvanize their partnership. First, a single Merrill trader lost $377 million by taking huge, high-risk positions in mortgage-backed securities. Schreyer calls the explosion "my Chernobyl."

Tully became the crisis manager, operating from a conference room near the trading floor. He found an appalling lack of controls. Each trading desk had its own homemade risk-management system. But what most nettled Tully was runaway arrogance. A group of traders, some of them from the department that suffered the loss, demanded that Tully assure them the disaster wouldn't affect their bonuses. Tully was livid. "I told them, 'This is not gambling. I'm setting up parameters here. If you go outside them, I'll break your legs.'"

To prevent another meltdown, Tully established a risk-management department that's become a model for Wall Street firms. The group reports not to the heads of the trading desks but to the president. The unit sets standards and monitors risk in every security. If it deems a position poorly hedged, it can order the trading desk to unwind it. As a result, Merrill hasn't suffered a major trading loss in almost a decade. Says Schreyer: "If I had any doubts about Dan's ability to replace me, they were totally erased by the way he handled the crisis."

After a second earthquake, the trauma of October 1987, Schreyer and Tully adroitly sidestepped a disaster and helped to hobble a competitor, in one deft stroke. In late 1987, a stricken E.F. Hutton had to put itself up for sale. Shearson, then owned by American Express, desperately wanted Hutton in order to become almost as big as Merrill Lynch. Recalls Tully: "We were the old, stodgy battleship, and Shearson was the destroyer coming up the Hudson." But Tully worried that Hutton came with dicey accounting methods and looming legal liabilities. He and Schreyer quickly decided not to bid. Tully told Hutton nothing until hours before the deadline, leaving the clear impression that Merrill would make an offer. Shearson put in the solo bid for Hutton—a fat one billion. A year later Shearson took a $165 million charge because of Hutton, and it continued to take write-downs in 1990.

The crash—and the two-year chill that followed for Merrill— prodded Schreyer and Tully to put shareholders first. By 1990 ROE had dropped so low that "my kids could have done a better job running the company," Tully recalls. That's when they set the goal that stands to this day: an average return on equity of at least 15%.

In the process, Tully and Schreyer tackled one of the perennial problems at Wall Street firms: Investment bankers and traders make huge amounts, whether shareholders win or lose. Tully helped design a formula that, like the risk-management system, is a path breaker on Wall Street. Today traders and investment bankers get their bonuses from a single pool tied to ROE and profit. Thus, bonuses for an investment banker with a salary of $200,000 could reach $800,000 or more, or fall to a sliver of that. "A lot of firms haven't done it, and they've paid the price," says Tully. "Shame on them."

DRIVING STRAIGHT TOWARD THE FUTURE

NO MATTER how tightly Tully controls costs, he knows that he'll never compete with a Schwab on price. Merrill Lynch supports not only an expensive branch network but a $200 million budget for research as well. By contrast, the discounters are stripped-down outfits that sell mainly through 800 numbers and don't employ analysts. Hence, they can sell stocks and bonds for a lot less than Merrill. But Merrill is striving to create a one-stop shop that untangles a well-to-do client's scrambled financial profile from retirement savings to mortgages, then provides an array of mutual funds, insurance products, trust accounts, and loans to put the picture in order. The advice and planning, Tully figures, will enable Merrill to keep charging rich prices for its products.

There's already a measure of competition offering similar services, and it's bound to multiply. But for its Cadillac service, Merrill Lynch isn't courting the masses. Instead, it's aiming at a narrow segment, the wealthy and near-wealthy. The target is "priority households" with $250,000 to $5 million in liquid assets: families headed by executives, doctors, lawyers, entrepreneurs, all too busy making money to manage it—or retirees who'd rather fish and travel than pick mutual funds.

It's no wonder Merrill covets the well-heeled. Its 534,000 priority households—20% of its total customers—generate 80% of its brokerage revenues. The big money is in the hands of people over 50. Fortunately for Merrill, 36 million baby-boomers lugging a trove of savings will cross that milestone by 2005.

As Merrill hands its brokers more new resources, it remains heavy-handed in making sure those brokers stay loyal. It requires new recruits to sign a draconian agreement pledging that if they leave Merrill, they won't contact their clients for a year. When a broker leaves, says Merrill, the firm typically keeps 60% of his accounts. That's extraordinary; usually brokers take their clients along. "It's a dirty little secret," says an attorney who represents ex-Merrill brokers, "but a brilliant strategy."

Tully is aiming as well to establish the firm at the top of the institutional business. By 2005, he wants trading and investment banking to generate $16 billion in revenue (in 1995 it was $3.8 billion).

BUT MERRILL has a weakness. It's still struggling in one of the most lucrative aspects of the business—advising corporations on mergers and acquisitions. Merrill is especially weak with the FORTUNE 200. Morgan Stanley and Goldman Sachs have spent decades establishing close relationships with the CEOs of companies like Ford and GM. "We don't have the school ties," grouses Tully. What's more, Merrill rarely raids other firms for star investment bankers.

Yet at raising money for corporations, Merrill is a titan. Because Merrill Lynch trades 13% of the shares in Wal-Mart, 11% in Chrysler, and 12% in Goodyear, it's a logical choice for someone seeking an underwriter. Its institutional sales force knows just who's buying and selling the stock, and why. Corporations rely on Merrill to place their shares with the big buyers, at the best prices. Another strength is its vast retail distribution. That appeals strongly to Callaway Golf, which Merrill took public in 1992. "If you want your stock substantially held by both the public and institutions, Merrill is tops," says CEO Ely Callaway. "They treated us like IBM." The computer giant likes Merrill too: "If there's a retail component to a deal," says its former CFO Jerome York, "you must use Merrill Lynch."

Roger Enrico, PepsiCo's new CEO, has traveled a career path as curious as they come. But then, he says, "I think 'career path' are the two worst words invented."

ROGER ENRICO: PEPSICO'S NEW GENERATION

BY PATRICIA SELLERS

ROGER ENRICO has done about everything you're not supposed to do to reach the top. The son of a small-town factory foreman, he never earned an MBA. He's drifted around PepsiCo, running a huge business, then a smaller one, then detaching himself altogether from operating management to become a sort of roving leadership guru. Nevertheless, one day in late January, PepsiCo Chief Executive Wayne Calloway, who is suffering from prostate cancer, asked Enrico to take over as CEO. Enrico didn't say yes. The proposition rattled inside Enrico's head for two full weeks.

"He's a reluctant debutante," says a close friend of PepsiCo's new man at the top. Another observer, Jeff Campbell, who used to be senior vice president of marketing at Pepsi-Cola, says, "It's like the Republican Party going to Colin Powell and saying, 'We need you to save the country from Pat Buchanan. You gotta do it.'" Campbell figures, "Roger Enrico's becoming CEO is great for PepsiCo. He's the embodiment of what Pepsi is supposed to be—aggressive, creative, in your face on a global scale, really tough. He's a stud."

The news that Enrico, 51, was Pepsi's choice to lead a new generation of management helped the company's stock market value bubble up by $2 billion the day after it was announced. How will Enrico change PepsiCo? Should we get set for Cola Wars II? Might he forge some big global venture to strengthen the company abroad, where lie the real profit margins and where Pepsi gets outsold by Coke three to one? Will he spin off PepsiCo's restaurants—Pizza Hut, Taco Bell, and KFC, all relatively low-return businesses? Some people believe that Enrico will be an interim CEO, a relief pitcher closing Calloway's game while a trio of PepsiCo all-stars—Craig Weatherup, Chris Sinclair, and Steve Reinemund—wait on the bench. Is the new boss in for the whole season? Who is Roger Enrico?

"I WANT PEOPLE TO WORK ON THE LEFT SIDE OF THE DECIMAL POINT."

PEPSICO'S NEW CEO is broad-minded, mercurial, hyperactive. Usually he's effective. Sometimes he's dangerous. Always he's surprising. "Big changes to big things is the way you build a business," Enrico says. "The CEO's role is to articulate that message, because change is unsettling. Change is risky. Change is going to result in failure as well as success. The CEO has to provide a safety net."

Personally, he tends to perform without one. Mr. Cola Wars during the Eighties, Enrico is regularly given credit for instigating the Pepsi Challenge. Actually, he's the guy who axed it. Soon after he became president of Pepsi-Cola USA at age 38, Enrico decided that the celebrated marketing campaign—Pepsi vs. Coke taste tests, which you-know-who typically won—was tired. He changed the strategy: Without consulting his superiors, he paid Michael Jackson $5 million, ushering in the age of celebrity soft drink endorsements. Some people thought Enrico was burning money (Jacko's hair got torched instead, remember?), but it turned out to be a great time for Pepsi. Enrico positioned the brand as the hip,cutting-edge alternative to Coke. Coca-Cola struck back with New Coke.

Enrico has blown a few too, though not on the scale of New Coke. "Madonna was a mistake," he says. He put the Material Girl in a commercial that did well overseas but so offended religious groups in the U.S. that it aired only once. Still, Enrico never shrinks from the big idea. "So many of us in business tend to overcomplicate things, making every single component right, squeezing out the last drop of profit," he says. "Sure, it's important to run a business smoothly. That's the art of management. But 'management' means working on the right side of the decimal point. I want people to work on the left side of the decimal point. That means taking chances."

CHALLENGE EVERYTHING; ASSUME NOTHING.

AUDACITY HAS REWARDED Enrico, but there's plenty more to his success. In 24 years at PepsiCo, he has rejuvenated each division—drinks, snacks, and recently restaurants. Every time, he simplifies the business, then passionately rallies supporters. "Roger is at once one of the warmest and most personable people, and so cold," says a former PepsiCo executive. "His strength is his ability to charm you and get you on his side, and also dispassionately evaluate a business and fix it. He never gets sucked into the culture, the history of a business. So he's not afraid to cut the fat, storm ahead, reorganize, shut the factory, kill the product line. He's agile and he's cunning."

He challenges everything and assumes nothing. For example, when Enrico took charge at PepsiCo's Frito-Lay division five years ago, the numbers looked fine. But Enrico smelled something rotten at the food company. Profits were rising, it turned out, because management was pumping up prices on Doritos and other snacks. Frito was scrimping on product quality. Enrico slashed costs, firing 1,700 workers and sweeping out management. He promised the employees who remained that he would funnel every penny of savings into making Frito grow.

"There's not a single thing that PepsiCo makes that anybody needs," he told the workers. To win back consumers, he lowered prices, cranked up product introductions, and spent heavily on fresh ads. He focused everyone on a single competitor, Eagle Snacks. Rubber chickens with pasted-on eagle wings hung, corpselike, around the factories. "You can't shadow-box your way to victory," says the veteran cola warrior.

Enrico did win the snack war, belatedly. This past February, three years after Enrico exited Frito, Anheuser-Busch, Eagle's owner, gave up on snacks.

Focused as Enrico is when he's fixing a business, he is astoundingly haphazard in managing his career. "That's quite correct," he says "I think 'career path' are the two worst words invented," he explains. "I've always believed you ought to go with the flow. Be a bit fatalistic. Don't overprogram yourself. A career adventure is the better way to think about life. You should do what seems exciting, even if there's a lot of perceived risk."

Enrico has led a wayward life since he was a kid in Chisholm, Minnesota, a small town in the Mesabi Range. As he recalls in his memoir, he wanted to be an actor at first, an idea that was unsettling to his father, a maintenance foreman in a taconite processing plant. When young Roger volunteered for John Kennedy's presidential campaign, he caught the political bug. It didn't last. He got his first job in the local soft drink bottling plant, but he never envisioned pushing pop for a living. After high school—Enrico was smart, not brilliant—he had no clue where to go. He simply wanted to get away from Minnesota. Babson College in Massachusetts offered him a full scholarship, and he was off.

Enrico sped through Babson in three years. Running his fraternity and editing the college yearbook, he never thought much about his future. He knew he was people-oriented, and he figured, "Why not personnel?" An opening at General Mills brought him back to Minnesota, where his high school sweetheart, Rosemary Margo, was living. But he decided the personnel department was boring; he wanted to be in the action. He didn't have an MBA, though, so he applied to business school. He was accepted, but at the last minute he was seduced by advertising: "Join the Navy and see the world." Enrico quit General Mills and enlisted.

In the Navy officer candidate program, he figured he'd soon be riding a ship across the ocean. But he flunked the Navy's test for colorblindness. Dreading a tour of office duty, he volunteered for Vietnam. This was 1967. Enrico, 23, got stationed in the northernmost part of South Vietnam. His assignment was to help transport millions of gallons of fuel from unreliable sources to hundreds of destinations. Mortars, rockets, and Viet Cong sabotage made the job terribly difficult. Enrico had a commander—Bill Aldenderfer, "the Supply Corps version of Rambo," he says—who taught him to break rules and pass on paperwork to get the job done. Enrico wrote that this was his first lesson in "delivering precious liquids to his consumers."

After Vietnam, Enrico returned to General Mills. He snagged a job in brand management, and he loved it. But he felt that he was being passed over for raises simply because he didn't have an MBA. So he plucked the names of headhunters out of the yellow pages and sent out his résumé. PepsiCo's Frito-Lay division, in Dallas, offered him a position. He and Rosemary, by now his wife, hesitated—because Kennedy had been shot there. But when Enrico took his first trip to Texas, he sensed that Dallas and Frito both were set to boom. So he began his PepsiCo career as a 27-year-old associate brand manager for a tiny brand of onion-flavored snacks, Funyuns.

Frito was a tough, unbureaucratic boot camp, and Enrico fit in perfectly. At 31 he was offered the presidency of PepsiCo Foods Japan. "People thought I was crazy to go to Japan, because the business was terrible," says Enrico. "And I didn't turn it around. I never saw Japan as a steppingstone. I saw it as a fabulous life learning experience."

While the Japanese operation lost money under Enrico, PepsiCo's top brass deemed that market too perplexing to be a fair test of managerial skill. So they moved him to the company's beverage division, where he served in Brazil and was boss to Sergio Zyman, now Coke's marketing honcho. He then went to the U.S., and thrived. John Sculley, Pepsi-Cola's president at the time, prized Enrico for his brash point of view on marketing issues. And when Sculley left Pepsi for Apple Computer, Enrico was appointed his successor.

The Eighties seemed to be a fabulous stretch for Enrico—he was the Cola King, clinking glasses with Michael and Madonna. But a couple of epiphanies dampened his desire. First, he got scorched in the spotlight surrounding his 1986 book, *The Other Guy Blinked: How Pepsi Won the Cola Wars*. The title refers to Coke's decision to change its formula after 99 years. As things turned out, *The Other*

Guy Kicked My Butt might have been a more accurate title. Anyway, Enrico's book got panned. He was branded an egomaniac. "I shouldn't have done the book," he says. "We did the book to sell Pepsi. It became a personal publicity thing. Now I'm really sensitive to not cross over the line." During the past decade Enrico has done only a handful of interviews. He rarely talks to the press about himself.

Also, there was the heart attack. Enrico had a coronary in 1990—in Turkey, during one of his many whirlwind tours for Pepsi-Cola. "I don't feel that my heart attack was such a dramatic life experience," he says. "It was a mild thing. But I suppose there has been some influence, subliminally." He quit smoking. And ever since the heart attack, Enrico has seemed less certain than ever what to do with the rest of his life.

For example, five years ago, after heading worldwide beverages, he jumped back to Frito-Lay, to run a much smaller business. Wayne Calloway says, "People outside PepsiCo were wondering, 'What happened to Enrico? Who has Roger made mad?'" The retiring chief executive puts Enrico's career in perspective: "At PepsiCo, we just don't have clear career paths. We never have. It's a little confusing when people join us, after they've read all sorts of books about career paths. Or they've been at other companies where you move from brand manager to group brand manager to vice president of marketing. We don't think that kind of progression makes for broad, freethinking leaders."

THE IRREPRESSIBLE MR. FIXIT TAKES THE PEPSI CHALLENGE.

ENRICO'S WEIRDEST career move—mystifying even to some Pepsi people—came in 1993. He quit operations and decided to be teacher/coach to the company's hotshot young managers. Enrico says that his mentor, Don Kendall, who was PepsiCo's CEO for 21 years before Calloway, called him frequently and hounded him, asking, "Are you working? What are you doing, Roger? Why does this make sense from your perspective?" Says Kendall, who is 75 and a sort of ambassador-at-large for PepsiCo: "I've needled the hell out of him." Enrico laughs and says, "Once Don understood what I was doing, I think he still thought I was a little flaky. But I had this idea that we should be doing a whole lot more to accelerate the development of our high-potential people. And I could contribute more to PepsiCo doing this than I could running a business on a day-to-day basis."

Enrico relished his time off the firing line, taking PepsiCo's young studs to offsite retreats. It was a brief vacation. Calloway asked Enrico in the summer of 1994 to take charge of the restaurants. Taco Bell was striking out. Pizza Hut was suffering. KFC wasn't doing any better. A friend says he didn't like going back into the pressure cooker, though Enrico says, "I didn't hate it when I got into restaurants." Once again he was an irrepressible Mr. Fix-It. Enrico decided that PepsiCo had been investing too much money in its restaurants, and he overhauled the strategy—more franchising, à la McDonald's. Big ideas in marketing, like stuffed-crust pizza, revived Pepsi's largest chain, Pizza Hut. Wall Streeters say the ongoing restaurant-division turnaround is the No. 1 reason for the recent rise in PepsiCo's stock.

Everything seemed to be humming along. Then, a couple of months ago, Calloway said to Enrico, "The time's come. Are you ready?" Calloway, 60, was getting sicker. "I needed more time to take on the challenge of cancer," says Calloway, who headed PepsiCo for ten years. When he asked Enrico to become PepsiCo's new CEO, Enrico replied, "Well, that's pretty daunting." Calloway urged him: "Think about the challenge, what it takes, the personal commitment, the joy and fun, the impact you can have. Roger, you should think of this in terms of how proud you'll be."

Why didn't Enrico want to be CEO? "It was never something I lusted for," he says. People who know Enrico intimately say this is the truth. A big consideration for Enrico was lifestyle. He and Rosemary really liked living in Dallas, and they treasured their escapes to Grand Cayman, a 22-mile sliver of sand south of Cuba. Enrico scuba-dives there. "It's another world to me," he says. "It's fascinating and extraordinarily peaceful. Time is suspended. I find it energizing in a cocoony type of way. When you're out there against a 6,000-foot wall, it's like being in outer space." Adds Pepsi ad veteran Alan Pottasch, who taught Enrico to dive: "More than most people, Roger has a disdain for well-traversed areas, where the tourists go."

Enrico also owns a ranch in Montana. He and Rosemary, whose one son, Aaron, is 24, simply didn't want to move back East near PepsiCo's suburban New York City headquarters. "The main question inside my head," says Enrico, "was whether I felt comfortable with an open-ended commitment—to be CEO for an indefinite period of time, until you get the corporation positioned in the right way for many years of growth after you're gone." He says, "In the wee hours of the night, I decided it's the right thing to do."

Investors are wondering: Will Enrico unload PepsiCo's 28,000-plus restaurants? They don't seem to fit well in the PepsiCo portfolio, and they generate much lower returns than snacks and soft drinks. They also require lots of capital. "A spinoff of the restaurants is on my radar screen because people keep asking me about it," says Enrico, smiling. "But it isn't in my consideration set." He savors international opportunities. In Asia, for example, PepsiCo has over 2,000 eateries. Its typical unit there brings in more than twice the revenues of its average outlet in the U.S. "On a global scale, no question, McDonald's is a better operator than we are," says Enrico. "But there's no reason that we can't do internationally what McDonald's has done."

PepsiCo's overall financial recipe is changing significantly. Since Enrico determined that restaurants eat too much of PepsiCo's capital, management has decided to feed more money to the snack division. "In the snack-food business, there is no Coke," says Enrico, who adores a rivalry but doesn't mind a rout, either. During the next few years, he's expected to spend billions to spread Doritos and Fritos and Cheetos around the globe.

Enrico doesn't anticipate earthshaking acquisitions or global ventures. But he needs to do something to strengthen Pepsi-Cola abroad. The profits Pepsi earns from selling drinks outside North America are less than 7% of revenues. Coke's international margin: about 30%. "Our margin is low because we're making big-time investments," says Enrico. "As they pay off, the margins will come up smartly." He won't sit still in the meantime. Enrico says he might overhaul PepsiCo's organizational structure. Currently, in snacks and beverages, domestic and international operations are run separately, each with its own CEO, marketers, and finance people. In a global corporation, which PepsiCo is supposed to be, does this setup make sense? "I don't know where we'll come out on this question," Enrico says.

EXPECT MAJOR management changes. The same day Enrico got appointed CEO, three people were promoted to PepsiCo's board of directors: Chris Sinclair, the international snack and beverage boss; Craig Weatherup, who runs Pepsi-Cola North America; and Steve Reinemund, the chief enchilada at Frito-Lay. "I hope we'll be the most powerful leadership team in American business," says Enrico.

Once Enrico gets his team aligned, a big question will be, How long is Roger in the job? "No way more than three years," says a close friend, who believes Enrico might move on to a position in the entertainment industry or perhaps teach at a university. "That's dead wrong," says Enrico. "I recognize this job is an open-ended commitment. I hope I have the wisdom not to shortchange PepsiCo. Or to stay too long."

Shareholders should hope he stays a good while. But what can anyone know about Roger Enrico, except that he'll surprise once again?

Critics once called for his head. Now Citi's boss is fully vindicated and pushing hard to create "a global growth company."

CITICORP: JOHN REED'S SECOND ACT

BY CAROL J. LOOMIS

THERE IS A DRAMA in two acts that plays out time and again in the affairs of corporations. First, poor management drives a company into deep trouble and its stock into ruin. Next, new management swoops in and, with purpose and resolve, begins the long haul of bringing the company back. At that turnaround moment, unsensed though it is by most investors, there arises a terrific stock market opportunity.

So it has been at Citicorp, with one perverse twist. It was CEO John Shepard Reed who dug the company into trouble in the late 1980s and early 1990s, and it is the same Reed, now 57, who has brought Citi back to a smashing recovery. From the disastrous days of 1991, when Citi lost $457 million, wallowed in bad real estate loans, and fought off suspicions that it might actually fail, the company has climbed to a 1995 profit of $3.5 billion and a return on equity of nearly 18%. The dollars earned were the best ever not just for Citi but for any U.S. bank.

As for the stock, you could have bought it at $8.50 a share in December 1991, and you could have sold it for ten times that in this year. You might even have sold it to Citicorp itself: Since last summer, Citi has been plowing big money—$1.5 billion through December—into repurchases of its stock, paying an average price through year-end of $66 a share and continuing at the higher prices that have prevailed since.

To some critics who remember how frantically short this company

78

was of equity capital only a short while ago, those buybacks smell of the arrogance for which Citi has long been known. Fact is, though, that Citi has excess capital today and therefore plenty of cash to spend.

But Reed's ambition reaches further still. In speeches to groups of analysts—he's too reclusive to do one-on-ones—he's persistently talking about a new vision, one entailing plans for high-powered growth. Citi's goal, he says, is to increase earnings by 10% to 12% a year. Evidence suggests that Reed is probably pushing for even higher numbers, trying to turn Citi into what he calls "a global growth company." Success in that quest would require a strong brand. So Reed has pulled in new management from outside the company to burnish the bank's worldwide image.

In this effort, Reed can harvest some Citicorp strengths he preserved when all was tumbling about him. Citi, for one thing, has arrived at this point with all its essential parts intact. During the tough years it continued to invest in promising emerging markets, and it is now operating in 98 countries with two more coming up. Something else didn't happen: Citi was threatened during the crisis with having to sell at least a part of its huge credit card business, and that danger was ducked. So the business was around in 1995 to supply $1.2 billion in profits, about one-third of Citi's total.

Reed can meanwhile claim vindication—and the power that goes with it—for having produced a comeback that decks all the critics who clamored for his head in 1991. Naturally he didn't care to lose it, nor did he think his exiting would serve Citi itself. Asked then by FORTUNE why he deserved to remain CEO, Reed said, "Well, you know, my sense of it is, I know what has to be done. I think I understand the problem. I think I have the right sort of response to it, and it is likely that I will get it done. Maybe more likely than anybody else. I would submit to you humbly—because I wouldn't want to say that I haven't been sort of forced to ask this—I've asked myself if I'm the right guy to do this, and I hate to tell you, I think the answer is yes."

And then he proved it was. That intricate comment is also

pure Reed: Deeply embarrassed by the events of that time, he nonetheless remained indestructibly confident that he was the fellow who could turn the ship.

THE NAME STAYS THE SAME.

TODAY HE'S THE FELLOW who's got eight years to Citi's retirement age, the Bermuda Triangle behind him, and those visions of growth on his mind. That's growth, not sheer size, a switch in emphasis that just happens to be convenient: Citi, though this year's FORTUNE 500 shows it once again the biggest U.S. banking company by most financial measures, is about to lose the lead in assets to the new combination of Chemical and Chase.

Once, this kind of demotion would have shaken Citi's halls. But the crisis years changed many a Citi attitude, pride of size among them. To a security analyst who presumed to ask at a January meeting how Reed felt about dropping to No. 2 in assets, Reed shot back an answer suggesting that gross size was irrelevant and the question stupid. "We don't think," he said acidly, "that we're the No. 2 bank."

It is an oddity that the chairman of a bank so recently mired in deep trouble can say that and get away with it. But it is a fact—vital to Reed in his growth ambitions—that Citi's crisis years do not seem to have done lasting damage to its image or name. In its New York retail advertising, Citi has actually been making hay with its name, pointing out the constancy of "Citibank" while all around competitors are reconstituting and relabeling themselves.

So the name is one horse that Reed drives today. It is that same "Citibank" that he proposes to turn into a worldwide consumer brand, establishing it in effect as the Coca-Cola or McDonald's of financial services. What goes with the brand equity that those companies have, and he covets, is the ability to set themselves above the competition, either in the prices they can obtain or quantities sold or both. What also attaches to brand-name companies is high price/earnings multiples, and in that respect Citi certainly comes across shy of brand equity. Coke's P/E is 35. Citi's is 11.

SECRET GOALS FOR STELLAR PROFITS?

YOKED TO REED'S wish for the brand is that announced goal of increasing Citi's profits by 10% to 12% a year and of also maintaining at least an 18% return on equity. He flunked the profits goal in 1995—growth was only 3%—but the reason was a much bigger tax charge in 1995 than in 1994. Pretax profits grew by a rousing 21%, helped especially by a bounceback in foreign exchange and other trading profits, and by near breakeven results in that graying albatross, North American commercial real estate. But investors won't put much of a multiple on trading profits, which are notoriously erratic. What Reed really needed in 1995 was strong growth from his bulwark consumer business, and all he got was 11%. Even so, you might say, that fits into the goal of 10% to 12%.

But there is a funny thing about that goal: It's probably bogus. At the very least, Reed is aiming straight-out for 12%—you can tell that by certain inconsistencies between his overall target and those for individual businesses—and the better bet is that he's set his sights still higher. "It's 15% he's going for. There's no doubt about it," says one man with a deep knowledge of Reed's thinking.

A 15% goal would be a traffic stopper. Fighting the fact that banking doesn't even begin to grow that fast naturally, Reed's predecessor, Walter Wriston, set precisely that target for Citi in the early 1970s and eventually got it to be the biggest bank in the biggest mess, LDC (less developed countries) loans. Because of this history, some investors would today view a Reed run for 15% as alarming.

That is probably why Reed sticks to talking about 10% to 12%, no matter what his private intentions. He virtually confirmed that conjecture by something he said this year at a Merrill Lynch consumer products presentation for institutional investors, at which he turned up to implicitly push the proposition that Citi is a consumer products company disguised as a bank. Reed was asked there why he said he was shooting for a mere 18% return on equity, when his huge consumer businesses return 20% to 30%.

Answering, Reed granted the inconsistency and said that about 85% of his business—everything but corporate banking in the developed countries—could legitimately shoot for 30% returns. But "psychology," he explained, was in the picture. "In our business," he said, "it's dangerous to embrace very aggressive return targets because the market interprets that as an appetite for risk." Investors, he averred, would react to the targets adversely, saying, "These guys are nuts. They're going to get into the derivatives business; they're going back into real estate and leveraged buyouts, and whatever the no-nos are."

So, said Reed, "we don't want to communicate to the market an appetite for risk we don't have," and that's why he talks 18%. From that explanation, we can also surmise that targets of 10% to 12% for earnings growth are a smoke screen and that 15% may well be the true goal.

Reed has turned down virtually every interview request since 1992, deciding to let Citi's results speak for themselves. In Reed's mind also, reports a Citi spokesman, is the conviction that he doesn't want to waste his time doing interviews when he's got so many things on his plate. That presumably would include building the brand and meeting those earnings targets (whatever they truly are) and perhaps something more personal: a relatively new marriage.

Having been divorced from his first wife in late 1991, Reed wed Cindy McCarthy, then 37, in September 1994. She was a flight attendant on Citi's corporate planes, and rumors about their romance were around as early as 1991. The Reeds now live in a New York commuting town, Princeton, New Jersey, and also, improbably, in a Greenwich Village loft. John Reed has told old friends that he is exceedingly happy and caught up in new interests, like cooking. So this is a man who in the past few years has been rejuvenated both professionally and personally

He has meanwhile been trying to whip up precisely the right mix of executives below him. Just this winter, Reed reshuffled his management team, ending up with a cadre of broadly experienced but still youngish executives in "one down" positions—

meaning in Cititalk that they report directly to Reed. Down the road, a successor to Reed could conceivably come from this group.

"OUR NAME IS CITIBANK, AND OUR COLOR IS BLUE."

GOING GLOBAL is what Citi has done for 100 years and simply wants now to do more intensely. A global brand requires a consistent image. So Citi has rapidly been building model branches—modern and user-friendly—around the world, with these numbering 439 out of a total of 1,203 branches. In every country, that consumer piece of plastic—the Citicard—looks the same, carrying two big blue arrows. It was not always so. Once, Citi operated around the world under an assortment of names and hues. But in the mid-1980s, Pei-yuan Chia (former vice chairman and chief of consumer business) decreed uniformity, reminding his troops that a parent gives two things to a child: its color and name. So, said Chia, "our name is Citibank, and our color is blue."

None of these things means that the Citi name resonates the same in all countries. In the U.S., where Citi has branches in eight states, it is no more classy than most banks. In many countries outside the U.S., however, Citi has a decidedly upscale image. It is viewed both as a bigtime, sophisticated place to work and as a harbor for serious money. In the Asia-Pacific area, for example, Citi does not solicit small accounts. What Citi sells hard in that part of the world is the Citigold account, which generally requires the customer to have assets lodged with the bank—either investments or cash—of $100,000 or more. In return, the customer gets special services, such as a daily sweep of his cash deposits into money market funds. A U.S. customer putting up the same quantity of assets—and also paying a $125 annual fee—can get a Citigold account too, but the concept is not aggressively marketed in the U.S.

Some of the company's cachet abroad has translated into impressive profits, particularly in the emerging areas of the Asia-

Pacific region, where Citi's commercial and consumer franchises last year made $781 million. That was more than one-fifth of the company's total profits and a leap of 34% from 1994.

That's in spite of tough competition, especially on the corporate side of the bank. In certain Asian locations—Hong Kong and Singapore, for example—Citi's commercial bankers are up against international players like Chase and J.P. Morgan. In all spots, they're battling local banks. One "local" name is particularly formidable: Hongkong & Shanghai Bank, a subsidiary of HSBC Holdings, which is very international. HSBC (whose big U.S. property is Marine Midland) operates in 71 countries, a number second in the banking industry only to Citi's 98.

In credit cards, Citi also faces American Express, which Reed thinks of as the "only other global brand" in financial services. But Amex has no great strength internationally. Its Asian profits, for example, are less than one-fifth of Citi's. One institutional investor noted the contrast between the two companies when he went to Asia to study Citi. He was impressed, but what jumped out at him, he says, was the weakness displayed by American Express.

You cannot leap from a specific competitive superiority to a conclusion that Citi can build a successful worldwide brand; too many important roadblocks stand in the way. But when FORTUNE asked three different marketing experts—none with any connection to Citi—what they thought of the company's brand prospects, each had something positive to say. David Aaker, a professor at the University of California at Berkeley, has only the barest mention of Citi in his new book, *Building Strong Brands*, and he does not slight the difficulties of a financial services company acting out that title. But he sees Citi as way ahead of its competitors, saying, "I don't think other people are going to be able to copy them."

Kenneth Roberts, head of Lippincott & Margulies, a corporate-identity consulting firm in New York City, believes Citi's long-standing focus on the consumer—two decades old now—gives it a real leg up in knowing how to burnish a brand worldwide. Also, he says, this brand and this bank, Citibanking and Citi, are synonymous and therefore relatively simple to market.

Consultants at the Optima Group in Fairfield, Connecticut, feel that the ultimate ability of any financial services company to establish a brand will depend on its technical ability to sort and manage data about its customer base, and to market the right products to the right customers. And here, says Kenneth Hoffman, head of Optima, Citi has a lead: "We talk to some of Citi's competitors, and they feel that Citi is ahead on this curve."

BUILDING BRAND EQUITY

I N THE END, Citi's ability to build a consumer brand of weight and power seems to depend on two unpredictable matters. One is the basic question about brand equity: Will consumers in effect "oversubscribe" to Citi's offerings, either by providing it with plump market shares or by paying premium prices for some service they might well get more cheaply down the street? It's worth remembering that brand recognition, which Citi certainly has, is not brand equity. No bank, in fact, has yet proved it can step up and grab that gold ring.

Moreover, today's never-ending advances in electronic communications are a distinct hazard for brands, particularly those financial. Reed himself got a close-up reminder of that point recently when he and Robert M. Howe, an IBM financial services expert, were speakers on the same panel at a Goldman Sachs conference attended by many bankers. Said Howe in his speech, with Reed two feet away: "In a virtual banking world, what is the value of your brand when I can page through my PC and see every financial institution that I want to deal with?"

For that matter, what was the value of Citi's brand a few years ago, when it tried to keep fees on its credit cards even as competitors all around it were dropping theirs? Not much: The company lost tons of market share and was eventually forced into what Reed calls its own Marlboro Friday, in which it started to phase out its fees, meanwhile accepting an annual loss of fee revenues of $300 million. That slide, of course, was the result of competitors' attacking a market of rich returns, and Citi can expect similar invaders in other profitable parts of its world. Says Reed: "The competition is unformed at this point. It will form."

The other question, as has ever been the case, is whether Citi can manage its big, sprawling bailiwick, including so many geographies that executives—or perhaps their speechwriters—can't keep them straight. At a recent Citicorp presentation for analysts, vice chairman Paul Collins spoke of Citi's plan to move next into Israel and then into Lebanon and Gabon. Whoops! Citi has been in Gabon for 20 years. It's Angola that Collins should have mentioned.

But that's a detail, and the brand-building exercise is fundamental. It will demand expert execution at all levels of management, including the one-down layer that has just been added to the cake. Reed has talked frequently about the need to get the right people in the right places, and there's no way of telling whether he's got an effective lineup in place at the moment. If he concludes he hasn't, there will surely be fast changes again, for he has shown absolutely no tolerance for so-so performance.

THREE YEARS AGO, with Citi clearly on the mend but not yet fit, some students of its workings worried that Reed would revert—slip back to the old Citi beliefs that it could do whatever it cared to, in any quarter of the world, at whatever pace was required. If he's pushing for 15% earnings gains, some covert form of reversion may already be rumbling around. On the other hand, Reed has spent the past five years bearing down on Citi's problems with unusual focus and consistency. The drill, he told analysts earlier this year, is to keep on that track, to put "one step in front of another, year after year." A swashbuckling style that's not. But a reasonable rule for building a brand it could just possibly be.

David Shaw's secret formulas pile up money.
Now he wants a piece of the Net.

WALL STREET'S KING QUANT: DAVID SHAW

BY JAMES ALEY

W AY UP ATOP a Manhattan skyscraper, inside the investment banking firm of D.E. Shaw & Co., is a tiny hexago-
nal room staffed by six people who look fresh out of college.
They stare at computer screens that cover the walls, clicking
their mice, occasionally talking calmly to one another or into
their phones. It is utterly unlike the typical Wall Street trading
floor (where scores of shouting, sweating Mylanta chuggers raise
a Dantesque din). In fact, it is utterly unimpressive—except for
the fact that Shaw's trading volume is sometimes equal to 5% of
the total volume of the New York Stock Exchange.

D.E. Shaw & Co. is the most intriguing and mysterious force
on Wall Street today. It's the ultimate quant shop, a nest of
mathematicians, computer scientists, and other devotees of
quantitative analysis who use their arcane sciences to monitor
the world's financial markets and squeeze profits out of places
most people would never think of looking. It's the answer you'll
get if you ask the question, What's the most technologically sophisticated firm on the Street? Many investment banks and
trading firms, of course, have stocked their ranks with hot-rod
quants plying their Ph.D.s to figure out the markets. But D.E.
Shaw doesn't just have lots of "rocket scientists." This place is
run by rocket scientists, starting with the 44-year-old chief executive and founder, David Shaw, Ph.D., a former Columbia

University computer science professor who used to design and build supercomputers for a living.

AN INVESTMENT BANK'S HUMBLE BEGINNINGS

FEW PEOPLE outside the world of finance have ever heard of D.E. Shaw, and until recently that suited him just fine. The firm's primary business—quantitative trading, using techniques like statistical arbitrage—is very esoteric stuff, and its other investment banking activities are done in obscure markets. But now Shaw and his scientists and mathematicians are pursuing a hugely ambitious plan to venture far beyond Wall Street. If they succeed—anything but a sure thing—D.E. Shaw could become as well known as Charles Schwab, if not Bill Gates. Shaw already has used his firm's computational muscle to offer free E-mail to every man, woman, and dweeb on the Internet. At a later date he wants to add online personal financial services, including home banking. He sounds more like the academic he used to be than the mogul he's become when he talks about his business plan. What he's aiming to do, he says, is "to identify ways in which technology has the potential to fundamentally transform our world, and to play a significant role in bringing about that transformation."

Shaw formed his company eight years ago as a hedge fund—an investment partnership designed to use everything from derivatives to shortselling to make money in any market environment—with $28 million in startup capital. The most prominent of the handful of original investors were Donald Sussman of Paloma Partners, another hedge fund, and Continental Casualty Co., owned by Loews Corp. Shaw started with six employees and leased his first office space in a loft near Greenwich Village. ("We have the distinction," he notes, "of being the only investment bank to be started above a communist bookstore.") The company made its first trade about six months after startup, turned a profit, and has been making money ever since. Today, D.E. Shaw & Co. has about 300 employees and more than $600 million in gross capital, ranking it

TYPICAL WALL STREET. AS IF.

Sitting at his 20-foot wing-shaped aluminum desk with a constellation of halogen lights hovering overhead, David Shaw is explaining why his company's headquarters looks more like an art gallery than a financial institution. "We don't want this to seem like a regular Wall Street firm," he says, "because it isn't."

No kidding. Shaw succeeded in making the place look different (photos of it were displayed in a design show at New York's Museum of Modern Art), and his statement also helps explain some other things, like the need for stacks full of academic journals and why the company has neither vacation policy nor dress code. So what kind of firm does D.E. Shaw & Co. seem like? How about: a well-funded research lab in the sky—a place where the avant garde meets artibrage, and intellectualism and profit-seeking mix harmoniously.

Like a top academic institution, D.E. Shaw spends a lot of time and money recruiting brainpower. The head of the talent spotters, Charles Ardai, spares no superlative when speaking of his mission. "We want people who make our jaws drop. We know a D.E. Shaw hire when we say, 'I can't believe this person did this at age 25,'" says Ardai (age 26).

The goal is to have a list of people the company might want in the future—and then to pounce when a need arises. If computer science Ph.D. students are any good, says Shaw, "we'll have heard about them by their second year in grad school." His firm typically offers low six-figure starting salaries to Ph.D.s in New York—and these can quickly turn into mid-six-figure salaries. Heady stuff for graduate students living off grant money and student loans.

among the top 25 securities companies in the country.

How has the company performed? Very nicely. According to one person familiar with his operations, D.E. Shaw has been averaging 18% annual returns since its inception. Numbers like that put Shaw well above the average, if not into the stratosphere, of money managers. But what really attracts hedge fund investors to Shaw is the fund's low volatility relative to the broader market. Last year, through December 1, the take was around 16%, well behind the S&P 500. But in 1994, a year when most hedge funds either lost money or barely broke even, Shaw delivered a 26% return.

Getting this kind of hard information about D.E. Shaw isn't easy. In fact, getting practically any information about the company is difficult. The paragraph you just read may well be the most detailed account of Shaw's finances that's ever been published. Shaw's penchant for secrecy is legendary; his attitude toward the press has been indifferent. The company not only refuses to discuss specifics of its investment performance—it even declines to reveal simple facts such as the names of all of its original partners, though they are listed on a publicly available document. (True, you have to track down the limited partnership papers at the Secretary of State's Office in Albany, New York.)

To make sure nothing gets out that isn't supposed to get out, Shaw has all his employees sign nondisclosure agreements, and these gag orders do their job well. Two former employees who initially agreed to be interviewed by FORTUNE changed their minds after sleeping on the decision, both citing the nondisclosure agreements. Only one would say anything at all, to wit: "I only have positive things to say anyway."

The secrecy is understandable when it comes to the firm's proprietary technology—what Shaw calls "our life's blood." Shaw's market-beating algorithms are so secret, even limited partners such as Morgan Miller (one of Shaw's earliest investors and an executive at National Spinning Co.) aren't entirely sure what's going on behind the curtain. "With most of the investments I have, I understand exactly what's going on. I don't with David," says Miller. "It does bother me in a way. But it's something I can live with." Shaw himself will give only a coarse description of the statistical-arbitrage trading strategies his mathematicians have invented, which are designed to exploit tiny pricing mismatches, taking a little profit here and a little more there, in the hope that by the time you add it all up, you come out well ahead. Shaw is quick to point out that this strategy is "market neutral," meaning the goal is finding these little profit pockets without actually betting on the direction of the market. "Although to be fair," he says, "if we did know how to do that, we would."

Given his reputation as an amalgam of Einstein, Midas, and Rasputin, Shaw in person turns out to be surprisingly unpretentious. Consider the unassuming way he explains himself and his firm. "Our goal," he says, carefully picking his words to get it right the first time, "is to look at the intersection of computers and capital, and find as many interesting and profitable things to do in that intersection as we can." He doesn't live extravagantly, either. A favorite restaurant is a Brazilian buffet joint across the street from his offices—"The last time I was here, a cockroach was walking across the floor," he tells a dinner companion.

BACK WHEN $100 MILLION
COULD REALLY BUY SOMETHING

SHAW GOT A COMPUTER SCIENCE Ph.D. from Stanford in 1980, very close—temporally and geographically—to the epicenter of the computer revolution. It took him eight years to earn his doctorate because he took a few years off to start and run a successful computer software company. He wasn't the only wallah-in-training at Stanford in those days. Leonard Bosack and Andreas Bechtolsheim, co-founders of Cisco Systems and Sun Microsystems, respectively, and Jim Clark, founder of Silicon Graphics and now chairman of Netscape—all were either faculty members or fellow students. "It was a fascinating time to be at Stanford, absolutely incredible," says Jerry Kaplan, a prominent Silicon Valley entrepreneur who was a research associate there at the same time. Although Shaw didn't have a reputation as a superstar, Kaplan

HOW QUANTS LIKE SHAW
MAKE THEIR MONEY

So what exactly is "statistical arbitrage"—the financial black art that D.E. Shaw & Co.'s mathematicians and computer scientists employ to make millions in the markets? In general, arbitrage is the closest thing that exists in finance and economics to getting a free lunch. You begin by noticing a price discrepancy—that shares of General Motors, say, are going for $49.50 in New York and $50 in Tokyo. Then you exploit it, by buying in New York and selling simultaneously in Tokyo, guaranteeing yourself a profit of 50 cents per share, minus transaction costs. You are being paid, as finance types would put it, for detecting and correcting a "market inefficiency."

The problem with making a living from arbitrage is that such price gaps are usually tiny. "Any one source of inefficiency may be so small that it wouldn't cover transaction costs," says David Shaw. Also, they don't last very long. Indeed, with computers and communication links spreading market information everywhere in nanoseconds, such price gaps tend to close up almost as fast as they open.

This is where statistical arbitrage comes in.

The basic idea, according to Andrew Lo, a finance professor at MIT's Sloan School of Management, is that you might be able to exploit these tiny inefficiencies some of the time, with no guaranteed profit at any given moment but with at least the confidence that in the long run you'll come out ahead. Continuing the above example, say you notice that while GM is going for $49.50 on the New York market, exchange rates keep fluctuating, causing the Tokyo share price to vary between $49 and $50.50. Now suppose that you've got a foreign exchange whiz on your payroll who tells you he can hedge the yen-dollar movement with currency options. As long as the hedging dampens the variation enough to make the Tokyo price equal $49.75 on average, or any number high enough to beat New York's price (after transaction costs), you've got a deal on your hands. Even if the bouncing yen makes the New York price slightly more expensive than the Tokyo price some of the time, you can still win over the long run.

That's an exceedingly simple example of statistical arbitrage. To find market anomalies to exploit in the real world, you have to dig much, much deeper into more complex relationships between securities, interest rates, exchange rates, and God knows what else. Andrew Schwaeber of Highbridge Capital, a trader who has dealt with D.E. Shaw both as customer and broker, says the company's computational powers help it find obscure, convoluted relationships in financial markets that elude almost everyone else. "You would never look at Microsoft's relationship to the square root of Genentech and Texaco or something completely obscure like that, but they might," says Schwaeber. "The weirdest relationship you can think of might show up as mathematically significant to them. They have computers crunching numbers all day long looking for non-chance relationships—for needles in the haystacks that no one else would even begin to comprehend."

recalls, "he was considered one of the core, competent people."

Fresh from Stanford, Shaw got a job as an assistant professor of computer science at Columbia, where he did research on massively parallel supercomputing. In 1986, Morgan Stanley lured him into its analytical and proprietary trading technology group, offering him six times his professor's salary and an environment where there were much greater financial resources at his disposal than he'd ever see in academia. The shift to Wall Street was a natural, says Shaw. "Finance is really a wonderfully pure information-processing business," he says. But he soon started coming up with his own ideas about applying computer technology to financial markets, and although he speaks admiringly of Morgan today, he found the place too restrictive. He wanted to build his own company, as he puts it, "designed from the beginning from a computer science perspective." A year and a half after joining Morgan, he quit to form D.E. Shaw & Co.

Despite all his success as a pathbreaker in these arcane forms of proprietary trading, Shaw—incredibly—says that if he were starting out today he'd probably stay out of the business altogether, simply because it's gotten so much harder to break into. As competition has increased, profit opportunities have gotten even tinier. Over the past eight years, D.E. Shaw has spent roughly $100 million developing its technology and uncovering new ways to beat the market. State-of-the-art computer hardware is everywhere, but the real soul of the operation is the software. Trying to re-create the systems it has come up with would cost much more today than the original investment. "For us, proprietary trading is still very important and very good," Shaw says, "but that's partly because we lucked out." In other words, they got into the statistical arbitrage game early, when it cost only $100 million to play.

The company already devotes two-thirds of its personnel to newer services aimed at outside customers, unlike proprietary trading, which is all for its own account. For the past couple of years, Shaw has been using his $100 million technological toolbox to build a financial services division. Among other functions, this new client-seeking enterprise specializes as a market maker for obscure, complex securities like Japanese warrants and convertible bonds. One reason these issues are attractive to Shaw is that they're hard for most people to figure out—

that is, those without his computational firepower find them more trouble than they're worth. Perhaps a more important reason, says Andrew Schwaeber, a trader of Asian securities at Highbridge Capital who has experience dealing with D.E. Shaw both as customer and broker, is that Shaw got into the Japanese warrant and convertible business at a time when the business was declining and other securities firms were scaling back because they weren't making enough money. The market opened up, Shaw jumped in, and now, says Schwaeber, "they're doing it better than anybody."

DOING BUSINESS IN CYBERSPACE

OKAY, SO SHAW built his firm into the quant shop other quant shops dream about, and since then has blazed a path toward bona fide investment bankdom. Then what's a smart outfit like D.E. Shaw doing flirting with that crowded no-profit zone, the Internet? "I'm embarrassed to tell anybody, just because everything in the newspaper seems to have the word Internet," Shaw admits. But, media drenching notwithstanding, he thinks cyberspace really is a place where he can do business—and where he can compete with the likes of Microsoft, Sun Microsystems, MCI, and every other high-tech company frantically trying to capture a market no one can even measure yet.

The first Net project—already up and running—is a spinoff called Juno, a free E-mail service. The simple, sensible pitch of Juno is right there in its advertising material: "E-mail was meant to be free." Users of the service don't pay a dime—not if they just want to send and receive E-mail to or from anyone anywhere on the Internet. "It has a huge potential," says Phoebe Simpson, an online analyst at Jupiter Communications. "There's a huge market for people who want to simplify the E-mail process, who go online just for their E-mail." The profits in this scheme will theoretically come through ads displayed onscreen as people use the software. "It's like network TV," says Charles Ardai, Juno president—a former pulp mystery writer with a background in marketing. "You want to watch *Seinfeld*? You get a few ads."

Optional fee-based services may be added later, like online shopping or the ability to attach graphics or spreadsheet files to your E-mail. "If you want to send pictures of your kids, God bless you, but it may not be free," says Ardai.

Even more audacious than Juno is the second venture, called Farsight. Essentially, Farsight's ambition is to become your online banker, broker, insurance salesman—whatever you do with your money, they want you to do it with them on their Web page. The service isn't ready for outsiders to test, although the prototype Shaw demonstrated for FORTUNE looks slick and easy to use. Shaw says he's lined up some partners; he's also talking to commercial banks and mutual fund companies, but (there's that secretiveness again) he won't say who. Will it succeed? Remember, a successful online personal finance enterprise has been the elusive dream of the entire banking industry for more than a decade. It's something no one from Citibank to Microsoft has figured out how to do yet. D.E. Shaw's Farsight could be the online personal finance breakthrough everyone's been waiting for. Or not.

ONE RECENT EVENING, Shaw whirled into his lobby, apologizing profusely. He was a half-hour late for an appointment because of a phone call from Richard Gephardt, the House minority leader and fellow liberal Democrat. Shaw is also an acquaintance of President Clinton's—they met while Clinton was still governor of Arkansas—and has served on presidential advisory bodies. Back in college he was an early anti-Vietnam protester.

Yet another persona. Could this quant among quants, with his massively parallel business ambitions, also have an incipient case of Potomac fever? Shaw laughs at the suggestion. He can't imagine going into politics. Or leaving the private sector, period. Or being bought out. "The most fun I've ever had has been serving as CEO of this company," he says. More he won't say, just as he's not about to tell anyone how he beats the market.

CHAPTER THREE

MANAGEMENT IDEAS WORTH A FORTUNE

THE NINE DILEMMAS LEADERS FACE
page 98

WHY VALUE STATEMENTS DON'T WORK
page 104

**HOW TO NEGOTIATE WITH
REALLY TOUGH GUYS**
page 110

RAMBOS IN PINSTRIPES
page 114

**HOW TO FIRE PEOPLE
(AND STILL SLEEP AT NIGHT)**
page 117

JOIN THE HEADHUNTER'S INNER CIRCLE
page 128

YOU INC.: THE ORGANIZATIONAL CHART
page 132

ARE YOU AFRAID OF SUCCESS?
page 135

*The hardest job a leader has is to navigate among often conflicting goals.
Identify them first, and you can steer a winning course.*

THE NINE DILEMMAS LEADERS FACE

BY THOMAS A. STEWART

M ANAGEMENT—the word—traces its origins to the arts of
horsemanship—from the Latin *manus,* "hand," via the
Italian *maneggiare,* "to train horses." But since most of us call
down to the stable to have the coach and four readied even less
often than we wear white tie, let's talk cars. When you're driving,
you do several potentially contradictory things at once. You want
to get to your destination quickly, and also safely. You must watch
the road and also look behind and around you. You can do one—
you can do the other—but you want to do both. These are dilemmas: a word from the Greek, "two assumptions or premises."
Dilemmas are what your boss talks about when he says, "You're
in charge, Fosdick, but make sure Susannah is on board."

Managing dilemmas is what you do.

However, you cannot manage what you cannot name. That's why,
when God gave Adam dominion over the fish of the sea and the
birds of the air and every living thing that moves upon the earth, He
brought the creatures before Adam, and had him name them.

A couple of years ago, an opportunity to define the dilemmas
of management presented itself when Canadian Imperial Bank
of Commerce decided to build an Edenic leadership center for its
managers and employees on a rolling 100-acre site 45 minutes
north of its Toronto headquarters. When Al Flood, the CEO of
the bank (North America's eighth largest, with 1995 assets of
$132 billion), okayed the plans, he did what any good banker

would: He told Michele Darling, head of human resources, and Hubert Saint-Onge, who was to run the center, to make sure that this asset performed.

Thus challenged, Darling and Saint-Onge responded with an extraordinary act of in-house journalism. To create a mission and a curriculum for the center, Saint-Onge interviewed CIBC's 27 most senior executives, one on one. He asked each of them five open-ended questions:

What factors in the business environment most affect CIBC's leaders?
What cultural changes does the bank need to be more successful?
What organizational capabilities does it need to build?
What are the most pressing management-development needs?
What features should leadership-center programs include?

Those questions elicited a wealth of ideas. Though some were predictable—what company's leaders don't feel they should "be more customer-driven"?— together they helped Darling and Saint-Onge define their mission. But there was more: The pages upon pages of notes made for an unusual chance to learn how leaders think and what they think about.

Poring over the interviews, Saint-Onge began highlighting phrases like "we must do a ... but also b," or "in going after x, we must not lose sight of y." When he was done, he found nine "core leadership dilemmas." They fit any business and any manager, though they may be felt most keenly at the top.

◆ BROAD-BASED LEADERSHIP VS. HIGH-VISIBILITY LEADERS. The bankers acutely felt the need for top executives to get out front, to rally the troops personally and even charismatically. With equal fervor they saw a requirement to foster leadership throughout the company. If top management dominates the airwaves, it will silence others; if it is too reticent, the others will fret and wither for lack of support. For example, experts say reengineering will fail if the CEO doesn't take a strong role, but add that its success depends on a broad cadre of leaders among middle managers, team members, and others.

◆INDEPENDENCE VS. INTERDEPENDENCE. We want entrepreneur-ship, a sense of ownership, and P&L responsibility, but we don't want one division badmouthing another, hogging shared resources, or refusing to take advantage of what the company has to offer. I was gored by the horns of this dilemma once: My then boss told me and a couple of peers that we had authority to make ad-budget decisions; we should consult with the marketing director but feel free to over-rule her. When a few months later I felt it was necessary to do pre-cisely that, he rapped my knuckles and said I should be more of a team player.

◆LONG TERM VS. SHORT TERM. The oldest dilemma in the book, but that doesn't make it easy to resolve. Several years back, I inter-viewed David Kearns, then CEO of Xerox. The topic: lessons learned from Xerox's failure to make successful businesses out of some of its inventions, like the desktop fax machine and the personal computer. Kearns had been wrestling with the problem of how to link labs more closely to the commercial needs of the business—while not gutting their talent for imagining and inventing a faraway future. As he showed me out at the end of our talk, he took a deep breath, shook his head, and settled his shoulders. He said, "We've been talking about five and ten years ago, and five and ten years from now. Waiting outside are a couple of security analysts, and the only thing they care about is the next quarter." What struck me most was the almost physical effort he needed to rearrange his mind.

◆CREATIVITY VS. DISCIPLINE. You encourage all those en-trepreneurial leaders to benefit from freethinking, but they still have to make budget and adhere to company policy. It's as if Mao Zedong had said, "Let a thousand flowers bloom—in a topiary garden."

◆TRUST VS. CHANGE. At first blush, trust and change don't seem to pull in opposite directions, but they do: Implementing organiza-tional change—whether it's moving offices around or massive reengineering—can damage trust and commitment. Old work groups are sundered, new bosses have new standards, the world's in flux, and it's Look out for No. 1. Even positive change can weaken trust: It was those wedding bells, after all, that broke up that old gang of mine. Yet without trust, change is impossible.

◆BUREAUCRACY BUSTING VS. ECONOMIES OF SCALE. Let's centralize purchasing to leverage our size to get a better price. Let's also destroy the costly bureaucracies that clog the corporate coronary arteries when they, for example, force me to buy stuff that doesn't fit the needs of my business unit. (If you're not noticing that these dilemmas fall into a pattern, you're not reading closely enough.)

◆PEOPLE VS. PRODUCTIVITY. Another chestnut, but one that's really in the fire these days: The need to maximize productivity, to get everybody contributing 110%, must be balanced against the demands of personal life and the realization that, in the long run, all work and no play makes Jack a sitting duck.

◆LEADERSHIP VS. CAPABILITY. The managerial and technical skills that enhance operations are quite different from the people-and-vision skills that produce leadership. The best strategy in the world won't work if it is poorly executed, but superb implementation of the wrong strategy simply means that Armageddon will come sooner than it otherwise would.

◆REVENUE GROWTH VS. COST CONTAINMENT. Once, in a hotel lobby, I saw a man carrying a coffee mug on which was printed BUDGETS ARE FOR WIMPS. "Where'd you get that?" I asked, hoping he would tell me a nearby shop had them.

But no: "My boss had them made for us."

"He a marketing guy?" I asked.

He said, "How did you know?"

NINE DILEMMAS that describe your job. What do you do with them? First, notice that pattern. Says Saint-Onge: "These are all different, but they form a single, central dilemma." Its name: empowerment vs. alignment, the never-ending balancing act of managerial Bongo Board in which you try to give people independence and authority while making sure they use it in a way you'd approve of if they asked, which you don't want them to do except, of course, when you do want them to. Lee Iacocca sent the wrong message in that TV ad. The right one is "Lead, follow, and get out of the way."

Second, you can make charts—always a good use of managerial time. Take each dilemma, and put one horn on a vertical axis and one on the horizontal. Draw a 45° diagonal to represent a balance between the two. Then on a scale of 1 to 10, 10 being best, locate your outfit (or yourself or your boss) on the grid.

Set these up with all the "empowerment" tendencies (broad-based leadership, independence, long-termism, creativity, etc.) on the vertical axis and the "alignment" group on the horizontal. What do you see? Are you usually below the diagonal (too controlling) or above it (too loosey-goosey)?

You want to be spot-on the diagonal line, and as far out toward the upper-right-hand corner as possible. This is because both sides of each dilemma are good: You want creativity, and you want discipline; in fact, to get the greatest benefit of creativity, you need to temper it with discipline, and vice versa. The goal is to manage better in both directions—you want maximum empowerment and maximum alignment, just as a figure skater wants perfect scores for both artistic impression and technical merit.

For the folks at CIBC, the most important lesson of the nine dilemmas was seeing that, fundamentally, leadership is about ambiguities, not certainties. Says Michele Darling: "The dilemmas helped us come to a different understanding of the roles a leader plays."

One role she calls "polarity management." Leaders often are mesmerized by the virtues of one side of a dilemma, and ignore its worthy alternative. "Successful leaders," says Darling, "explore both ends." If you get your jollies from bureaucracy busting, force yourself to love economies of scale: Who better to reap its benefits than an honest skeptic? Polarities can also help you diagnose and deal with a group's resistance to change—chances are they're hung up on one horn of a dilemma, and you can help by showing them that they are right, but only half right.

Twinned with polarity management is ambiguity management. Too much thinking about leadership has a hortatory "set a vision and march on toward it" feel. But big strategic facts aren't always so clear—something that both leaders and their followers have to understand. Embracing ambiguities can be a powerful way to learn about a changing world.

A third role emerges from polarities and ambiguities: making meaning. Says Darling: "The defining role of a leader is to sort out a message" from these mixed signals and cross-purposes. The new customer-satisfaction scores have just come in, and they show problems, but you also just received a market-segmentation analysis that shows that some customers demand so much service they are actually unprofitable. Your job is to take those dilemmas and make sense—and sensible plans—out of them. Otherwise it's all Greek.

You can blather on endlessly about teamwork and trust, but if your people don't see what's in it for them, don't expect them to listen.

WHY VALUE STATEMENTS DON'T WORK

BY THOMAS A. STEWART

SEVERAL YEARS AGO I happened upon an employee-attitude survey taken at a FORTUNE 500 industrial. Part of it asked workers about the company's statement of values—a fairly typical list of six, articulated a year or so previously, that included quality, integrity, respect for individuals, and profitability. The survey asked employees whether they had heard about each of the values and if they believed that the company meant and did what it said—if it walked the talk.

Nearly all the employees were aware of the company's value statement, but only 60% believed the company actually meant it. Surprised by the low numbers, I described the survey to a consultant who specialized in employee-attitude surveys. What he said shocked me: "Those are really high scores."

Looking more closely, one could divide the list into "hard" values (profitability, e.g.) and "soft" ones (integrity, respect). For the soft values as a group, only 45% of employees believed the company lived its creed—and just one in four thought it sincere about respecting individuals.

The workers were probably right: At another company I saw (again confidentially) a study that compared what its top executives said with its published values—a list quite similar to the first company's. It turned out that the brass talked about the "hard" values all the time, while "soft" values were discussed far less often; the company's equivalent of "respect for individuals" showed up scarcely at all. The executives didn't think about it in the ordinary course of business.

Yet, said the person who showed me the data, that is the value employees care most about. If the company can't promise a long and safe career, employees truly need to know that management will treat them fairly; that their work will prepare them for the future, whether it's with their company or with another; and that it's permissible, even desirable, that employees take overt steps to prepare for life beyond its walls. The new employer-employee contract boils down to this: The employer won't promise security, but it will support your individual development. If you think your company believes that, ask yourself a Hobbesian question: How comfortable would you be if you went to your boss, or if a key subordinate came to you, and candidly said, "Since lifetime employment is no more, I want to discuss how to change what I do here so that I will be more attractive to the next company that hires me"?

Assume—perhaps naively, but assume nonetheless—that executives really do want their companies to promulgate values and their people to live by them. How do you go about it? How do you set forth values that work—that people see as more than just words on a wall plaque, that they see as beliefs both they and the organization as a whole live by?

Certainly it makes logical and intuitive sense to infuse a corporate culture with a set of values. As we empower people, as we flatten hierarchies so that supervisors have 20 direct reports instead of eight, the boss can't look over your shoulder to monitor you—at least not as much. Moreover, in a fast-changing world, it's foolish—even reckless—to delay a decision while it makes its studied way up and back down the chain of command. Almost all workers are making decisions, not just filling out weekly sales reports or tightening screws. They will do as they think best. If you want them to do as the company thinks best too, then you must hope that they have an inner gyroscope aligned with the corporate compass. In this environment, says celebrated management cerebratician Charles Handy, "the vision and values stuff really matters."

VALUES AND TRUST are interdependent, and trust is a two-way street: employer trusting employee, employee trusting employer. Warren Bennis, the leadership expert at the University of Southern California, points out that bureaucratic organizations need not rely heavily on trust. Hierarchy is the Olestra of trust—a substitute that tastes almost like the real thing. In a hierarchy, you know the boss likes you because he just gave you a bigger office and grander title; you know the guy down the hall will deliver on his promise because he works for you or because his boss will see to it; you know secrets will be kept because only trustworthy people know them.

When a network becomes the means by which a corporation works, those hierarchical crutches are knocked away. Networked organizations have fewer promotions to give out. Far from getting a bigger office, you might start working from home. Rewards may go to teams, not individuals. Those teams are likely to be interdepartmental—so that hierarchical power, position power, can't guarantee that work gets done. And as anyone who has hung around networks knows, lots of secrets are available to damn near anyone; some of them are even true. Trust in a network has to be real.

It's curious that the trust gap has widened at the same time hierarchy has flattened. Nowadays you call the CEO Jim, not The Chairman, and on Fridays Jim wears a sweater to work. Beneath the surface egalitarianism, however, is a strong sense that rewards are very unequal and that, though executive job security is low too, the character of the insecurity is different. If I get fired, I get a few weeks' severance per year. If my boss gets fired, he gets a million bucks.

TO REACH ACROSS the trust canyon to find and instill shared values, you have to understand how value systems work. A fundamental fact: People don't buy corporate values; they roll their own. This is one lesson Brian P. Hall, president of Values Technology, a Santa Cruz, California, company, has learned in 30 years of studying values. Hall, a former professor of psychology at the University of Santa Clara, working on an in-depth study with the Maltese sociologist Benjamin Tonna and others, found that 125 different values underpin all human behavior. They are things like prestige, success, independence, control, and belonging. Of this universe of 125, however, each individual operates according to perhaps 15. For example, some people want to belong; some want to be independent—but it's unlikely that those two clappers would ring the same bell.

Now, when the company's high panjandrums and their consulting firm go up to the mountaintop and come down with a tablet of values, I will buy into only those that in some way match mine. I don't have to agree entirely; I do have to see that the corporate values don't stifle mine—indeed, that I can fulfill mine in the corporate context. Also, I will interpret the value statement according to my own beliefs. If you tell me to respect every individual and my personal value system says Look out for No. 1, then I will understand that the company should respect me—but I might miss the part that says I should respect my co-workers.

Values must fit the corporate culture. You can't descend from Sinai and proclaim something that sounds great in the clear mountain air but doesn't fit conditions in the valley. Take General Electric. In the past decade GE has done a brilliant job of tearing down bureaucracy and replacing it with a culture of just-do-it teamwork. The tools GE uses—the Work-Out program, in which employees propose changes in procedures, process mapping, sharing best practices—were developed in the industrial parts of GE. They rely on encouraging ideas to bubble up from below and on making bosses see that their success is yoked to the success of their subordinates. All kinds of events—Work-Out's requirement that leaders say yes or no to employee suggestions on the spot, 360-degree evaluations—are explicitly designed to cut the boss down to size. A couple of years ago Jack Welch even proclaimed that managers who make their numbers but don't live GE's values would get the sack—a bold statement in a company that has never been abashed by profits, but one that underscores Welch's belief that profitability and productivity result from collaboration rather than machismo.

Those tools and values don't translate well into businesses

that have a star system. They might work fine for technicians at NBC, but when Tom Brokaw's agent negotiates a new contract, does how well he works in a team figure in the talks? Did traders at Kidder Peabody care about process mapping? The mismatch is part of the reason GE finally sold Kidder. People like rogue trader Joseph Jett saw that personal success and the organization's success weren't coupled: As Welch put it, Jett operated "a phantom trading scheme, by a single employee, directed not against customers but against the firm itself." Look at what happened at Salomon Brothers when Warren Buffett tried to impose respect for shareholders on superstud Wall Street cowboys. It didn't work. You can make a leopard be a better leopard, but you can't change its spots.

OVER TIME, SELF-INTEREST distorts corporate values. Give me a value, and I will subtly redefine it so that it fits my world view. The organization's values will gradually evolve away from what the company wants. To bring them back, top management must constantly reiterate, refresh, reinterpret, and rename.

Take GE again. In February, I attended a conference where someone from GE Capital spoke. The slides he was showing were all about GE's brand-new initiative, total quality management. It had a characteristic GE twist—satisfying customers at a profit—but it was still TQM, with stuff about reducing the cost of poor quality, eliminating rework and inspection, etc. I was nonplussed. GE, fecund mecca of new management ideas, is just discovering TQM? But as he went on, I began hearing familiar GE language. There was "speed, simplicity, and self-confidence." There was "be No. 1 or No. 2 in your business or you'll be fixed, sold, or closed down." There was "boundarylessness."

GE had decanted its vintage stuff into a TQM carafe, presenting the same ideas in slightly different packaging, from a slightly different point of view. This isn't fad-of-the-monthism, because the message remains the same. It is, instead, a refreshment and revitalization of fundamental beliefs. It's also a way to get more people to hook their values to the corporate ones. If collaboration isn't my thing, I might not respond to "boundary-lessness." But if excellence is a value of mine, and GE can show me that quality comes from boundarylessness, count me in.

We have a start, then, toward understanding how to make corporate values work. They have to be compatible with the culture that's already there; pretty words won't bloom in the wrong soil. And you have to guard against value mutation. Values are living things. You can't just stick them in a vase and leave them. You have to manage them. Work with them. Keep them alive.

*Advice from the U.S. point man on how to prevail during
potentially hostile negotiations.*

HOW TO NEGOTIATE WITH REALLY TOUGH GUYS

W HEN THE U.S. needs to negotiate with hostile governments for the release of political prisoners, the task usually falls to **BILL RICHARDSON,** a seven-term Democratic Congressman from New Mexico. The former pro-baseball prospect has played hardball with the likes of Saddam Hussein, Fidel Castro, and General Sani Abacha of Nigeria. In most cases he walked away a winner. Richardson engineered the return of two American defense contractors who wandered across the Iraq-Kuwait border, prevailed upon the North Korean government to release a captured U.S. helicopter pilot and turn over the body of his co-pilot, and persuaded Castro to free three political prisoners. He also held a critical meeting with Raoul Cedras of Haiti to try to smooth Jean-Bertrand Aristide's return to power. Richardson spoke with FORTUNE's Justin Martin about the art of negotiating.

What does it take to be a good negotiator?
You have to be a good listener. You have to respect the other side's point of view. You have to know what makes your adversary tick. Certainly you want to have a goal. You want to come out of a meeting with something, even if it's only a second meeting. And basically you have to use every single negotiating technique you know— bluster, reverence, humor.

How much leverage do you have when you're negotiating to release a hostage?
I can't really offer the other side any concessions. I have to be clear

at the outset that we're not going to resolve differences between our countries. Just building in the minds of some of these dictators that they'll have somebody to talk to whom they can trust is helpful. I let these governments, especially unfriendly ones, know I can pass messages. They know I'm going to end up talking to the White House. There's now the perception that the United States is the only superpower out there. Any entity associated with the U.S. government automatically has a leg up.

How do you prepare for a negotiation?
I talk to people who know the guy I'll be negotiating with. I talk to scholars, State Department experts, journalists. Before meeting with Saddam Hussein, I relied a lot on Iraq's ambassador to the U.N. He told me to be very honest with Saddam—not to pull any punches. With Castro, I learned that he was always hungry for information about America. Sure enough, he was fascinated by Steve Forbes, fascinated with the congressional budget impasse. He fancies himself an expert on U.S. politics. With Cedras of Haiti, I learned that he played good cop and that a top general, Philippe Biamby, played bad cop. So I was prepared. During our meeting, Biamby leaped up on the table and started screaming, "I don't like the U.S. government to call me a thug... *Je ne suis pas un thug.*" I remember turning to Cedras as Biamby was doing this and saying, "I don't think he likes me very much." Cedras laughed and laughed. He said, "All right, Biamby, sit down."

What else can you do if negotiations get dicey?
Dictators often try to take advantage of you at the outset. They try to catch you off guard. At the beginning of my meeting with Saddam Hussein, I crossed my legs and the soles of my feet were visible. He got up and left the room. I asked the interpreter, "What did I do?" He said, "The President was insulted that you crossed your legs. To an Arab that's a nasty insult, and you should apologize." I asked, "Is he coming back?" The interpreter said, "Yeah, he'll come back." When he did, I made the decision not to apologize. I wasn't going to grovel, say, "Hey, I'm real sorry I crossed my legs." I planted my feet and said, "Mr.

President, let me resume." And I think he respected that, because the discussions got better. You try to show that you're a humble person, but at the same time you can't back down. You can't show weakness. You keep coming at them.

What other techniques do you use?
I try to appeal to the leader's advisers, the ones I've talked to in advance, to cut a deal. I did that in Cuba. I said to Castro, "Look, I just talked to your assistant here, and I thought we had an agreement." I turned to Carlos Lage, a vice president, and said, "Come on, help me out, will you?" Finally he did. And so we kept the conversation alive.

A lot of these leaders are isolated. They're told only what they want to hear. So you bring them a dose of reality. If they think you're honest, sometimes they'll respond to that. With Castro, it was nearing midnight, and I said, "I came here to negotiate an agreement. I'm going to have to go back to the United States empty-handed. I'm going to have to say to the press when I leave that I got nothing. Is that the message you want?" I started making inroads after that.

When you finish a negotiation, can you tell right away whether you achieved your objectives?
You always know by the end, when you get either a pleasant or a perfunctory goodbye. With Saddam there was a grudging respect. There was definitely a rapport with Castro over baseball and Latin culture. I spoke with him in Spanish, and he gave me five cigars; he said they were the best—Cohiba.

You wound up smoking a cigar with Castro?
No, he doesn't smoke anymore.

Have you ever walked out of a negotiation?
Yes, in Nigeria four months ago. My objective was to secure the release of Moshood Abiola, who was imprisoned after he won the 1993 election. But General Abacha was taking such a hard line that I didn't even get to visit Abiola. Finally I said, "Mr.

President, I'm leaving the country. Let me know if you change your mind." You want to keep the channels open. And I've been contacted since then. They've sent messages, and I've coordinated with the State Department. I think eventually Abiola will be released.

Who are the toughest people you've ever negotiated with?
The North Koreans. They're the most relentless, the most dogmatic. They can't make any decisions on the spot. They always have to check with their superiors, but you don't know who the superiors are. Saddam Hussein is tough too. He starts out with a very menacing image. It sets you back a bit. I remember looking at my hands, and I was sweating. I was conscious that he knew what his reputation was. And he knew that I knew his reputation.

Why are so many CEOs lousy leaders? Research shows they tend to be impatient, impulsive, manipulative, dominating, self-important, and critical of others.

RAMBOS IN PINSTRIPES

FOR MORE THAN A DECADE, executive-development consultant **RICHARD HAGBERG** has been advising chief executives on the fine points of leadership. His firm, the Hagberg Consulting Group, has compiled a database on the characteristics of 511 CEOs that delivers intriguing insights into why so many fail to inspire loyalty in their troops. Based on CEO personality tests and evaluations from thousands of their co-workers, Hagberg's research shows that many who stumble are impatient, impulsive, manipulative, dominating, self-important, and critical of others. Moreover, Hagberg has concluded that the number of Rambos in pinstripes is increasing. Five years ago only half his CEO clients were classified as loners; today the figure is closer to 70%. He spoke with FORTUNE's Linda Grant.

Your studies have found that many CEOs don't have what it takes. What exactly is it about their leadership skills that's lacking?
We find there are three pillars of leadership: One is to be the inspirational evangelist for a vision. A lot of CEOs, we found, are mechanical and machine-like, and it's hard to be inspired by a problem-solving machine. Another pillar is to manage implementation—which many are good at—and a third is to build relationships with subordinates. We discovered that many CEOs are very egocentric. They don't think the third step is important, because the world doesn't exist beyond them. Therefore, they have a hard time developing talent. They are Rambo-like individualists who create a survival-of-the-fittest atmosphere.

How do these CEOs get their companies into trouble?
Under the stress and pressure that go with the job, many CEOs become reactive, listen less, and act impulsively without thinking. Their impatience drives them to focus on financial goals, which means they fail to build relationships with boards or their employees. One result is that people stop buying into their solutions. As a group, CEOs tend to be domineering and strong-willed; they state their opinions forcefully. As they distance themselves from others, it becomes harder for people to disagree with them. When that happens, they stop getting bad news or the benefit of a give-and-take conversation.

Why does that matter?
Teamwork, which you need in any corporation, suffers. When CEOs disconnect emotionally—which, by the way, may be a personal survival technique—they end up making decisions in a vacuum because they are alienated from others. Good leaders are demanding, but they maintain a connection to their people and therefore build a sense of loyalty. It's hard to be loyal to a machine.

Why do so many become alienated?
As a group, CEOs tend to be very independent and have high needs for autonomy. The more entrepreneurial they are, the stronger their need is to be in control. But many are poor communicators. They are good at developing a vision, and they think they have communicated it, but frequently their strategy isn't widely understood. As a result these leaders get confused and frustrated, because their people aren't doing what they think they've told them to do. They become critical of others and suspicious. This creates more barriers.

Many are also hobbled by self-importance, which keeps them from hearing feedback and prevents them from being objective about their own strengths and weaknesses. The head of one large company recently told me about an incident that occurred as he and his wife waited in line to get his driver's license renewed. He was frustrated at how long it was taking and grumbled to his wife, "I have a lot to do. Don't they know who I am?" She replied, "Yeah, you're a plumber's son who got lucky." Her remark really got to him. It drove home how far he had gotten caught up in his sense of self-importance.

How do they get to the top?
They produce financial results over the short run. A lot of companies reward independent cowboys who are not in it for the long haul. I see this in Silicon Valley, where the rate of change in high-tech companies is so fast and people often get promoted because of their technical skills. Great companies like Hewlett-Packard realize they have a lot of technical people, so they need to create a culture that reinforces management by walking around. HP, for example, uses open cubicles so people can't isolate themselves in offices, and spends a ton of money on training and development. It's almost a recognition that if they let automatic pilot take over, all those engineers won't communicate.

Are these CEOs capable of change?
Some are, if they get good feedback. But who's going to tell the emperor he has no clothes? It can limit your career. I think a lot of times consultants get hired because somebody thinks that a message needs to be delivered. But CEOs didn't get where they are by being stupid. If given credible feedback, they frequently run with it. But if they are too self-important, they will be defensive because they have a vested interest in maintaining an image of themselves as omnipotent. And that can be an absolute killer.

Shedding employees is something almost every manager dreads.
But if you don't think hard about the process, you and your
company could be headed straight for a world of woes.

HOW TO FIRE PEOPLE
(AND STILL SLEEP AT NIGHT)

BY KENNETH LABICH

TALES OF BADLY TIMED, thoughtless, and even cruel corporate executions are everywhere these days. A man finds out he has been let go when a restaurant won't accept his company credit card. A woman manager gets the news via a note placed on her chair during lunch. Employees at a high-tech firm learn of their fate when their security codes no longer open the front door of their office building.

Sheer numbness may account for at least some of this nasty behavior. The great corporate restructuring fever has held pitch for over a decade now—some 400,000 hapless folks got the boot during 1995 alone, and some executioners may be too desensitized by now to stand on ceremony. But any company that ignores the human wreckage involved, that halts people's careers and threatens their financial security carelessly, is taking foolish risks. Lawsuits are the most obvious threat; high-six-figure awards for wrongful dismissal or discrimination are ever more common.

Harder to measure, but at least as corrosive to any organization, is the effect on survivors of a mindless corporate purge. Any mass layoff somehow tarnishes a company, and the damage can be permanent if the deed is done without care. Says Jim MacLachlan, director of change management operations at the Deloitte & Touche Consulting Group: "One thing is certain: If

117

you treat people like pieces of meat, it will come back to haunt you."

TO FIRE—OR NOT

T HE EXPERTS—human resources executives, outplacement specialists, corporate hitpersons themselves—all agree that managers ought to question their own motives hard before they institute layoffs. The stakes, human and otherwise, are just too high. Don't pull the trigger, they say, if you are simply trying to cover up for your own management lapses. Says Frederick Reichheld, a director at the Bain management consulting firm and author of *The Loyalty Effect*: "Too often a layoff is viewed as some sort of virile gesture, a way of saying that senior management is hard-minded and serious."

Nor should top corporate brass view restructuring as a quick fix for a slumping stock price. True, Wall Street has often responded nicely to layoff announcements. But companies have gone to that well too often; security analysts and investors now grouse that repeated restructurings, resulting in supposedly nonrecurring charges, have thoroughly muddied earnings at giants like AT&T, IBM, General Signal, and many others.

It's also becoming clear that investors' ardor for stripped-down payrolls fades quickly. A recent Mercer Management Consulting study of 1,000 of the largest U.S. companies found that the compound annual growth rate of market capitalization for downsizers was about 11% from 1988 to 1994. For the companies that concentrated instead on revenue growth, the figure was 15%.

Top managers would also do well to consider the multiple costs involved in firing people, say the experts. That's true even if just a single individual is involved. Boston outplacement specialist Laurence Stybel estimates that the average U.S. company spends at least $25,000 to replace an executive getting a $70,000 salary. Far better, he argues, to find ways to improve a faltering employee's performance. "Rehabilitation is better than replacement," says Stybel.

SMART FIRING

◆It used to be that if you replaced an older worker with someone 40 or above, you'd be safe from age discrimination suits. The Supreme Court has decided that no longer holds.

◆You generally can't fire an alcoholic unless you've first offered him counseling or a leave of absence. But be careful: Accusing an employee of alcoholism could result in a defamation suit.

◆Just because the person you fire is straight, white, male, and under 40 does not preclude a lawsuit.

◆Don't even think about jettisoning anyone who refuses to perform some part of his job because of religious beliefs.

◆You typically can't fire someone for frequent absences due to a medical condition—even allergies or backache.

◆A jury could decide you have publicly defamed someone if you boot him (or her) for sexual harassment. Instead, encourage the employee to draw up a resignation letter detailing his own reasons for leaving.

He cites one client, a large hospital, that contemplated axing a director of radiology who had become increasingly rude to co-workers. Instead of firing him, the hospital's managers put him on probation and assigned him a consultant who counseled him on interpersonal relations. To everyone's surprise, the doctor appeared delighted to tone down his act. Result: The hospital saved the slew of money and effort it would have taken to replace him.

Then there are the human costs to consider. The toll on people losing their jobs is obvious enough. "These are wounded people, often battered by exactly what they had been loyal to," says Richard Levin, a Massachusetts psychologist who works with corporate executives who fire people. For purely practical reasons, top managers might consider even more the potential pain and guilt survivors of a big layoff suffer; they are, after all, the people who would have to carry the ball forward. Almost everyone is likely to be affected in some way, but the managers who do the actual firing are often hurt the most. Alan Downs, a confessed corporate assassin for years before turning to human resources consulting, recalls the hideous feeling of walking into a headquarters building the day after a round of layoffs had begun. This was his greeting from a survivor: "Are we clubbing baby seals again today?"

BEING THERE

T HE HARD TRUTH IS THAT, despite whatever soul-searching senior managers can muster, some firings are inevitable. There will always be individuals who don't hack it, and increasingly, there will be companies that are forced to restructure to stay competitive. When an AT&T deconstructs into three smaller companies, there are bound to be casualties. When banks or utilities are deregulated, employee rosters are all but certain to shrink.

But whenever heads roll, particularly during a large layoff, top management has to be an active and visible presence. Among the worst sins corporate leaders can commit during a restructuring is a Pontius Pilate maneuver—placing the job with outside consultants or their own personnel department and then washing their hands of it. Ralph Johnson, who trains managers in proper firing techniques for the American Management Association, recalls an East Coast manufacturer who sent a low-level human resources executive around to announce a series of plant closings. Workers started hurling spools of thread at her, and she completed her tour accompanied by security guards.

Top management's proper role before a restructuring is, first and most important, to develop and disseminate a rational explanation for what's taking place and where the company is headed. Those who are leaving are far less likely to be angry (and litigious) if they understand why their company is changing. Those who stay are more likely to pitch in with a full heart if they believe they are working for a more competitive organization.

Management, working with the legal department, should also draft a profile of the new work force, one that matches its vision of the company's future. The idea is to take a close look at your total labor group—age, sex, competencies, length of service. There will eventually be legal issues to consider; your lawyers won't let you even think of wiping out most minority workers or employees over age 40.

But most important at this stage is to hold your labor force up against the precise future needs of the company. Says Eileen Canty, an organizational psychologist who labored through layoff battles at ITT during the 1980s and now works as a consultant with William M. Mercer Inc.:"It sounds simple, but you'd be amazed how often people screw it up. You have to ask yourself two questions: What are the skills you need to run the business at the end of this tunnel—and what are the skills you won't need?"

GET SERIOUS

ONCE MANAGEMENT has a clear grasp of its future labor needs, the next step in the layoff process is preparing the troops for the coming storms. Top management should issue clear, repeated warnings that a downsizing is possible; informal advice from line managers can help too. The employee who has been tipped not to take on a big financial burden—a new house, say—will be grateful to have been warned when the ax falls.

Actions, however, rattle way more cages than words. Workers

all over the U.S. have been living with the threat of downsizing, and they are unlikely to take verbal warnings seriously unless they are backed up by concrete changes in the status quo. The best methods serve two purposes. First, they proclaim, loud and clear, that change is inevitable. Second, they demonstrate that involuntary layoffs, when they occur, are a last resort.

Depending on the nature of the business involved, salary and hiring freezes often get people's attention. Reduced overtime, shortened workweeks, pay cuts, unpaid vacations—they all make it obvious that this particular ship is changing course. One of the trickiest moments in the cruise comes when management contemplates asking for volunteers to walk the plank. Since you've promised to offer a package to anyone who steps forward during a voluntary layoff, there's always a danger that too many people will leap at the chance. This could make it appear that the ship is sinking, or cause a lot of those employees you'd rather keep on board to go ashore. Still, say the experts, if management has communicated its vision of the future properly, voluntary layoffs are the proper initial step.

There's nothing wrong, of course, with trying out special inducements to get more people to walk out voluntarily. Smart managers, those with close links to their work force, sweeten severance packages to match the tastes of each particular employee. "You never know what buttons you have to push unless you are in touch with your people," says Canty of William M. Mercer. She worked with one company that helped persuade a number of older workers to retire voluntarily by promising them membership in a 25-Year Club, even though they were a couple of months short of the requirement. Another company got the body count it wanted by allowing departing employees to remain in the corporate gun club for an extended period.

When deciding who's going to stay, it's crucial to receive feedback from employees. At AT&T, the decision this winter to eliminate some 40,000 jobs took place only after months of furious planning and internal communication. Management first defined the core competency of each of the company's three new businesses, then polled supervisors to gather information on

WHAT NOT TO DO

Don't forget you're a member of the family of man. The head office of a steel fabrication company instructed an employee to fire his father. The son, having no choice, followed orders but tempered the bad news by giving Dad six months' severance pay. For his generosity, the son, a few weeks later, was unexpectedly fired. Mom, who worked as a part-time bookkeeper, also got the boot. The son sued. A jury agreed he had been fired wrongfully.

Don't use your employees as pawns in a corporate chess game. A supervisor called a meeting with his waitresses to say that someone was stealing from the restaurant. In order to establish the identity of the thief, he told the assembled women, he would begin firing them, one by one, in alphabetical order, until someone fessed up. The company was found guilty of intentional infliction of emotional distress.

Don't fire en masse. As part of a sales agreement, the original owners of a medical collection agency were instructed to winnow its staff by half. The 1,000 employees were assembled in the company parking lot and the names of the 500 to be laid off were read aloud. The original owners then told the remaining employees they were lucky they still had jobs, but their medical insurance had been terminated.

Don't be a hypocrite. A division within a FORTUNE 500 company issued a memo encouraging employees to increase their global competitiveness by taking foreign-language instruction during the workday. Six months later all those who had availed themselves of the offer were fired. Management had apparently concluded that anyone who had the time to take a course during business hours was obviously underemployed.

each worker's skills. Employees were asked to fill out a highly structured résumé, including job preferences and geographical limitations. No one was left in the dark about how the old work force would fit into the new, streamlined company.

The final decision about who would go was left up to a team of supervisors and HR staffers; each employee was evaluated for specific posts that needed to be filled, and there were no unilateral decisions. Says Linda Villa, the AT&T human resources VP who led the team masterminding the company's recent layoffs: "It was of utmost importance to us that everyone was treated with dignity and respect."

KINDER, GENTLER

THAT ATTITUDE ought to carry over to the climactic meeting when a firing takes place, often a life-changing moment for the victim. "This isn't rocket science—you treat people the same way you would want to be treated," says Dan Nagy, a longtime outplacement specialist who now runs the placement office at Duke University's Fuqua School of Business.

But doing it right takes careful preparation. The experts say a firing should take place on neutral ground, in a quiet, uncluttered office; they warn managers who do the firing against using their own office because it's too hard to walk away if things get sticky. Early in the day is better than late—it gives the victim time to get important career questions answered—and you should make sure the fatal meeting doesn't fall on the victim's birthday or some other special day.

Bob Swain, chairman of Swain & Swain, a New York consulting firm, says managers facing the job of firing people ought to prepare a script beforehand, perhaps even reading it into a tape recorder a few times to ensure the proper empathetic tone. Your remarks should simply summarize the individual's severance package and outline how it's to be implemented. Avoid angering people by making gratuitous remarks about their shortcomings. Says Swain: "In trying to compensate for their own guilt, executives often say too much, highlighting specific reasons that led to the dismissal."

It's all right to express regret about the situation and concern about the employee's well-being, but don't get defensive or indicate in any way that the decision is negotiable. Maintain eye contact, don't fiddle with papers or pens, and never, ever fire anyone with alcohol on your breath. After 30 minutes tops, you end the meeting by standing up and escorting the employee directly to a counselor. Don't expect to be viewed as any kind of hero; even if you've done everything by the book, chances are excellent that at least some people will make sure their grandchildren curse your name.

Though the actual act of getting fired will stick with most victims for the ages, what happens to them afterward is at least as important. No company should attempt to guarantee new employment to the workers it lays off, but all should at least give its discards a fighting chance to start again. The best practice is offering flexible outplacement packages, geared to the specific needs of each individual. Some technical workers may want retraining to broaden their skills. Some laid-off executives may want help in starting their own businesses. Many large companies have put together job fairs, sometimes in their own cafeterias, during big layoffs. William M. Mercer's Canty recalls one ITT division that found new positions for 75% of its firees by using such job fairs as well as other methods.

Consultant Alan Downs is a special fan of certain layoff plans used at Hewlett-Packard, Levi Strauss, and elsewhere. Under these plans, employees are notified that their jobs are to be eliminated but that they will remain on the payroll for a specific amount of time—usually six months. In essence, their job becomes finding a new job, inside or outside the company. Retraining opportunities are offered. Placement specialists are assigned to aid each of the endangered employees, and in some cases no new outsiders are hired until the program has run its course.

SO SUE ME

THE DOWNSIZING CRAZE has ignited a frenzy of lawsuits from layoff victims alleging everything from age and race discrimination to sexual harassment. And more and more, cases that reach the courtroom are resulting in lush awards to employees. Says Ronald M. Green, a Manhattan attorney who often defends corporations against discrimination charges: "Juries walk in there ready to put employers' feet to the fire. Legal issues often give way to a sense of shared humanity with the plaintiff."

The basic law involved in laying people off sounds simple enough. In lieu of some contractual agreement, union or otherwise, all workers are so-called employees at will. That means they can leave whenever they want and can be let go at any time for any sound business reason. But things aren't nearly that simple when you are shedding anyone in a protected group—including women, minorities, the disabled, and anyone over 40 years old. To get rid of folks in any of these categories, you may have to prove that their sex, age, race, or physical condition was in no way a factor in the decision.

That has proved difficult for many downsizing employers recently, particularly when it comes to charges of age discrimination. Tens of thousands of such cases are being filed every year, and Green estimates that at least three in four result in a settlement or jury award for the plaintiff. Jury awards are often substantial because the law allows plaintiffs who win their cases to be reinstated and collect double the amount of wages and benefits they would have earned during the time they were unemployed—plus all legal fees. If the aggrieved is a $100,000-a-year executive who has been grounded for three or four years, you approach seven figures fast.

The proper defense against charges of unfair treatment, whatever the basis, begins on day one of an employee's tenure. "You make no guarantees about longevity of employment," says Ralph Johnson. "The only thing you promise people is a chance to use their skills and talents." Regular, formal evaluations are also a must; you've got to lay a paper trail if you want to claim an employee's work has been unsatisfactory all along. In doing so, however, the experts emphasize that supervisors must avoid any language that implies that age or sex or race was an issue. Plaintiff's attorneys trying age-discrimination cases salivate when they turn up smoking-gun evaluations that say things like "this employee is less efficient than his younger colleagues." A manager's offhand remark about a worker's graying hair or arthritic knee could be equally damaging.

WINNERS/LOSERS

T HE WORKERS WHO REMAIN after a big downsizing are filled with a range of emotions—relief, guilt, fear over their own future. They will almost surely identify closely with departing colleagues and react accordingly if an employer appears callous and arbitrary. As John Parkington, a consultant with Watson Wyatt Worldwide in San Francisco, puts it, "If you've seen all your buddies bum-rushed out the door for no particular reason, you start thinking that maybe the same thing will happen to you."

Employers can ease survivors' fears by striving to create stability after a big layoff. Nothing eviscerates morale among survivors more readily than repeated downsizings. Workers can develop a sense that management has run out of new ideas and is instead subjecting employees to some sort of never-ending pogrom. Says Bain's Reichheld: "Churn simply for the sake of churn is evil; it destroys knowledge, trust, and growth." All semblance of connectedness between employers and workers vanishes, and true teamwork is impossible. At companies where layoffs have become a way of life, says Reichheld, you rarely find the energy and cooperative spirit necessary for success. "Business becomes a transaction between strangers," he says.

Eventually, companies in continuous turmoil can succumb to what Peter Scott-Morgan of Arthur D. Little calls "change fatigue." By hammering away at workers' sense of security—Rambo reengineering, Scott-Morgan calls it—management winds up with a labor force full of overly timid zombies. Conflicts are forced underground, there to fester like so many untreated wounds in the corporate soul.

Fully aware that no one is immune in a downsizing world?
Don't just sweat it out. Start networking before you need to.

JOIN THE HEADHUNTER'S INNER CIRCLE

BY MARSHALL LOEB

WORRIED THAT YOU MAY be bounced out of your job to-morrow? Well, I have some good news for you: Even as they dump their loyal longtimers, companies are eagerly looking to hire outsiders who have particular talents. The result is that headhunters are busier than ever. Break onto their short lists, and you have a nifty chance to make a large leap up. Ah, but how do you do that?

Your first step is to be proactive: Find and cultivate headhunters before you need them. Attend conferences of the trade association in your field and look for the headhunters. Many of them attend to scout the talent. You can get the names of the most reputable retained recruiting firms by consulting a recruiters' directory. The four largest U.S. firms are Heidrick & Struggles, Korn/Ferry, Spencer Stuart, and Russell Reynolds Associates.

When you spot someone whose tag announces he is with a search firm, introduce yourself with the magic words, "I'd be happy to help you with information when you're searching for someone in my field." Recruiters live by their sources; become one, and you may well be recruited in the future.

When she screens potential sources, Manhattan headhunter Linda Bialecki rates their responsiveness on a scale of one to five: "Five is so high that almost nobody gets it, four means you're terrific, three indicates you gave a good try to help us, two means so-so, and one says you were really rude." Anyone who scores two or lower is blackballed—"We don't recruit jerks"—if his name ever comes up as a candidate in a later search.

Targeted mailings can help you more than you think. "Send in your résumé," urges CEO Paul Ray Jr. of Paul Ray Berndtson in Fort Worth. "Three or four years ago it was a waste of time, but no longer. Résumés are looked at more by search firms than in the past, because the new technology lets us scan in and store your information and get it out to every searcher in every one of our offices in the country."

Find the searchers who focus on your industry and profession. (Yes, it is ethical to deal with several firms at once.) More than 1,000 are listed by specialty and location in *The Directory of Executive Recruiters* ($49.95, Kennedy Publications, 800-531-0007). Or buy the $55 directory of the Association of Executive Search Consultants (212-398-9556) for an elite listing of 125 top search firms. Then what? If you're a health care manager, for example, send your résumé to both the head of research and the head of health care practice at various search firms.

Enclose a three-paragraph letter highlighting your current work and a one- or two-page résumé. Your industry, your company, your pay, and your most recent two or three positions are all flagged by the searcher for future reference. Most headhunters focus on the past five or ten years of your career. Says Dale Winston of Battalia Winston International in Manhattan: "Show me accomplishments—increasing sales, raising profitability, cutting costs, turning a business around." For example, don't merely say you can work the Internet; explain how you made the Net useful in marketing your company.

Another tip: Call your college, ask which alums are recruiters, and write to them. Says Bialecki (Stanford MBA '79): "I will see any Stanford MBA."

Don't waste your time cold-calling headhunters for an interview. Instead, look for people who are acquainted with headhunters, and have them call for you. That group probably includes many high-ranking executives with whom you are acquainted. Outplacement executive Robert Swain of Swain & Swain confides, "Some of the smartest executives I know have

RECRUITERS AND SEARCH FIRMS

Y OU CAN GET THE NAMES of the most reputable retained recruiting firms by consulting a recruiters' directory. The four largest U.S. firms are Heidrick & Struggles, Korn/Ferry, Spencer Stuart, and Russell Reynolds Associates.

Find the searchers who focus on your industry and profession. More than 1,000 are listed by specialty and location in *The Directory of Executive Recruiters* ($49.95, Kennedy Publications, 800-531-0007). Or buy the $55 directory of the Association of Executive Search Consultants (212-398-9556) for an elite listing 125 top search firms. Then what? If you're a health care manager, for example, send your résumé to both the head of research and the head of health care practice at various search firms.

Executive Recruiter News (Kennedy Publications, $187 per year, 800-531-0007) is a monthly newsletter that covers trends and developments, key personnel changes, fees, mergers, defections, legal questions, ethics, and association news.

hired recruiting firms that they figured might eventually help themselves get placed."

Once you make contact with a searcher, keep her updated. Write her whenever you get a promotion; send her a letter at least once a year with your latest accomplishments. And drop her a note whenever she bags a big trophy: "Dear Jane, Congratulations on recruiting the new chairman of General Motors!" You can discover such nuggets by subscribing to a head-hunters' newsletter, such as *Executive Recruiter News* ($187 per year, Kennedy Publications, 800-531-0007).

On the other hand, if you're fired, don't conceal it. Indeed, persuade your company to announce it. Headhunters scour the press for names of people who have decided to "seek other opportunities." And it cannot be repeated too often: Firing these days doesn't carry the stigma it once did.

Finally, be kind to colleagues who leave your company. "If I want to find out who's good at First Boston," says Linda Bialecki, "I call 20 people who used to be there."

It pays to be pleasant. And patient. Six years ago, recruiter Pendleton James clipped a FORTUNE article about three young up-and-coming executives. One was Ronald Burns, who had just become president of the Gas Pipeline Group of Enron, the oil and gas company. Eight months ago, James placed Burns, 43, as CEO of the multibillion-dollar Union Pacific Railroad.

For those of you who decide to bag the big corporate arena and focus your talents and energies on your own business—or for those of you who dream about it—here's an organizational chart to help you assemble your "staff." Almost certainly—until you're up and running, and maybe long after that— you will be filling these slots with friends and family. Their official capacity might be limited to an occasional call for advice. You might never hold a staff meeting; you might never write them a paycheck. But as CEO, you are only as good as your employees, even if they are only employees in your mind.

YOU INC.: THE ORGANIZATIONAL CHART

BY THOMAS A. STEWART

YOUR CHIEF EXECUTIVE OFFICER. Only you can provide the vision, values, and leadership for You Inc. Make sure that your board and staff support your vision and values and understand how they further You Inc.'s strategic plan.

YOUR FINANCE FUNCTION: TAX, TREASURY. Chances are you act as your own chief financial officer, and your tax department (accountant), treasurer (broker), banker, and insurance company report directly to you. That setup may be inadequate as the company grows. If the job gets so time consuming that you are making money but not managing it, bring in a professional financial planner.

YOUR GENERAL COUNSEL. Your mouthpiece, of course.

YOUR CHIEF OPERATING OFFICER. This is your boss. She works for you. Her job: managing your day-to-day, quarter-to-quarter, year-to-year operations, making sure things run smoothly. She is not responsible for your long-range planning or decisions to enter new markets, though COOs often give valuable advice in these areas.

Relationships between CEOs and COOs can be delicate. Often the COO thinks she really runs the place. To keep your COO happy, it's best not to disabuse her of this illusion.

Note that if your boss works for you, it follows that you work for your subordinates. What have you done to help them meet their strategic objectives?

YOUR CHIEF TECHNOLOGY OFFICER. If you look for Lotus Notes on the botany shelf at Barnes & Noble—if you think SAP goes into maple syrup or if you don't know the difference between Yahoo and yippie-kiyay—get with it. You Inc. is in perpetual competition with Them Amalgamated. Being savvy about information technology can be the difference between winning and losing.

Unless technology is your field, you can't keep up with it; you need a guide to tell you if you're cool or out in the cold. Your son or daughter is a good candidate for the CTO job, especially if you can get him or her interested in business computing. Otherwise, take a nerd to lunch.

YOUR VP FOR MARKETING. Actors have them (they're called agents), and you should too: one or more people who make it a point to steer opportunities your way. The marketing VP might be a senior person in your company, a mentor, who touts your skills and puts you up for challenging projects. A headhunter who placed you once and would love to move you up. An ex-boss. Or best of all, a satisfied customer.

Good marketing VPs are rare. One way to find one: Be one. Start shilling for someone you admire. He might be so surprised that he returns the favor.

YOUR BOARD OF DIRECTORS. An important and often neglected structure of You Inc., your board of directors has three responsibilities: giving you advice, keeping you honest, and respecting the confidentiality of boardroom discussions, i.e., clamming up. Board members serve without pay, and often without knowing it.

You Inc.'s board includes insiders and outsiders. Joining you, the chairman, should be these insiders: your spouse (who is also a major shareholder), a parent or an adult child, and your boss, who, as already mentioned, is also chief operating officer. If your relationship with your boss isn't such that she can serve wholeheartedly on your board, consider whether some other senior person at your place of work can fill the role.

As corporate governance experts will tell you, you should pick outside directors with care. At least one should know your business well. They all should know you and be people who, as it says in the old song "Bosom Buddies," "will sit down and level—will give you the devil—will sit down and tell you the truth." Says Richard Moran, a partner at Price Waterhouse consulting: "Often people get all their career advice from people who love them, who might be unable to face facts or unwilling to make you face them." Good candidates: a co-worker whose judgment you admire; a professor you keep up with; a couple of peers—maybe that tough customer who has become a friend or a B-school classmate in your industry.

Moran's own "board" includes an imaginary member who is called in when the CEO needs private counseling. Says Moran: "Usually I imagine the advice Bob Newhart would give me. But sometimes I call on Clint Eastwood."

Manager, know thyself.
A surprising number of talented people sabotage their own work
performance because of a deep-rooted fear of doing well.
You can overcome it. Step one? Own up to it.

ARE YOU AFRAID OF SUCCESS?

BY ANNE B. FISHER

FAR AND AWAY the biggest moneymaker in pro golf, Greg Norman wins and wins and wins—until he gets to a major tournament. At the 1996 Masters, he took a six-stroke lead and the next day, in just five holes, handed his six strokes and then some to the guy behind him. He's done this not just once, not twice, but over and over and over again.

You don't have to be a sports fan to see the parallels between golf and business. The same phenomenon is far from rare in corporate life: the talented person, with everything going for him or her, who self-destructs for no reason that anyone can fathom. Some of these tales—and everybody knows a few—are as spectacular in their own way as Norman's, although they mercifully aren't broadcast live via satellite around the world.

Robert Meuleman, president and CEO of Amcore Financial in Rockford, Illinois, tells of a bright young banker with a solid marriage who, shortly after his promotion to the presidency of a division, began an affair with an employee, whom he then knocked down a flight of stairs. "We don't know why he destroyed himself that way," says Meuleman, who fired him. "His career has never recovered." Then there's the executive at Union Pacific in Pennsylvania who, despite his $500,000-a-year salary, claimed lavish business outings with imaginary customers on his

135

five-figure expense reports. "Even after he was spoken to, he kept doing it," says another Union Pacific executive. "In fact, he did it more." He too was fired.

HOW TO TELL BAD LUCK FROM SELF-SABOTAGE

YOU'D NEVER BE SO RECKLESS, you say? Probably not. But hold on. Most often, being your own worst enemy is a far more subtle thing. You're in line for a promotion you've worked toward for years, and suddenly find you can't get to work on time. Or you start losing your temper in meetings with higher-ups where cool is the rule. Or you somehow misplace the data for a client presentation that could make or break your team. Or maybe you haven't made any obvious blunders, but you haven't been doing your best work for quite a while now, and you don't know why.

Any of these examples may share a common cause: fear of success. It's strange to think, at a time when so many people are struggling just to hold on to what they've got, that fear of succeeding could be much of an issue or do much damage. It is and does. "Fear of success is a terrible problem in this culture," says Brian Schwartz, a psychologist and consultant in Greenwich, Connecticut. "The vast majority of people I see are afflicted with it." What is so treacherous about this anxiety is that the people who suffer from it most acutely are usually not aware they have it. Those who do know are not eager to own up in print, at least not by name. In an ever more Darwinian business world, an admitted weakness is a dangerous thing.

The dread of doing well in life is rooted deep in the unconscious. Nobody deliberately sets out to wreck his or her own career. And people are so adept at rationalizing their own mistakes, or misinterpreting those of others, that fear of success can be hard to distinguish from, oh, let's see, incompetence, arrogance, inattention, burnout, or any of the 101 other gremlins that can send a career into a tailspin. Often fear of success shows up in the exceptionally talented as a long pattern of underachievement, of schlubbing along in the same old rut. "People who have an unconscious fear of success won't set ambitious goals for themselves, so they achieve far less than they're capable of," says James O'Connell, a psychologist at the outplacement firm Drake Beam Morin. "And this is the tragedy of it, because ultimately it stops people from getting what they really want or even from asking for help."

If this is an unconscious fear, how can you tell if you have it? Shrinks have been studying the problem since 1915, when Freud wrote an essay called "Those Wrecked by Success." He noted the "surprising and even bewildering" tendency of some people to fall apart "precisely when a deeply rooted and long-cherished wish has come to fulfillment ... as though they were not able to tolerate happiness." As with the Illinois bank president, a spate of self-destructive behavior—often involving drinking, drugs, sex, or all three—immediately before or after a major triumph is a dead giveaway. Says Elissa Sklaroff, a therapist in Philadelphia who treats success-fearing executives: "Being on the brink of success brings a crisis, and all of our neuroses pop right up to the surface. On some level, success-fearing people are running from change—especially from having to change their secret self-image as an unsuccessful or undeserving person." Sometimes, Sklaroff says, people about to take a big step up in their careers become convinced, without any medical evidence, that they have a grave illness, usually cancer.

Donnah Canavan is a psychology professor at Boston College, a practicing therapist, and co-author of a textbook called *The Success-Fearing Personality*. For 15 years she's taught a course on this subject; many of her classes are full of business people. "I keep expecting to run into some skeptic who'll say, 'Fear of what? Oh, come on,' " says Canavan. "But I never have. Everybody seems to know exactly what I'm talking about."

That's probably because, at one time or another, most of us have had occasion to ask, What was I doing? Maybe you once procrastinated until a crucial deadline sailed by, or inserted foot firmly in mouth at the worst possible time, or had one cocktail (or was it six?) too many at the office Christmas party, or showed up inexcusably late for a big job interview—well, hey, nobody's perfect. Over time, though, too many of these missteps should be telling you something.

Likewise if you, or someone you know, has been stuck in the same job despite obvious talent. "Often people who fear success do succeed, eventually," says Canavan. "But it takes them longer than they or their peers may have expected. They get less far. And it causes them a lot more mental turmoil and emotional pain than it does someone else to get to the same level."

EXPLORING YOUR FORMATIVE YEARS

WHERE DOES all this angst come from? Ah. Please lie down on the couch, get comfortable, and we will proceed. Freud postulated an unconscious need to fail (not just a desire, but a need) that arises from the unresolved competition between parent and child—mainly father and son—for the approval of the opposite-sex parent. Because a child cannot distinguish between thinking or wishing something and actually doing it, he is afraid to express, even to himself, his rage at his father, for fear that his father will die. So he represses his anger, which in the murky brew of the unconscious alchemizes into guilt.

By this reasoning, success in any competitive realm is a blood sport. Beating one's father, vanquishing the primal foe, is, in the complex metaphorical world of the unconscious, an unspeakable act. It is not merely murder but patricide. (And all this time you thought you just wanted the three-window office and stock options.) This is why, according to Freud, some men feel terrible unease at the prospect of getting ahead in business, in sports, or anywhere else. It's guilt.

Today's shrinks acknowledge that, compelling as Freud's theory is, most fear of success springs from less dramatic sources—mostly the bad stuff that happened to you as a kid and hammered your opinion of how good you are. "People will only achieve the level of success that their image of themselves can absorb," says Brian Schwartz, the Greenwich psychologist.

If, long ago, somebody important to you—a parent, a teacher, a sibling—told you that you aren't very smart, or very competent, or very likable, or that nothing you do is ever quite good enough, you will have the devil's own time believing that you're capable of doing well in life or that you deserve to. This conviction of unworthiness is rarely something people take out and examine, except in therapy. It's just there, lurking around the edges of life like a creature out of a Stephen King novel, spoiling everything. People with rotten childhoods do become successful, of course, but often they can't enjoy what they've achieved. The archives of American popular culture (Marilyn Monroe), politics (Richard Nixon), and sports (Dennis Rodman) are crammed to bursting with examples.

A childhood belief that what you are is never enough, that you must live up to others' lofty expectations of you, can lead to a lot of self-sabotaging behavior later on at the office. Sometimes successful people don't want to be where they are. They're there because someone else—a parent, a spouse—expects them to be. They can't imagine how to extricate themselves except by messing up. If I provoke my own firing, the unconscious logic goes, I'm off the hook. I can get out of here, and the decision can appear to have been someone else's. The ex–railroad executive who partied himself right out of a job, says an erstwhile colleague who knew him well, "didn't want to be here so bad, he didn't even know how bad he didn't want to be here." He got his unconscious wish, but in a way far more damaging than if he'd been able to figure out his motives beforehand and leave the company on his own steam.

Even if you manage to get through childhood unscathed, along comes adolescence. Alas, when Kurt Vonnegut remarked that "life is high school," he wasn't kidding. Much of our grown-up self-image is formed at a time when, let's face it, most of us are no prize. "Does anybody not remember how godawful those teenage years were?" asks a well-known CEO who has wrestled with a deep distrust of his own accomplishments. "Everybody feels ugly and inadequate. I think that as a result, a sense of peace, the idea that 'I am good enough,' eludes most of us." There may be many adult moments when doubts about your achievements are nothing more or less than your old high-school self coming back to nag that you'll never be (or date) the football quarterback or the head cheerleader because you're just too tall, or short, or smart, or dumb, or teeth-braced, or—fill in the blank. Dennis Rodman perfectly captures this vague feeling of inadequacy in his autobiography, *Bad As I Wanna Be*: "I wasn't accepted there [in his Dallas neighborhood]. I was too skinny, too ugly, too something."

The trouble with teenage self-loathing is that a severe case of it may make you spend the rest of your life with a chip on your shoulder—or to put it in shrinkspeak, suffering from a compensatory disorder. This can be a dandy way to wreck a career. Steven Berglas, who teaches psychiatry at Harvard Medical School and specializes in treating fear of success in executives, tells of a CEO who is very short and who has been self-conscious about it ever since he was ruthlessly razzed back in high school. As part of a lifelong campaign to prove his masculinity, this CEO started sleeping with a board member's wife. Yes, that's right. Out of all the women in the world, he got mixed up with the wife of a member of the only group of people with the power to fire him. And sure enough, they did. "Compensatory disorders use success as a vehicle for masking or suppressing old traumas," says Berglas. "Succeeding—being CEO—can't fix or cover up a painful feeling of inadequacy. You have to deal directly with the feeling itself and put it behind you, or it will sabotage you."

Few things cause more fear of success than a sense that if you follow your dreams, you will betray the people who love you. The loss of love, and of the security it engenders, is the mother of all unconscious terrors. In adolescence, when you're trying to figure out what you want to be when you grow up, this fear can stop you in your tracks, or it can set you up for some major self-defeating stuff if you pursue your ambitions in spite of it. Pete Hamill, an accomplished journalist and fiction writer, tells in his memoir

A Drinking Life of growing up in a working-class Brooklyn neighborhood where factories were closing, the good life was moving to the suburbs, his own dad's job had been relocated to Georgia, and "in the daytime, there were more men in the bars, drinking in silence and defeat." Hamill's father urged him to learn a blue-collar trade, but he wanted to be a writer. He feared it was an arrogant wish: " 'Who do you think you are?' some collective voice from the Neighborhood called to me. 'Who the hell do you think you are?' "

It turned out that Hamill was exactly who he hoped to be: a talented guy who went far. But as a kind of penance he drank too much for years, often "in the company of friends who thought they were failures and I was a success. Who could accuse me of snobbery, a big head, deserting my friends, if I was just another bum in the men's room throwing up on his shoes?" Getting drunk, he writes, "was a way of saying I would never act uppity, never forget where I came from." Meanwhile, whole decades flashed by in an alcoholic blur. Eventually Hamill realized that despite his feelings of guilt about leaving, he didn't owe the Neighborhood an early death from cirrhosis—or even one more hangover—and he quit drinking altogether. Not everybody in his situation does. Psychiatrists say that excessive drinking and fear of success are often closely linked, especially in people with one or more alcoholic parents.

WHEN IT'S RATIONAL TO JUST SAY NO

The generation of women now in middle and upper management has had to grapple with the same personal and cultural aspects of fear of success as their male peers—plus a few marked Women Only. Long before there was anything like Take Our Daughters to Work Day, girls were routinely taught that being too capable, too smart, or too ambitious would make them unfeminine, unlovable, and unmarried. The primal fear of abandonment, of success as a road map to loneliness, hits women hardest of all. Obliged to choose between success at work and fulfillment after hours, some women consciously or unconsciously choose the latter.

Conscious choice is a wonderful thing—the Holy Grail of therapy. It's where the shrinks separate the neurotic from the normal. If you decide you really don't want to scale the corporate or professional heights, good for you, as long as you know what you're doing and why. Jill Natwick Johnston, a trademark lawyer at Stroh Brewery in Detroit, just turned down a far better job at another company to spend more time with her 8-year-old twins than the new position would have allowed. The decision wasn't easy. "It's a job a lot of people would have killed for," says Johnston. "But I decided it's not worth it if it's going to kill you." Economist Juliet Schor, author of *The Overworked American*, discovered last year in a survey of 1,000 men and women that 28% had downshifted—that is, voluntarily accepted a lower income and less stress to do a better job at life outside the office, especially raising kids.

This is not fear of success. Steven Berglas, the Harvard psychiatry professor, wrote *The Success Syndrome: Hitting Bottom When You Reach the Top*, based on years of clinical sessions with business people who needed help figuring out what success really is. "What we call success may have consequences that you know you don't want," says Berglas. He suggests that if the idea of the next promotion makes you queasy, do a cost-benefit analysis. "Approach it as you would any other business decision," he says. "What are the pros and cons? What will you have to give up to get this? Is it worth it?" Are some losses, such as having to spend weekends in the woods with a beeper strapped to your fishing pole and a portable fax in your pack, not worth a new title and a bigger paycheck? If not, say, "No, thanks," and let somebody else sweat it. As Berglas puts it, you're being "rational and adaptive."

Or think about this: Do you have the right personality and the requisite skills to take on the role of the person above you? If the idea of getting promoted is keeping you up nights, it may be that you ain't got the chops, as jazz musicians say, and you know it.

142

RECOMMENDED READING

Your Own Worst Enemy: Understanding the Paradox of Self-Defeating Behavior, by Steven Berglas and Roy F. Baumeister (Basic Books, $21; hardcover).

Why Smart People Do Dumb Things, by Mortimer Feinberg and John J. Tarrant (Fireside/Simon & Schuster, $12; paperback).

Success and the Fear of Success in Women: A Developmental and Psychodynamic Perspective, by David W. Krueger, M.D. (Aronson, $25; paperback).

The Fear of Success, by Leon Tec, M.D. (Signet, $3.95; paperback).

That's not fear of success, it's fear of failure, and it may be a realistic fear indeed. Berglas believes the long-standing American career path of promoting people from technical to managerial jobs is wrongheaded for lots of reasons. Some people have terrific technical skills but the personality type known as "empathic." These are folks for whom the task of controlling someone else's fate, which is what management comes down to, is, in Berglas's words, "stressful to the point of toxicity." If that applies to you, turning down the Big Management Job is no sign of neurosis; it's common sense.

WORK KEEPS GETTING more precarious, more complex, more demanding. The last thing you need is a jumble of unfinished psychological business to trip you up. Before you can decide whether you're a success fearer or a common-sense downshifter—or neither—and then act accordingly in

143

your own best interest, you have to know yourself, including those parts of your psyche that you might rather ignore. You have to like yourself too. And that, initially, can be even harder.

Chapter Four
Investment Strategies for a Secure Future

BE A TAX-SAVVY INVESTOR
page 146

GLOBAL STOCKS TO BET ON
page 153

66 REASONS TO BUY BOND FUNDS
page 157

A STRATEGIST TAKES STOCK OF THE MARKET
page 159

FORTUNE-TELLING:
WHAT THREE EXPERTS EXPECT
page 162

REAL ESTATE:
A SMART ALTERNATIVE TO STOCKS
page 166

HOW TO LEAVE THE TAX MAN NOTHING
page 169

Most of us ignore the impact of taxes on our investments. That's a mistake. Measuring the bite can radically change the way we buy stocks, bonds, and mutual funds. Here's what to do.

BE A TAX-SAVVY INVESTOR

BY SUSAN E. KUHN

ARE YOU HEADED for an unhappy surprise? To find out, take your portfolio and calculate what you give up each year to Uncle Sam. A 28% capital gains payment here, a 39.6% or more swipe there from taxes on income or short-term gains—it adds up mighty fast. Bite by unseen bite, the tax worm might be feeding itself full at your portfolio's expense. There's a reason this may come as news. Research on tax-wise investing has been conducted only in the past few years, and rarely are after-tax returns seen in print.

The results of a new study by SEI, a global investment management firm in Wayne, Pennsylvania, shed some light on tax-efficient investing. SEI asset allocation strategist Susan West has come up with a model tax-wise portfolio for individuals. It includes an oversize exposure to international investments and a zero allotment to actively managed large-cap U.S. mutual funds, favoring index funds instead. Without falling back on tax shelters or other risky stratagems, it differs markedly from the typical tax-ugly portfolio most of us hold. Before taxes, the average annual expected return of the tax-ugly portfolio is 9%, beating the tax-efficient model. But in real life, after taxes are paid, the efficient model returns significantly more.

This disparity is big enough to warrant the attention of even us taxpaying peons; the rich, to whom taxes matter more, are already

TAX-WISE PORTFOLIO		TAX-UGLY PORTFOLIO	
40%	Municipal bonds	40%	Taxable bonds
32%	Index of U.S. large-cap stocks	50%	Actively managed U.S. stocks
12%	International stocks	5%	International stocks
6%	Emerging market stocks	5%	U.S. small-cap stocks
5%	U.S. small-cap growth stocks		
5%	U.S. small-cap value stocks		
	Pretax return: 8.6%		Pretax return: 9.0%
	After-tax return: 6.5%		After-tax return: 5.8%

Portfolios are sold after 20 years. Annual returns are projected, derived from historical averages. Assumes a 39.6% income tax rate and a 28% capital gains rate.

FORTUNE/TABLE SOURCE: SEI.

starting to holler. "They realize taxes are a hidden bomb in a portfolio that can go off," says Charlotte Beyer, founder of the Institute for Private Investors in Summit, New Jersey, a trade forum for the wealthy and their advisers. According to an institute survey, only 19% of advisers say they provide prospective clients with after-tax results. Further, 94% say the industry has not fully identified the implications of managing taxable money.

Money managers can be accused of ignorance at the very least. Says Robert Arnott, president of First Quadrant, a money management firm in Pasadena: "Most people managing taxable money manage it as if taxes don't matter. They ignore the tax consequences of active trading. I think it's shocking." Richard Rogers, director of consulting services at Family Office Exchange, an Oak Park, Illinois, wealth management consulting firm, is not surprised: "No money manager wants to be evaluated this way. To outperform on an after-tax basis, you have to be a truly exceptional manager."

In that light, it behooves individuals to be their own wise counsel. We live in a taxable world, a reality unlikely to change no matter what happens in Washington. Current proposals to cut the capital gains rate do not negate the fact that every year investors face the tax ax. By investing wisely, we can safeguard our gains and make our portfolios grow.

The first rule of tax-efficient investing: Own a lot more equities than bonds or cash. Most people know that stocks return more than bonds over time. But they don't understand that this difference widens once taxes are paid on the chunky income that bonds and cash generate. Historically, domestic stocks held for one year have returned 11% before taxes and 7.65% after. Taxable bonds, however, see their returns shrink from 6.5% to 4.02%. Throw in the bugaboo of inflation, at 4% per year, and bonds barely break even, making stocks the clear choice.

Stocks win out over muni bonds too, which over time have averaged just a 4.39% annual return. Even so, within the bond universe, munis are hard to beat. SEI recommends that individuals

HOW TAXES HURT RETURNS

	Pretax return	After-tax return	Percent lost to taxes
Large-cap growth stocks	10.50%	7.34%	30.10%
Large-cap value stocks	10.50%	6.89%	34.38%
Small-cap growth stocks	11.75%	8.36%	28.85%
Small-cap value stocks	11.75%	8.10%	31.06%
International stocks	12.00%	8.40%	30.00%
Emerging-market stocks	15.00%	10.54%	29.73%
Taxable bonds	6.50%	4.02%	38.15%
Cash	5.00%	3.02%	39.60%

Based on SEI's expected long-run returns, annualized. Taxes are calculated assuming a one-year holding period. Ordinary income tax rates are 39.6%; capital gains, 28%.

FORTUNE/TABLE SOURCE: SEI.

who pay more than 33% in combined federal, state, and local taxes choose muni bonds over any others. In general, intermediate munis maturing in five to seven years generate higher returns, after taking risk into account, than bonds with longer terms. But remember that inflation can make holding munis for a long time a wealth-shrinking strategy. Use bonds for needed income, not growth.

The reality is that most of us don't own enough stocks. While

SEI's model allocates 40% of the portfolio to munis, there is a case to be made that the proportion should be less. For example, a 50-year-old is typically advised to hold 50% to 60% of her assets in stocks, based on the simple rule of thumb of subtracting age from 100 or 110 to determine equity allocation. But after taxes are considered, says David Pear, president of Beecher Investors in New York City, "we typically end up increasing the allocation by ten percentage points, suggesting 60% to 70% in stocks."

Once you decide to go with stocks, which do you buy? Ideally, you want a handful of stocks that you can take to your deathbed. Then taxes, at least the capital gains variety, vanish like a ghost. At death, there is a step-up in basis on the value of your stock, meaning the $5 stock that is now worth $500 passes to heirs with a new cost basis of $500, period. The embedded capital gain of $495 is forgiven.

Nice as that is, there's news that's even better: You don't have to die to benefit from a buy-and-hold strategy. Look at Warren Buffett. He holds stocks for decades, so his net worth grows and grows. He's no fan of dividends and pays none to the holders of Berkshire Hathaway stock. Pear of Beecher Investors follows a similar buy-and-hold strategy in the individual accounts he manages, looking to buy only 20 stocks that can be tucked away for at least ten years. Over the past five years, annual after-tax returns on Beecher's composite account have averaged 25.3%, vs. 11.2% for the S&P 500. (For the tax calculation, it is assumed that stocks in the S&P 500 index were sold and rebought annually.)

Simple math proves the advantage of holding stocks instead of trading them. Take a hypothetical $100,000 stock portfolio returning 10% a year and paying no dividends. The stocks are held for 20 years, accumulating to $672,750, then sold. After forking over to the government 28% in capital gains tax, the investor is left with $512,380, equivalent to an average annual return of 8.5%. Now suppose that the stocks are traded annually, with the portfolio still generating a 10%-per-year return. Because the taxes paid along the way reduce the size of the portfolio on which gains build, the portfolio's effective average annual return drops to 7.2%. The investor is out more than $100,000.

Individuals assembling a portfolio of stocks for the long haul should consider companies that will dominate their niche for years, so there won't be a need to sell the stocks too soon. Further, discount dividends and the annual taxes owed on them. This strategy favors growth stocks over value stocks: Growth stocks typically generate most of their total return in the form of stock-price appreciation, while value stocks often sell at steep discounts and offer generous, but taxable, yields. Over the past 27 years, notes Brown Brothers Harriman, growth and value stocks have returned a nearly identical 11% per year. But after taxes, growth stocks return 8.9% per year and value stocks 7.8%.

Buy and hold is not a very attractive strategy for money managers: It's hard to justify your fee when you buy a basket of stocks and then do nothing year after year. Many argue that through superior stock picking they can generate returns high enough to overcome the tax penalties. But in a landmark paper in the *Journal of Portfolio Management* in 1993, "Is Your Alpha Big Enough to Cover Its Taxes?," authors Robert Jeffrey, president of Jeffrey Co. in Columbus, Ohio, and Robert Arnott of First Quadrant proved how difficult this is. They concluded that to offset the tax consequences of active trading, a fund manager needs to generate two to three percentage points more in pretax returns every year than a comparable index fund. Most managers don't, so they fail the performance test.

An interesting facet of Arnott and Jeffrey's research explores the relationship between portfolio turnover and taxes—and suggests just how difficult taxes are to avoid. Turnover is a measure of trading activity as a percent of a portfolio's assets. When the turnover is 100% that effectively means that the entire portfolio was traded during the year; in a buy-and-hold portfolio, turnover is zero. Arnott and Jeffrey found that at a relatively low turnover rate of 25% (each stock is held on average four years), portfolios incur fully 80% of the tax liability accrued by an active trader who turns over his entire portfolio annually.

For folks who invest in mutual funds, this all adds up to one thing: In most cases, index funds are a better bet than actively managed stock funds. On average, mutual funds sport a turnover rate of 80%, implying that the managers typically hold each stock for 16 months. While some funds achieve an annual turnover of 25% or less, most don't. In general, only index funds regularly post a turnover rate below 25%—they also consistently post among the best after-tax returns.

Index funds don't simply win the race; they do so by a comfortable margin. From 1990 through 1995, equity funds with assets exceeding $1 billion returned on average 16.3% per year pretax, roughly equal to the return of the Vanguard Index 500 portfolio. But after taking taxes into account, the actively managed funds showed average annual returns of 13.3%, well below the index fund's 15.2%, according to Beecher Investors. While 41% of managers outperformed the index fund nominally, only 16% managed to do so after taxes.

Looking at a larger universe, SEI found that over the seven-year period ended September 1995, only 33% of large-cap fund managers in its database beat the Russell 1000 index after taxes. Managers in less efficient markets did better, however. Among international fund managers, a whopping 86% beat their index over SEI's seven-year period. Similarly, 55% of small-stock fund managers beat their index. So here's an important exception to the index rule:

When it comes to foreign markets and small stocks, actively managed mutual funds can be a better bet than index funds, even after taxes.

There is hope for investors in large-cap stocks. In a paper published by the Center for Economic Policy Research in April 1993, entitled "Ranking Mutual Funds on an After-Tax Basis," Stanford professors Joel Dickson and John Shoven studied the pretax and post-tax returns of 150 growth or growth and income funds. A consistent winner was the Vanguard Index 500 fund, which ranked in the 78th percentile from 1983 to 1992 before taxes, and the 85th percentile after. All this may not surprise you now, but here's the kicker: The professors found that by offsetting much of the capital gains realized every year with capital losses, further reducing taxes paid, the return would have jumped to the 91st percentile.

What Shoven and Dickson were advocating is a strategy anyone can employ: matching capital gains with capital losses. To capture the loss in a favored stock that has fallen, sell it and then buy it back 31 days later—just enough time to avoid incurring a penalty under the IRS's "wash sale" rule. Then apply the loss to offset an equivalent capital gain. Firms like J.P. Morgan, Northern Trust, and Sanford C. Bernstein use this maneuver regularly. SEI advocates it, and individuals can do it as well.

Vanguard adapted the suggestion and launched three tax-managed index funds in September 1994. Charles Schwab & Co., which provided funding for the research, has three index funds that employ the same strategy. Vanguard's tax-managed funds require a minimum investment of $10,000, while Schwab's require just $1,000.

An international big-wheel tells you how to put a global spin on your portfolio. . . . Morningstar's publisher narrows the field for investors interested in bond funds. . . . Smith Barney's equity strategist evaluates the risk in today's market. . . . Three experts gaze into the future—and tell us what they expect.

ADVICE FROM THE PROPHETS OF PROFIT

GLOBAL STOCKS TO BET ON

MARK HOLOWESKO, 36, is still best known for his day job. In the brutally competitive arena of money management, Holowesko is a star global fund manager—the Bahamas-based skipper of three of Templeton's flagship mutual funds, including the Growth fund, which was founded by legendary investor John Templeton 41 years ago. By canvassing the globe for the best bargain stocks, and holding on to them for years, Holowesko has thrived. Over the past five years, the Growth fund averaged 15.1% annual returns vs. 10.9% for the MSCI World index.

FORTUNE's John Wyatt talked to Holowesko about smart value plays around the world.

Let's start with Japan—it's kicking in with real signs of life, and sentiment is vastly improved. Are you a buyer?
No. We think Japan's market will continue to lag for some time, [despite] startling economic figures. [GDP jumped 3% in the first quarter of 1996, the largest gain since 1973.] Many analysts are expecting net profit margins to rise from today's 2.5% up to the very high 3.5% that Japanese companies earned in the late Eighties, which we think is unlikely. Those margins were artificially bolstered

by the speculative bubbles in the stock market and the real estate market. Though the excesses have been working off for some time now, there is still a lot of bad debt left over from those days. Japan has more debt relative to GNP than the U.S. It has a $400 billion banking problem. The S&L problem in the U.S., huge as it was, totaled $100 billion. And look at the steep stock valuations: The P/E on the stock market is still at least 80, and that is adjusted for accounting differences. Even if earnings double and the P/E drops to 40, I'm not sure you should be paying that.

Are there any Japanese stocks that you like?
We are very keen on Sony. Its ADR, listed on the Big Board, trades at 35 times March 1997 earnings estimates—compare that with the Tokyo market's P/E of 57 times expected 1997 earnings—and the P/E could fall even more over the next two years as earnings begin a huge turnaround. The yen is starting to work more in the company's favor, and management has also done a better job at getting costs in line by reducing head count and controlling inventory. The brand name is phenomenal—perhaps the most recognized in the world after Coke. And people talk about the wonders of high technology—Sony is poised to take advantage of the fusion that is going on in technology at the retail level: They just introduced a computer, and the upcoming digital versatile disk (DVD)—which stores music, video, and computer data and is due out in 1997— could be the next Walkman or CD player.

Recently, emerging markets have been trading well below the dizzying peaks of 1993. Is the bloom off that story?
Not at all. The growth story is intact, and what is fantastic today is that the prices are so much cheaper than they were then. While the U.S. and the World indexes trade near all-time highs, almost all emerging markets are still well off their peaks—many, like Taiwan and Mexico, by 40% and even 50% in U.S. dollar terms.

Consumerism in developing countries is exploding. It's pretty simple to grasp. Between India and China alone there are two billion people, and the standard of living in Asia most of all is improving dramatically. In China, more people earn the equivalent of $15,000 on a purchasing parity basis than the entire population of Canada—and that group represents only a fraction of the total population. In Indonesia, less than 10% of the people live in poverty—it was 60% in 1970. I could go on, but the picture is clear.

What would be a smart way for U.S. investors to cash in on these developments?
Though we are generally downbeat on U.S. stock market valuations and have cut our U.S. holdings from 55% in 1993 to 22% today, there are a number of ways to get in on emerging markets' growth through selected U.S. stocks—like Boeing. Boeing is the dominant supplier of commercial aircraft, and orders for new planes are on the rise. Travel in Asia is growing 20% a year, and airlines in Asia are incredibly wealthy. Singapore Airlines, which has some 485 million Singapore dollars in cash, can literally write checks for new aircraft. The number of aircraft in Asia is very low relative to its population and the growth in travel. Cathay Pacific Airways, for example, one of the region's major carriers, has only 50-odd planes, vs. over 600 for American Airlines.

Other such U.S. stocks include American International Group, which derives more than half its earnings from overseas and is one of only two foreign companies licensed to sell insurance in China; and Citicorp, which has a huge emerging-markets presence, particularly in Latin America.

Speaking of Latin America, the declines in those markets scared the pants off most investors. What's your take on them now?
We have been buying into markets like Brazil and Argentina ever since they imploded last year, along with most emerging markets in the wake of Mexico's currency devaluation. People don't realize that a normal bear market in the U.S. means that you lose 20% of your money over 13 months, and that it takes 21 months to get back to where you were. Most investors would be terrified in such a situation. In emerging markets it is much more violent and condensed. Take Mexico. In this most recent decline, the market fell 78%. Such a fall was actually pretty normal. In 1987, for instance, it lost 84%

of its value, and in 1981–82 it lost 81%. And despite the falls, a lot of money has been made riding the market back up. Overall, we have increased our Latin American stake from 2% in 1994 to 10% today.

We like the telecom stocks, which were the first stocks people bought, and the first sold; even though very little changed in the underlying businesses, many of the stock prices dropped 50%. Brazil's Telebrás represents over half of our entire Brazilian position. The stock is one of the cheapest of the telecoms in terms of what you pay for each line of service. Telebrás's market cap per line is $1.5 billion, vs. $2.3 billion for Telefónica de Argentina, for example.

Energy seems like a logical fit to your investing strategy. Does the group appeal to you?
Very much so. Oil consumption in India and China amounts to less than one barrel per person per year. In the U.S. it is 23. If India and China get to five barrels—just half the level of Taiwan—the demand would equal OPEC's total current output. That won't happen overnight. But you can chart the rising consumption, and with so many people, only marginal increases in use lead to dramatic increases in demand. Around the world we like Argentina's YPF and France's Elf Aquitaine. French stocks in general have been beat up tremendously, and we found the French oil stocks to be a useful way to invest in energy. We also like U.S. refiners—namely Texaco and Sun—and Valero Energy, a refiner of residual oil, the black-sludge byproduct of refining oil into gasoline. There hasn't been a major refinery built in the U.S. in over 15 years, and with increased demand, capacity utilization is on the way up.

Aside from the stocks you've mentioned, are there other areas with value in Europe?
Europe is very much like the U.S. in the early 1980s. Costs are too high, the companies employ too many workers, and the products aren't as good as they should be. But there are significant hidden assets, and companies are beginning to restructure. We

like Sweden's Volvo, which tried to be a conglomerate, failed miserably, and is finally focusing on cars and trucks; and Philips Electronics, in the Netherlands, the consumer electronics giant that also has a major stake in PolyGram. We think both can successfully turn things around, and their stocks trade at terrific discounts to their major competitors'.

66 REASONS TO BUY BOND FUNDS

TO WHICH OF THE MORE than 3,000 bond funds should you entrust your hard-earned dollars? To find out where the high scores are likely to be, FORTUNE's Bethany McLean talked with mutual fund maven **JOHN REKENTHALER**, publisher of Morningstar, the Chicago-based fund-rating company.

With so many bond funds out there, how do you shorten the list?
In the Morningstar database, there are 3,516 funds. That's about 3,450 too many. The major issue is fees: The typical bond fund carries annual fees of about 1% and a performance that, before expenses, is no better than a bond-index fund's. So the first question to ask is, "Why should I buy such-and-such fund rather than Vanguard Bond Index Total Market?" In nine cases out of ten, you won't be able to find a good reason. The expenses on this fund are 0.18%, which gives you about a 0.8% head start on the typical competitor. The fund has a three-year annualized return (after expenses) of 5.5%. This compares favorably with the 4.6% return from the average high-quality corporate bond fund.

What about the other 65? When should you buy an actively managed bond fund?
When there's a lot of risk on individual securities, then a fund that offers diversification and the selections of a smart, experienced manager provides something you can't replicate on your own. The Loomis Sayles Bond fund, a no-load fund based in Boston that has

returned 11.6% (annualized) over the past three years, and FPA New Income, a load fund based in Los Angeles that's had a 6.9% annualized return (before sales charges), are the two best actively managed bond funds in existence. FPA has an expense ratio of 0.68% and a 4.5% sales load, and Loomis Sayles has an expense ratio of 0.79%, but you're getting your money's worth. Both these funds mix government securities, lower-grade corporates, and convertibles. Loomis Sayles is on the aggressive side, while FPA is more conservative: FPA is great in bear markets and acceptable in bull; Loomis Sayles is the opposite. There's no such thing as a bull-bear great.

What about specialized areas, like municipal bonds and short-term funds?
Joe Deane at Smith Barney runs five muni funds, including Smith Barney Managed Munis A, which has a 7% three-year annualized return after expenses of 0.71%. The fund imposes a sales charge of 4.0%. Deane has gotten a lot of press, but justifiably so—he calls interest rates correctly. If you're looking for a short-term fund, try the no-load Sit Tax-Free Income or Sit U.S. Government Securities, run by Michael Brilley in Minneapolis. Over the past three years, he's delivered annualized returns of 5.9% on the tax-free fund and 5.7% on the taxable fund by exploiting odd corners, like mobile-home mortgages. He gets high yield and very little share price fluctuation. The mass-market fund industry has spent millions of dollars hunting that holy grail while this funny little firm in Minnesota just plugs away. No one has found these funds, and the yields beat what you'll get in the money market: Right now, the muni fund yields 5.7%; the taxable, just under 7%.

Do you recommend any high-yield funds?
This year the lowest-credit-quality funds have led the high-yield category, but with corporate profits weakening, now is not the time to play around with credit risk. Stick with the better-rated funds. American High Income and Oppenheimer High-Yield are two of the more conservative; on an annualized basis they've both

returned about 9.5% over the past three years (before the 4.75% sales charge). For a no-load, go with Vanguard F/I High-Yield Corporate, which has a three-year return of 8.8%.

What about international funds?
Jack Bogle at Vanguard argues that these funds shouldn't exist, because you'll get at best comparable returns to the U.S. with a heck of a lot more risk because of currency swings. Since Vanguard is the best bond shop in the country, and Bogle tends to be right, you have to listen to him. If you own everything else and you're looking for maximum diversification, buy a fund that's unhedged: Embrace the currency risk. T. Rowe Price International Bond fund has turned in consistently above-average performance relative to its peers—8.6% annualized over the past three years—with an okay expense ratio of 0.98%.

Do you see a disaster coming?
No, we don't think there is one. You need a boom time first, and today's bond fund investors are veterans who survived 1994.

A STRATEGIST TAKES STOCK OF THE MARKET

IS THE GREAT BULL MARKET in danger of an abrupt end? Some big one-day swings in the Dow, a long-bond yield playing footsie with 7%, new jobs cropping up at double the expected rate, and simmering inflation concerns leave investors wondering. For some seasoned insights, we turned to **MARSHALL ACUFF,** Smith Barney's equity strategist, who in 30 years has made more than his share of sage calls. In 1992 he beat a timely retreat from tech stocks right before they hit the skids, and loaded up on natural gas stocks just in time to watch gas prices soar. Since 1994 he's wisely been betting on multinationals like Coca-Cola. Acuff discussed his predictions with FORTUNE's Andrea L. Prochniak.

What do you make of the recent volatility in the equity market?
Certainly there's more risk today in this market than there has been since 1994. Interest rates may be working against stocks more now than they have in the past, and that comes at a time when the longer-term outlook for corporate profit growth is downshifting relative to what we've been experiencing. This is all in the context of a more speculative stock market. So you put it all together, and it's natural to be more cautious.

In our asset allocation mix, we have positioned ourselves for a corrective period [that stretches to mid-1997] but aren't predicting an end to the bull market. We're recommending an asset mix of 50% equities, 35% bonds, and 15% cash, vs. early March, when we were at 60% equities and 5% cash.

How serious a correction do you expect?
Perhaps 10%, but not necessarily a full-fledged bear market, which would be a decline of 20% to 30%. We've gone an extraordinarily long time without a 10% correction. The monetary climate's been quite good: Inflation and interest rates have been low, we've had good profit growth, and it's been a very good period for equities. To some degree that may be shifting, and the market's volatility reflects the recognition of that shift.

What areas of the market are most vulnerable to a drop?
Small- and mid-cap stocks have done very well, but it strikes us that that sector has become increasingly speculative and is therefore taking on greater risk than the larger-cap stocks. If the market were to correct, all stocks might fall, but the small ones will fall further.

What are the safest stocks to own?
In a market like this, we have not only the potential for weakness triggered by rising interest rates, but also the potential for profit growth on a multi-year basis to slow. Profits in 1994 were up over 20%; last year they were up 12% to 15%. Yet we estimate that over the next five years profit growth will be just 5% a year. So our market strategy is focused on larger-cap growth companies. Our favorites right now are the companies that are selling more and

160

more outside the U.S., like McDonald's and Procter & Gamble. And despite the volatility of high tech, we like Intel and Hewlett-Packard. We also like companies that fit our capital-conservation theme—those that can weather both a bump in the economy and a slowdown in their industry's earnings momentum. These companies are redeploying assets and focusing on the higher-returning assets. In the process they generate more cash, which they use to buy back shares and raise dividends. BankAmerica, which recently raised its dividend by 17% and plans to buy back 7% of its market cap this year, fits that theme, as does Allstate, which is moving away from business insurance to focus on its more profitable auto insurance specialty.

We also like drug companies that have large pipelines of new products: Eli Lilly and Pfizer, specifically. While these stocks have recovered in recent years, their valuations relative to their prospective growth are still not that high. Look at Lilly and Coca-Cola: The two companies have comparable growth rates, 18% to 20% for Lilly over the next five years, vs. 17% for Coke. But Coke's P/E is about two times its growth rate, while Lilly sells at 1.2 times its growth rate and so seems to be a pretty good value.

What emerging investing theme looks exciting but safe?
Long term, we're most excited about the wireless area. The major companies like L.M. Ericsson, Motorola, and Nokia are still down in price—though up from recent lows—and we predict compound earnings growth of 20% to 30% for them over the next five years. It's now estimated that by the end of the decade the number of cellular subscribers worldwide will be 350 million to 400 million, compared with about 85 million currently. There's going to be tremendous infrastructure buildup around the world, which will benefit Ericsson most because they have the largest share—about 35% of the global market—and they generate about 70% of their earnings from that service.

FORTUNE-TELLING: WHAT THREE EXPERTS EXPECT

ABBY JOSEPH COHEN
GOLDMAN SACHS

Co-chair of investment policy committee. Earlier this year Cohen accurately foretold a stronger economy and more robust corporate profits. She is bullish, if not exuberantly so, on the stock market's future course.

MUCH OF THE RECENT RISE in long-term interest rates has already been factored into the equity market. Look at the market's choppy trading range since the middle of February, when we began to see evidence that the economy was better than expected and interest rates began heading up rapidly. Before then, stocks went up like a moonshot. But five times since February 15 we've seen big declines followed by rebounds.

It's been a real tug of war between those who interpret the evidence of a strong economy as good news for corporate profits, as we do, and those who see that as bad news because of inflation. We think that inflation fears are premature and that the rise in rates has already more than accounted for it.

Look at intermediate- and long-term interest rates, for example, which are already up more than a full percentage point in just three months. With the long bond at 6.9%, yields are nearly four percentage points above the inflation rate, which is a historically high spread. Typically it is closer to 2.5 percentage points. We do expect inflation to rise modestly over the next few months, but only to about 3% for the year, up from 2.8% in 1995. Such high real rates just simply aren't warranted.

My conclusion is that equities will be okay. We continue to like technology stocks like Microsoft, Intel, and Compaq Computer. Long-term growth for tech companies remains phenomenal, and the U.S. companies stand head and shoulders above the international competition. We also like small-cap stocks. Investors are most comfortable owning small issues when they feel that profit growth will be strong for a long time—which happens to be our own expectation. A current favorite is Williams-Sonoma, which is in an appealing niche, retailing high-quality home-related items.

BYRON WIEN
MORGAN STANLEY

U.S. investment strategist. At the beginning of January, Wien correctly saw that U.S. Treasury yields would climb above 7%, and stocks would begin the year with a powerful rally. He recently predicted that a sharp stock market correction would push the Dow down by 1,000 points.

THOUGH IN THE VERY NEAR TERM we may see a short rally, between now and the end of the year we will have the first major stock market decline since 1990—a correction on the order of 15% to 20%. The short-term rally will provide a good opportunity to sell in order to raise reserves for the forthcoming decline.

The economy is still stronger than people think. At the beginning of the year, people were nearly unanimous on six points: (1) the economy was hovering near recession, and the Fed would ease several times; (2) long-term interest rates were headed even lower, to 5.5% or 5.2%; (3) corporate earnings would be flat to down; (4) inflation, for all intents and purposes, was dead; (5) the market would be dull after 1995's big returns; and (6) the Fed never tightens in an election year. To a certain extent people are still holding on to those old views. I expect interest rates to go to 7.5% and maybe beyond, because the economy is still growing and inflation is increasing faster than what is priced in the market. For most of this cycle, unit labor costs grew at a modest 1% to 2% annualized rate. Now it's 3%. Since labor makes up 70% of manufacturing costs, increases are quickly reflected in inflation.

Corporate earnings will improve, but not enough to offset the rise in interest rates. The Fed's next move will be to tighten rather than ease—bull markets don't die of natural causes; they are killed by the Fed. The Dow could fall 1,000 points.

At the beginning of the year, as bond prices fell and the stock market went up, people thought that they had "decoupled." In fact, the link was still tight because stocks were 25% undervalued when compared with bonds. That has since changed: Stocks are up 7%, while the long bond has fallen some 8%, and the market is far less attractive.

Within this negative context, we continue to favor economically sensitive cyclicals like airlines and semiconductors, among others, because of our view that the economy is likely to be strong. We like AMR, UAL, and Intel, for example. We also like the consistent earnings trends in selected health care stocks, particularly American Home Products and Eli Lilly. Still, with the changed dynamics, it's not only going to be tougher to make money in the stock market, it's going to be possible to lose.

WARREN SHAW
CHANCELLOR CAPITAL MANAGEMENT

CEO and chief investment officer. Under Shaw's watch, Chancellor, which runs $32 billion of institutional money, bolstered its market-beating returns early this year by overweighting equities when many of his peers were pulling back. Shaw expects a correction but still looks for stocks to go up 5% to 7% into early 1997.

CONTINUING CONCERNS over commodity prices and inflation could easily push long-term bond yields to 7.5%, which might be the catalyst that causes a 10% to 15% correction in the market. But there is enough that is sound about the market's fundamentals for stocks to recover. As interest rates go up, particularly at the long end, overall economic activity slows. The slowdown should appear in the second half of the year. With a slowing economy, inflation fears abate, and stock prices rise in response. It's a self-correcting process.

The backdrop to this scenario is a relative absence of serious structural imbalances. Inventories aren't out of line, capacity utilization is at midcycle levels, and inflation is not abnormally high. Also, neither monetary nor fiscal policy is stimulative now. The Fed's real funds rate [the rate after inflation] is over 2%—if it were stimulative, it would be closer to zero. Budget deficits have declined, which means the government is borrowing and spending less money.

Clearly, by many absolute valuation measures, like dividend yield and price-to-book, the stock market is at an all-time high and looks over-valued. But when you consider relative valuation measures like our own dividend discount model, where you factor in current interest rates and earnings growth rates, the market looks to be fairly valued or just slightly overvalued, so we are not too concerned.

Much of the heavy underwriting of new shares is canceled out by stock buybacks and absorbed by mutual funds. Merger and acquisition activity is less noticed but remains strong and has shrunk the supply of equity by some $80 billion to $100 billion a year for the past two years. Fundamentals overall may not be as attractive as they were, but they are still strong enough that even after a correction, stocks can finish 1996 5% to 7% higher than where they were six months before.

We like banks in particular: They are cleaning up balance sheets, cutting costs, and repurchasing shares. We also like aerospace, and the networking area of technology has terrific growth potential.

Smart investors are turning to real estate—for gains and portfolio protection.

REAL ESTATE: A SMART ALTERNATIVE TO STOCKS

BY SUSAN E. KUHN

T HE FINANCIAL MARKETS are flailing. Stocks are seesawing, bonds are acting badly, and the prospects for international investments are wavering under a strengthening dollar. Fears of inflation are growing as commodity prices rise and the economic expansion ages. With bargains getting harder to find, smart investors are turning to real estate—for gains and portfolio protection. Morgan Stanley investment strategist Barton Biggs recently cut his global equity exposure to 56%, while recommending a 10% allocation to real estate. On the left coast, San Mateo, California, money managers Bailard Biehl & Kaiser recommend a 20% commitment.

Most of us haven't considered investing that much in real estate, but the high yields, steady returns, and financial safety net are hard to ignore. Better, recovery from the real estate lows of the late 1980s still has years to run. Says Biggs: "We'll have high returns in commercial real estate, well in excess of their 8% yield." Adds Art Micheletti, Bailard's chief investment strategist: "Real estate is a nice anchor, like a cash position. We think it looks attractive for the next four years."

There are plenty of ways to invest right now, whether you want to buy a building outright or invest a few dollars in real estate investment trusts. Called REITs, these bundled properties pay out cash from rents and trade like stocks. Real estate research firm

THE ROAD AHEAD FOR REITS

TOTAL RETURN TO INVESTORS

Property type	1994	1995	12-month projections (5/96-5/97)	Recent div. yield
Hotel	–10.6%	30.8%	17.6%	7.5%
Office	2.9%	38.8%	16.6%	5.9%
Apartment	2.4%	12.3%	19.2%	7.5%
Industrial	17.7%	15.9%	15.3%	6.8%
Diversified	-7.3%	21.2%	14.9%	7.3%

SOURCES: NAREIT; ALEX. BROWN & SONS

LaSalle Partners calculates that for the first time since 1978, cash yields generated from real estate are exceeding yields on ten-year Treasuries. Total returns, which include yields plus share price gains, are expected to average 12% per year in the future. Says Jeffrey Everett, manager of the top-performing Templeton Real Estate fund, a global fund with 35% of its assets in U.S. REITs: "Now is the perfect entry point, since the popularity is not there yet and the real estate market is undervalued." Morgan Stanley estimates that REITs on average are trading at 10% discounts to the market value of the properties they hold.

So far this year, REITs have been overlooked in favor of the rampant stock market; they rose 2.3% in the first quarter, vs. 5.4% for the S&P 500. In 1995 most REITs had a similarly tough time keeping pace, though some sectors surpassed equities in the dark days of 1994. Among the groups with momentum, REITs specializing in hotels, up 10% in the first quarter, remain on a roll. Salomon Brothers analyst John Litt reports that U.S. lodging demand rose 3.1% annually between 1991 and 1995, while total supply increased by only 1.4%.

REIT managers are keen on full-service hotels like Marriott or Hyatt. Patriot American Hospitality, a Dallas-based owner of 31 such hotels, has little debt and is acquiring properties below their replacement costs. Keith Pauley, co-head of investments for LaSalle, estimates the REIT, selling for $27.75, is worth $29. Plus, it's paying a dividend of 6.9%, and cash flow is growing 20% per year.

Two other hotel REITs worth checking into are FelCor Suite Hotels, an operator of Embassy Suites, and Starwood Lodging. FelCor's REIT zoomed 43% last year but could return 20% more, says Franklin Real Estate Securities fund manager Matt Avery. FelCor, based in Irving, Texas, recently sold for $29.25, with a 6.3% yield. Starwood Lodging is a unique two-for-one investment: one part is the REIT, which owns the hotels, and the other is the corporation, which runs the business. Starwood's soon-to-be 53 properties include everything from Marriott to Embassy Suites, making it the largest U.S. hotel REIT. Based in Los Angeles, Starwood sold recently for $33, with a 5.7% yield. Robert Frank, head of real estate securities research at Alex. Brown & Sons, believes it could return 12% over the next 12 months.

The apartment market is also soaring, particularly in San Francisco—thanks to expensive property, tricky hilltop construction, rents rising at twice the national rate, and vacancies as low as 1%. Bay Apartment Communities, headquartered in San Jose, is the REIT to buy; at $24.38, the dividend yield is 6.6%. Spieker Properties, which owns suburban offices and industrial properties, is another fine California REIT. Tim Reynolds, manager of the United Services Real Estate fund, predicts a 15% annual return over the next two years. The REIT was recently $26.13, yielding 6.4%.

With the bountiful options available to savvy estate planners, paying any tax at all may be optional. But you always believed that old saw about death and taxes? Read on.

HOW TO LEAVE THE TAX MAN NOTHING

BY EILEEN P. GUNN

WHILE NONE OF US want to contemplate our death, or that of our spouse, we all need an estate plan. If you need motivation to reach this decision, remember that every dollar you keep from the folks in Washington goes to someone you like a heck of a lot better—such as your kids, your younger sister, or your alma mater.

Jim Lumpkins, now 76, a retired president of a Florida bank, drew up a new will back in 1990. He says he started wondering what would happen if he didn't outlive his estate, which was worth roughly $2 million at the time. "I didn't see any point in going through the fortress of the damned to make that money just to die and leave it to the government," says Lumpkins. "I wanted to leave it to my family to the extent that I could."

At the advice of Marshall Gunn, his financial planner, Lumpkins set up an **"I love you" will**. Among other things, this enabled him and his wife, Norma, to use up the whole $385,600 available to them in so-called unified tax credits.

You can do the same thing. The trick is to divide the first $1.2 million of your assets between you so that you and your spouse have separate estates that can each receive the tax credit. The standard individual credit is $192,800, essentially the tax that would be due on an estate of $600,000. If everything is jointly owned, you'd get that deduction only once because the tax man considers jointly held assets to constitute a single estate that isn't taxed until the second death. After you've divided your assets, you need to write into both of your wills a mechanism for a bypass, or credit-shelter, trust.

Here's how a bypass trust works: Say the husband dies first. At his death, everything except the $600,000 in his name goes to the wife, tax-free, under the unlimited marital deduction. The husband's will directs his $600,000 into the bypass trust and his unified tax credit covers the tax due. The wife receives the income from the trust and, with trustee approval, can access the principal. When she dies, the trust bypasses her estate and goes to the kids. She gets a tax credit on her own $600,000. If that's all she leaves, the children inherit the lot and the government gets zero.

Getting the picture? There's more . . .

Now let's suppose you've been an industrious nest-egg builder—helped by a home that, perhaps, has appreciated wildly since you bought it all those years ago and by a plump retirement plan. Another way to keep estate taxes from impoverishing your heirs is to set up an **irrevocable life insurance trust**. It, in turn, buys a second-to-die insurance policy, which covers both spouses and pays the benefit only after both are dead. This can cover any estate taxes that will loom when the surviving spouse passes on. The reason to buy such a policy through a trust rather than on your own is to keep the benefit out of your estate, where it would be subject to taxes.

Suppose a couple has a $3 million estate and splits off two $600,000 portions to get full tax credits. The husband dies, and the wife retains a $2.4 million estate. At her death, even after her tax credit, her estate will have a tax liability of $784,000. The cost of buying insurance to cover that would be about $115,000 for a 60-year-old couple with a normal life span, says financial planner Gunn.

You can fund the trust outright at the beginning. But it might make better sense to pay the premiums annually. That way, what you pay the trust for the premiums could qualify as a very respectable tax-free gift. The IRS lets each spouse give away up to $10,000 a year to any number of beneficiaries, meaning a couple with three kids could hand the trust $60,000 tax-free, enough to buy that $784,000 policy in about two years. Conversely, if the couple paid the $115,000 premium in one go, they'd pay a gift tax on $55,000. (You can also give away your money in $10,000 chunks as run-of-the-mill gifts, of course. Tidy sums on their own, they soon add up to small fortunes for your beneficiaries.)

Perhaps you already have a second-to-die insurance policy but no trust. In that case, you can create one and move the existing policy into the trust to avoid estate tax on it when the surviving spouse dies. Yes, you'll pay gift tax on its current cash value, but that should be far less than the estate tax would be later. Be aware that you miss out on this if you die within three years of the transfer. In that case, the full policy payout will be taxed.

. . . or should we say less (to pay)

You can escape even more taxes if you use trusts and partnerships to transfer control of business ventures, houses, and other investments to your loved ones. Moreover, you can do this while building in ample protection for yourself down the pike. Say that the bulk of your wealth is in real estate, a large house in the suburbs plus a vacation home such as a ski chalet in Aspen, Colorado, or a beachfront home overlooking the Pacific. A **qualified personal residence trust** (QPRT) would enable you to transfer their titles to your heirs with some special tax breaks. Each residence requires its own trust, but you can continue to live in your home and use the vacation spot.

When setting up a QPRT, you establish a life span for the trust—you want to be around when it ends or the property reverts back to your estate. If you outlast the trust (that's the idea), the residence passes to the trust's beneficiaries, escaping estate taxes. You could then rent it from the new owners. You'll pay a gift tax on the house's value at the time the trust is set up, but the value of the place is discounted by the IRS because the beneficiaries don't benefit from the gift during the life of the trust. Thus, your gift tax should be relatively modest. Once the house is in the QPRT, any appreciation is out of the IRS's reach until the trust ends, the place is sold, and the capital gains tax kicks in.

These trusts aren't cast in stone, either, and leave room for you to change your mind. If you later decide you want the house back, you can buy it from the trust provided the trustees agree. Occasionally, buybacks happen because of disagreements between the original owner of the house and its future proprietor (the beneficiaries). The transaction is free of taxes, but you must pay full market value.

Now let's assume that you've been sitting on all kinds of assets, most likely stocks, that you believe will appreciate wildly before you die. The goal is to freeze their value now so that your heirs don't get hit by big estate taxes later on. You can do this via a **grantor retained annuity trust** (GRAT), which lets you pass the assets on while continuing to enjoy some of their fruits. As with a QPRT, you must outlive the trust, or the assets go back into your estate. Within IRS guidelines, you can be paid an annual percentage of the trust as an annuity.

When you establish a GRAT, you'll pay a gift tax on the sum the IRS expects to be left at the end, a calculation based on a usually conservative growth rate. This assumed rate of return is also what the IRS uses to set limits on your annual payouts. Ideally, the trust's growth will be better, and all that extra total return will also escape the tax knife. As Jonathan Blattmachr, a partner at Milbank Tweed Hadley & McCloy in New York City, points out, "The best GRAT is the one that grows the most, because it means you've gotten the most tax-free."

What to do if there's anything left

Okay. So you've shifted as much out of your estate as you can, paid some gift taxes, given your kids more than their fair share, and still have more left over than you want to offer up to the tax man? Think about charity, as Jim and Norma Lumpkins did. Much of their worth was in highly appreciated regional bank stocks that paid low dividends. In other words, the stock was not a good source of income, and Lumpkins was unable to tap the big capital gain in these stocks because he'd lose too much of it to tax. His solution was to set up two charitable remainder trusts, which sold the stocks and reinvested the money. This left the folks who collect those onerous capital gains taxes whistling in the wind. Jim and Norma Lumpkins receive lifetime income from the trusts, and what's left of the capital after the survivor dies will go to charities, their two grandsons' prep school among them.

Leaving nothing is always one way to outwit the tax man. If you want to do better than that, says Cohen, "the sooner you start planning your estate, the less you'll have to pay the IRS."

CHAPTER FIVE

HOW TO RETIRE WELL: A GUIDE TO PROSPERITY

HOW TO PICK YOUR ADVISERS
page 174

CREATING A HIGH-POWERED 401(K)
page 180

HOW PREPARED ARE YOUR PARENTS' FINANCES?
page 185

WHERE TO INVEST YOUR NEST EGG
page 187

Don't leave it to luck. To keep your retirement plan from becoming a financial nightmare, start assembling your financial experts now. Here's how.

HOW TO PICK YOUR ADVISERS

BY JOHN ROTHCHILD

ONCE, YOU COULD RETIRE with a garden hoe or a stack of novels and tell your ex-employer and Social Security where to mail your checks. Not anymore. Personal finance has gotten so complicated that no one can hope to prepare for retirement without employing a large and rather expensive advisory team. Says Roy Ballentine, a consultant who assembles such teams: "We long ago concluded you'll never find a single expert with all the answers."

Chances are you already have a money manager or a broker stocking your portfolio, and you've hired an accountant to keep score. Maybe you're already playing *You Bet Your Life* with an insurance agent. Once you build up your assets, you'll be talking to a lawyer about how to scatter them along with your ashes. Sometimes you'll need an expert you didn't know you needed, as I recently discovered.

I'm an early boomer, 51, with the usual smattering of assets and two file cabinets full of financial paperwork. My accountant does a fine job with the taxes, throwing out my imaginative deductions to create harmony with the IRS. But he's not a pension expert, so it didn't occur to him to recommend a defined-benefit plan that allows a self-employed writer like me to shelter more income. I stumbled onto that strategy in a magazine, then hired a defined-benefit specialist to draw up the papers.

Financial teams are often built in this accidental fashion. The friendly neighborhood agent who sold you auto and home insurance becomes your life insurance adviser. The law firm that won you a settlement in the case against the neighbor's dog handles your trusts, your will, and your estate. Your investment counselor is the broker who put you into Wal-Mart 15 years ago. Soon enough, you've assembled a lineup of familiar faces, none of whom has any particular expertise in the tax strategies, insurance strategies, or investment strategies that will maximize your return in old age.

Finding a Team Leader

Even if our ad hoc collection of experts is qualified, without a team leader to provide guidance and strategy, the members are likely to work in isolation and sometimes at cross purposes. This is where the U.S. health care system, for all its faults, is superior to the wealth care system. Medicine is a far more complicated subject than money, which is why it takes six years to become a full doctor and six months to become a stockbroker. Yet to the average person, having money has become more confusing than being sick. That's because people who get sick have a family doctor—usually a general practitioner or an internist—to lead them to the right specialists and explain the various procedures. When it comes to money, however, there's been no obvious GP of finance.

Earlier in the century, the banker seemed the logical choice for financial GP, but thanks to the Glass-Steagall Act, banks weren't allowed to sell stocks, bonds, or mutual funds to the general public. This cut them off from key areas of investing and limited their role as coordinators. Anyway, bankers never gained the public confidence the way doctors did. Too many banks went bankrupt.

More recently the financial planner has emerged as the most likely candidate to play the family-doctor role. At present, this profession claims about 300,000 practitioners in the U.S., but just because they hang shingles over their doorways and buy ads in the yellow pages doesn't mean they're qualified. Financial planning sneaked up on the regulators before they got around to setting up a nationwide licensing and rating system.

Finding a qualified financial planner is not as hopeless as it sounds. Of the 300,000 people who claim this expertise, about 10%

have a designation that means something. These are the certified financial planners, who must complete 24 months of study and have up to five years of practical experience before obtaining their title.

You can get a list of qualified planners in your area by calling 800-282-PLAN. To find out whether a planner is certified on the one hand or has been publicly censured for misconduct on the other, call 888-CFP MARK. Or, on your first visit, you can ask a planner to show you a copy of Form ADV, in which he is supposed to reveal any black marks, describe his qualifications, and tell how much he charges for his services.

Planners make a living on commissions, fees, or both. Everything else being equal, pick a fee-only planner, because those who earn commissions on the investments or strategies they recommend may be swayed by the potential payoff. This is the same sort of conflict of interest that can exist in brokerage houses.

If you connect with a good financial planner before you hire the rest of the team, you may be able to save yourself some bother and some money. In the GP role, the planner might talk you out of buying life insurance you don't need or an annuity that is a poor substitute for a 401(k) plan. And whenever you do need another specialist, the planner may be able to help you choose a good one. This is a job that most of us try, and often fail, to accomplish ourselves.

Choosing the Rest of Your Team

Most how-to articles on this subject suffer from an overdose of optimism: Do research and ask a few questions, and you're bound to find capable and honest planners, brokers, and accountants. This ignores the fact that few people besides Bob Woodward have the time or the energy to run background checks on their housekeepers and babysitters, much less their financial team.

Roy Ballentine offers this suggestion: "Look at education, professional affiliation, and the type of firm a person belongs to. You can also ask for references, but we don't put a lot of stock in that. These days people are gun-shy and afraid to say anything bad about anybody. Also, when was the last time you called a reference who said something critical about the person who provided the name?"

If you have the luxury of shopping around, another useful technique is to ask a variety of experts for a review of your financial setup to date. Most likely they'll provide the review free. This will accomplish two things. You'll get a second opinion on the current status of your portfolio, trusts, and plans, and you'll learn something about the expert that will help you decide whether to put him or her on the team.

What follows is a quick rundown on things to look for and avoid with various types of advisers.

THE ACCOUNTANT. If you're like many retirees, you'll get involved in some kind of part-time business, consulting maybe. In that case you'll need a good tax-return person who knows something about freelance deductions. Or you may be able to get two experts in one by hiring one of the 8,000 certified public accountants who specialize in planning. Among them is an elite group of 1,600 personal financial specialists, each of whom has passed a comprehensive test in planning and logged 750 hours of hands-on experience with real-life clients. For a list of personal financial specialists in your area, call the American Institute of CPAs at 800-862-4272 and hit No. 5 on the voice menu.

THE BROKER. There's no monopoly on bad advice anywhere on Wall Street, but the most useful broker is one who tempers enthusiasm with experience. Seasoned brokers know a great deal, but not about everything, so if you take advice from a broker, take it from one who is knowledgeable about your kind of investing. It doesn't do much good to sign on with a utilities expert when you plan to traffic in aggressive-growth mutual funds.

Beware the know-it-all who claims expertise in mutual funds, annuities, small stocks, large stocks, foreign stocks, and financial planning. Merrill Lynch calls its brokers "financial consultants," but this doesn't mean they are qualified to play the role of team leader.

It never hurts to do some investigating before signing on with a broker or a firm. You can do your own homework with the help of the National Council for Individual Investors, at 800-663-8516. For $5 the outfit will send you its annual survey, which rates 40 of the main brokerage firms on such things as commissions and disciplinary history.

The survey also gives the specialties of the different firms, which should enable you to identify those that do the sort of investing you're interested in—technology, say, or blue chips. As Nancy Smith, director of the SEC's office of investor education, points out, "It's a good idea to look for somebody in your area. Usually you want to get to know them and have a face-to-face relationship."

THE MONEY MANAGER. There is no shortage of excellent independent money managers, and most are honest as well as capable. The odds of your money manager going bonkers and running off to Brazil with your assets in his briefcase are quite slim, but it does happen—and this is an extra risk often overlooked. If your broker at Smith Barney absconds with the funds, Smith Barney's insurance policy will cover the loss. No such coverage exists for an account with an independent money manager.

THE TRUST AND ESTATE LAWYER. Did you know that lawyers are given ratings, just like bonds? A company called Martindale-Hubbell sends out surveys in which thousands of lawyers grade other lawyers A, B, or C. The results are published in the *Martindale-Hubbell Law Directory*, found in most libraries. All three ratings are positive; imagine the lawsuits if they weren't! "C" stands for "fair to high" legal ability, "B" for high to very high, and "A" for very high to preeminent. This is all highly subjective, but if you're looking for a lawyer for your team, the A list isn't a bad place to start.

The problem is, even an A-rated lawyer can be a whiz at personal-injury lawsuits, real estate closings, and wills but a dunce at trusts and estates. It takes an estate specialist to keep up with the frequent changes in the statutes.

A good place to look for legal advice on estate planning is the American College of Trust and Estate Counsel. This organization keeps a list of 2,700 member attorneys, with at least ten years' experience in trust and estate work—all of them recognized by their peers as topnotch. To get the names for your area, write the American College at 3415 South Sepulveda Boulevard,

Suite 330, Los Angeles 90034.

THE RETIREMENT PLAN ADVISER. When Keoghs, IRAs, 401(k)s, and other such plans were introduced, the idea sounded simple: Put in the money, let it multiply tax-deferred, then retrieve it at retirement, when you're in a lower tax bracket. But it turns out there are many types of plans and many wrinkles within each, and the rules are ever changing and devilishly complex.

Some people use a pension adviser to handle the paperwork for their retirement plans. This works okay if the plans are the simple, boilerplate variety, but it may not work with plans that are unusual or complex. In that case, the pension expert might not be up to the task of modifying the plan a step ahead of the bureaucrats who change the rules. Iris Roth, my current defined-benefit adviser, thinks an individual can get better service from a boutique firm that specializes in retirement plans, as opposed to a full-service money management firm, in which individual cases are often handled by clerks and not the top strategists.

THE INSURANCE AGENT. Here's a refrain I've heard from a chorus of insurance experts: Avoid buying policies from part-time sales reps. These are the schoolteachers, bus drivers, etc., who supplement their incomes by moonlighting as insurance salesmen. Your chances of getting informed advice are much greater with a full-time practitioner. Like many things, insurance is not something that can be mastered as a hobby.

The basic certification for an insurance agent is chartered life underwriter (CLU), a title held by roughly 30% of the agent population in the U.S. Many insurance agents are also certified as chartered financial consultants, which means they've passed the same test as many financial planners.

Every state has an insurance commissioner's office where you can find out whether complaints have been lodged against a particular agent, but these databases are far from infallible. Before you choose any insurance experts for your team, find out how much training they have had and whether they continue to take insurance courses.

Sorting through the choices in your 401(k) can make retirement planning seem more like a curse than a blessing. Here's a little help.

CREATING A HIGH-POWERED 401(K) STRATEGY

BY SUSAN E. KUHN

O NCE UPON A TIME, your company promised you a retirement. Now it hands you a 401(k) plan and lets you figure out how to allocate your future stash among some funds that may or may not have legs. Sound rough? Get over it. It's an unfair world, and the best revenge is getting rich.

The way to exact such pleasure with your 401(k) plan is to create a portfolio that performs well over the long haul, minimizing the rollercoaster ups and downs of today's markets. But achieving that requires some keen detective work. According to Buck Consultants, the typical 401(k) plan offers six funds: a GIC (guaranteed investment contract); a balanced fund made up of stocks and bonds; growth and growth-and-income stock funds; an index stock fund; and a money market fund. Many also throw into the mix company stock, assorted bond funds, stock funds of foreign or small-cap companies, and more esoteric options.

With all that to choose from, the first step is untangling the jargon: deciphering, for example, that a "stable value" fund is simply another name for GICs. And then figuring out that GIC funds behave a lot like a Treasury fund, throwing off regular interest payments that add up in the long run.

You might expect that your plan offers choices that have been carefully thought out. Sorry. Some companies opt for funds like Fidelity Magellan because they think employees will be less likely to sue for disappointing performance if they've invested in a famous fund. Plans built on that kind of logic are far from perfect. Their funds don't complement one another, making your package more a mishmash than a comprehensive whole. "I see a lot of duplications among fund offerings, and some holes," says Jim Sullivan, a principal with Arthur Andersen's individual services practice in Chicago. "That doesn't help you construct a diversified portfolio."

Some companies, of course, do find ways to help you make smart choices. But they can only do so much. It's against the law for your employer to tell you what to do with your money; instead, the company is obligated only to provide enough data for a reasonable "education."

No wonder that intelligently arranging your 401(k) is hard. But you can make your task easier by following a few key guidelines. First of all, remember that the primary goal is not to have a great return one year followed by crumbs the next, but to be a winner no matter what's in favor on Wall Street.

Diversify, Diversify

The road to that diversification begins with a decision on how to divide your assets among stocks, bonds, and cash. According to academic research, this one call is responsible for over 90% of investment success—or failure. Since stocks historically return 10% per year, twice as much as bonds, a heavy dose of equity is the clear path to wealth. But given the risks of a bear market, you should bank heavily on stocks only if you can wait a decade or more before cashing out. If you plan to withdraw funds in five years or less, focus on GICs, bonds, or money market accounts.

Let's say you decide to put 80% of your 401(k) in stocks. You then have to decide which stock funds to select. Your company will probably supply reams of fund literature, most filled with babble. You want to cut through the dreck to answer three questions:

1. Does the fund invest in U.S. or foreign companies?
2. Does it buy stocks in big companies, like Coca-Cola, or smaller companies, like Netscape?
3. Does the fund own more growth stocks or value stocks?

Getting answers to the first two questions isn't that tough. Most funds that invest in foreign stocks say so specifically. And a blue-chip fund probably invests in FORTUNE 500 companies. On the other hand, a fund that talks about "emerging growth" is hunting smaller fry.

Answering the growth vs. value question is harder. Many funds market themselves as both to lure investors. To cut through their marketing spiel, start by seeking out key words in the literature. Besides the obvious ones—"growth" and "value"—look for "strong earnings gains" (i.e., growth) or "cheap stocks paying high dividends" (i.e., value). Better yet, check out the fund's largest holdings (funds are required by law to list all their positions). Look the stocks up in your local newspaper. If the shares are trading at a P/E of 30 or higher, you're not looking at a value fund.

For a more detailed report, check out Morningstar, based in Chicago, or Value Line, from New York City. These services classify publicly traded mutual funds by analyzing portfolios security by security.

How to Slice the Pie

Once you're confident of the makeup of your plan's funds, all you have to do is construct a portfolio that will maximize returns with a minimum of risk. Easier said than done, right? Well, take a pointer from SEI, a global investment advisory firm in Wayne, Pennsylvania. SEI has come up with a model equity portfolio: It advises that you shoot for 60% of assets in large-cap U.S. stocks and 10% in small caps, each half growth, half value; and 30% in international equities, with one-third of that devoted to emerging markets.

You're unlikely to match those fine cuts exactly in your 401(k). But many plans make it possible for you to approximate that mix: You could, for example, put 60% of your 401(k) in an S&P 500 index fund or in a general stock fund; 10% in a small-stock fund; and 30% in an international stock fund.

You need to give just as much thought to how you mix the bond funds in your 401(k). Money market funds are fine for cash that you might need in the next year or so. But if you can wait a little longer,

A GUIDE TO 401(K) LINGO

Balanced Fund. No, it's not a gymnastics event. It's a fund that typically invests 60% of assets in stocks and 40% in bonds. The bonds supposedly cushion investors when stocks dip—but when both fall, watch out.

Equity-Income. Perfect for *Wheel of Fortune*: almost indecipherable. A yield-oriented stock fund, this could be mostly stocks paying high dividends or a mix of preferreds, convertibles, and Treasury bonds. Read the fine print.

Growth. Like, who'd want a stunted portfolio? These funds typically hold blue-chip stocks, but if you see the word "aggressive," look for small stocks. Another surprise: Fidelity Magellan, ostensibly a growth fund, owns bonds. Be wary.

Stable Value. Sounds like a bank CD. But it isn't. It's a GIC fund, full of guaranteed investment contracts that tend to pay out more than cash. Warning: The guarantee comes from insurers or other providers, not Uncle Sam.

Life Cycle. Dog food? Exercise equipment? No. The trendiest offering is a premixed blend of stocks, bonds, and other investments, designed to match an investor's age or tolerance for risk. But how many investors are exactly alike?

consider a GIC fund or an intermediate-term bond fund—according to Buck Consultants, over 50% of all 401(k) plans offer these. Since 1983, according to research conducted by John Hancock, intermediate bonds and five-year GICs have returned about 10% per year on average, vs. 6.4% for money market funds.

Owning bonds protects your portfolio. SEI calculates that over a typical five-year period, a globally diversified portfolio of stocks stands to earn, on average, 11.3% per year—but that same portfolio could lose as much as 5.5% annually. Slotting 40% of those assets into a specific bond mix—65% in intermediate bonds maturing in about five years, 20% in high-yield bonds, and 15% in foreign bonds—cuts your maximum annual loss in half while reducing your potential annual gain by less than two percentage points.

If you can't mix bond funds, consider a "balanced" fund. Many of them automatically allocate 40% or so of assets to bonds, with the rest going to stocks.

No matter what you do, you can protect yourself only so far. Bonds can be as volatile as stocks. In 1994, for instance, the average balanced fund lost 2.7%, according to Morningstar, more than the average U.S. stock fund.

Going for Brokerage

Brokerage companies are aware of how confusing this all is. In fact, they regard chaos as a great marketing opportunity: They're constantly proffering new products that promise to resolve all your worries. One such product has already found its way into many 401(k) plans.

Called a life-cycle fund, it professes to be a one-stop 401(k) shop. These funds are made up of investments that supposedly mimic the perfect blend needed by investors of a certain age or risk tolerance. In other words, when you're a rock-climbing slacker, you get a hefty slab of risky equity, but by the time you're a grandparent, that same fund may have nothing but Treasury bonds. One small problem: No two life-cycle funds are quite alike. "The financial services industry seems to need a new product every couple of months," says Andersen's Sullivan. "I like the idea, but to tell the truth, sometimes we overcomplicate things when a simple balanced fund will do the trick."

Self-directed brokerage accounts, on the other hand, are a great way to fill in holes in your 401(k) plan. They allow you to go outside the standard offering to purchase a wide range of

HOW PREPARED
ARE YOUR PARENTS' FINANCES?

Ask yourself the following ten questions, prepared with the help of Ernst & Young's personal financial counseling division, to measure your intergenerational financial IQ.

1. Has your parents' will been reviewed in the past three years?

2. Do you know where to find all your parents' financial and legal papers and advisers?

3. Do you know the approximate annual cost of maintaining your parents' current lifestyle in retirement, and do you know if they have sufficient financial resources to do so?

4. Have you reviewed their assets to ensure there will be enough cash readily available to pay the estate taxes due within nine months of the date of death?

5. Do the trustees of your parents' estate have the health, financial acumen, and willingness to perform the required duties?

6. Are you concerned about the mental or physical health of your parents? Consider the use of a durable power of attorney.

7. Have you or your parents considered the use of trusts as a way to manage and transfer assets to avoid either estate taxation of life insurance proceeds or the hassle of the probate administration process?

8. If your parents' estate is worth more than $600,000, have you made provisions to fully use the "unified credit" available to shelter gift and estate taxes?

9. To reduce estate taxes, have your parents considered a formal program to make annual gifts to children and grandchildren?

10. Have you reviewed the tax consequences of your parents' retirement plans, including the plan balances and beneficiary designations?

funds. So if your employer offers a self-directed brokerage account but no international fund, you could invest some money in a top-performing worldwide fund. Many of the accounts even let you use your 401(k) stash to buy individual stocks. If your employer is one of the 120 companies that offer the new Schwab Personal Choice Retirement account, you can get a particularly broad choice. The Schwab plan includes all listed and OTC stocks, 1,000 mutual funds, CDs, and bonds.

Of course, brokerage accounts have their own particular headache: the bill. Merrill Lynch, which has offered a brokerage option to 401(k) plan clients since 1982, charges an annual fee of $50 to $150 per account. You'll probably have to pay that yourself—as well as the commissions on any trade you execute.

No one ever said it would be easy. But if you stay focused on the basics and invest wisely in a blend of stocks with a dash of fixed-income thrown in, your 401(k) soufflé may pouf perfectly by retirement time.

Big fund companies want your money. Sure, individual fund managers are important, but you need to know about the firms they work for. Investing styles, trading practices, and bonus plans can all affect your returns.

WHERE TO INVEST YOUR NEST EGG

BY RICHARD TEITELBAUM

TAKEN TOGETHER, the ten largest fund companies manage $1 trillion in assets—not even counting money markets. That's fully half of all such fund dollars. Surprisingly, people who buy shares in mutual funds usually know very little about these huge companies to which they entrust their savings. What they do know generally centers on the fund manager, who often has a high PR profile. When you invest, you're buying not just the fund manager's services but often those of dozens of analysts who feed him ideas, traders who execute his purchases and sales, and managers who set the terms of his compensation. Know it or not, you may also be buying into a house investing style that can reward you richly in one market but punish you severely in the next. Says John Rekenthaler of Morningstar, the Chicago fund research firm: "The manager is a product of the organization he works with."

To size up the ten giants, FORTUNE had Morningstar rank their performance in seven stock fund categories chosen to reflect portfolio-management skills. Bond funds were omitted: A firm's composite return in bonds tells less about its bond-picking talents than about its mix of long- and short-term bond funds. Morningstar's figures point up important differences—and tell fascinating stories, from the ascent of once sleepy Putnam to the surprise success of Twentieth Century's foreign funds.

FIDELITY. The Boston shock troops of aggressive investing are starting to look a lot like the Keystone Kops. Fidelity's growth funds—for decades the industry's premier franchise—have been slipping. They finished second over five years, sixth over three years, and a depressing eighth in the past year.

Why? In Fidelity's freewheeling, free-spending culture, portfolio managers get ample freedom and oodles of research, trading, and technological backup. They also get blamed when things go wrong. In April, heads rolled. The company shuffled the managers of 27 funds in a restructuring that Bill Hayes, chief of equity investments, improbably described as "evolutionary." Eric Kobren, executive editor of the *Fidelity Insight* newsletter, says the changes made eminent sense: "So many of these fund managers were trying to fit a square peg into a round hole."

Example: Thomas Sweeney, as manager of Capital Appreciation, should have been buying aggressive stocks but instead had invested heavily in utilities and energy. Michael Gordon of Blue Chip Growth sank 35% of its assets into technology last August and turned over its holdings at a hectic 235% annual rate. Now Sweeney runs the tamer Canada fund, and Gordon was switched to aggressive Retirement Growth, a fund for IRAs and 401(k)s, where the tax effects of his restless trading would be minimized. (Gordon later left to join Jeffrey Vinik, the former Magellan manager, at Vinik Asset Management.)

Hoopla over the restructuring and over Vinik's abrupt resignation obscures Fidelity's resilience in other areas. Its more conservative growth and income offerings—such as the Market Index and Fidelity funds—have bested all competitors for one- and three-year periods. Naturally, the managers at these funds emerged unscathed in April.

VANGUARD. Buying shares in a Vanguard fund means buying a chunk of the business: Fund investors, not stockholders, are the owners of this uniquely structured Pennsylvania giant. The benefit to you is that your fund is managed to minimize expenses rather than maximize corporate profits, a strategy that helps boost your returns. Vanguard employees receive bonuses when they keep expenses low. The company's average expense ratio of 0.31% is less than a third that of the industry.

The best way to benefit from this skinflint-opoly is to invest in

Vanguard's equity-index and bond funds. Its actively managed funds typically are not run in-house but farmed out to firms like Wellington Management and Schroder Capital Management. Does Vanguard pick fund managers better than you or I? Not necessarily. The famed Windsor fund lagged badly in 1994 and 1995. But Vanguard does react when long-term performance falters.

AMERICAN FUNDS. A heart attack might cause some people to see their lives flash before their eyes. But during his brush with death in 1953, Jonathan B. Lovelace saw his stock portfolio instead. Worried about succession, Lovelace, founder of American Funds parent company Capital Research & Management, divvied responsibility for his fund with three other managers. Thus was born one of the world's strangest, and most successful, money-management systems.

Today, each fund's mammoth portfolio—its Investment Co. of America fund alone teeters at $25.7 billion—is split among three to 11 managers. A quarter or so of each fund is reserved for the company's 65-member research staff to manage. (Imagine, analysts get to pick stocks!) Each manager typically works on several funds and may buy and sell as he or she sees fit, taking care to remain faithful to a fund's basic philosophy and various guidelines. Does all this cross-managing lead to mass confusion? No, because an investment-review department oversees buy and sell decisions and keeps managers from tripping over one another. Explains senior vice president William Grimsley: "The system may seem cumbersome, but it works."

Apparently so. Capital Research has three of the ten largest stock mutual funds and ranks as the third-largest fund manager in the U.S. Over the years the company has cooked up a lot of ideas that are now truisms, such as that most investors should put their money in stocks (some 70% of assets are equity) and should diversify by investing overseas (the company's EuroPacific Growth helps it top the five-year foreign ranking). Low stock turnover of under 30% a year marks Capital Research as a buy-and-hold investor, and it has figured out how to make conservatism pay.

MERRILL LYNCH. As the house-brand products of the nation's largest brokerage, Merrill's funds are set apart by a couple of things. Says asset management president Arthur Zeikel: "Our job is, first, to preserve and protect the reputation of Merrill Lynch and, second, to maintain confidence in the brokerage force." That explains why, with more than 250 funds, the most in the business, Merrill has no aggressive growth or small-capitalization growth offerings. Such funds shine brightly in bull markets but are more likely to flame out in bear ones, hurting investors and leaving the giant brokerage embarrassed. So if customers are suited for riskier fare, brokers peddle funds of such well-known companies as AIM or MFS; when clients are in need of a conservative investment, the firm's 11,000 salesmen will likely steer them to Merrill's buttoned-down offerings, like Basic Value. Naturally, this strategy dampens Merrill's performance in a bull market, and in our U.S. diversified equity fund rankings.

Despite his company's aversion to risk, Zeikel lets Merrill's managers run their portfolios pretty much as they see fit. Stick within the guidelines of the prospectus and, Zeikel claims, you're on your own. Do you want quantitative research? Buy some. Need assistants? Hire them. The managers help design the benchmarks upon which their bonuses depend. Says Zeikel: "This system isn't something McKinsey came up with. I designed it to create an atmosphere in which I would want to work."

FRANKLIN TEMPLETON. Four years ago, Franklin was known only as a massive, dominating player in bond funds. That very success undermined the San Mateo, California, company's efforts to build equity funds. "We'd ask ourselves, 'Why keep trying to push a rock up a hill?' " recalls Chuck Johnson, now president of Franklin's Templeton Worldwide division. "We could raise four times as much money rolling out a fixed-income fund as we could an equity fund."

Johnson and his family, who own more than a third of parent Franklin Resources, decided to tackle the problem with a checkbook. In 1992, Franklin spent $786 million to buy John Templeton's famed family of international funds. Rivals gasped at the price, but the timing was nearly perfect: Demand for stocks has helped the Templeton funds more than triple in size, to $60 billion.

Even so, it is too soon to tell how the acquisition will pan out. Franklin retained the Fort Lauderdale company's unique research department, whose analysts are assigned a new industry and country every couple of years. To screen stocks, they use much the same analysis developed by Templeton himself. No buy is allowed unless a stock qualifies for the company's so-called bargain list. But some Templeton managers, even after receiving fat salary increases, were irked to find their bonus pool linked to that of their fixed-income counterparts in California. President Thomas L. Hansberger quit and took a handful of employees with him to found a rival institutional business. A few others have defected since employment contracts expired.

The Johnsons seem to like acquiring fund companies: In June, Franklin flashed its checkbook again, offering to buy another famous name: Michael Price and his Mutual Series funds. The price could reach more than $800 million, if Price succeeds in boosting assets over his five-year contract. An expensive move for Franklin? Perhaps. But its stock rose 3.7% the day of the announcement. And its performance in the growth and income category—dead last among the fund giants over the past three and five years—will likely soar.

T. ROWE PRICE. Advice to graduating MBAs seeking positions at T. Rowe Price: Limber up your throwing arm. The Baltimore company is home not just to some of the industry's best performing and most even-keeled funds but also to 19 softball teams. T. Rowe puts a premium on collegiality and teamwork—in order to gauge employees' willingness to share ideas, research director Jim Kennedy designed a computer program to track each suggestion and follow-up remark publicly uttered or E-mailed by an employee. Results of the monitoring affect bonuses.

Many T. Rowe fund managers are likely to receive advice from veterans like equity head M. David Testa or portfolio manager Jack Laporte. That's T. Rowe's informal "friendly uncle" system at work. The oldsters are mostly survivors of the dark days during the 1970s and early 1980s when—partly due to founder Thomas Rowe Price's penchant for large-cap and natural-resource stocks—the business lost 40% of its assets. The graybeards help greener managers avoid

191

common pitfalls, like compromising the quality of a portfolio in a quest for bargains.

T. Rowe has a reputation for strength in small-cap stocks yet always seems to have a top-performing fund or two in every category. Two funds—New Horizons and Small-Cap Value—have attracted so much business that they were recently closed to new investors, a rarity in big families. T. Rowe has rounded out its offerings with topflight foreign funds, like International Stock, which it co-manages in a joint venture with Robert Fleming in London.

PUTNAM INVESTMENTS. Consistency helps Putnam's stable of U.S. diversified stock funds stand out. According to a recent Morningstar study, Putnam's funds hew more closely to their stated objectives than those of any other big-fund group. The conservative Equity Income is heavily invested in just the kind of high-yielding utilities and energy companies you'd expect. Aggressive funds—like OTC Emerging Growth—keep their portfolios chock full of small-cap highfliers. This makes Putnam an appealing choice for financial planners, who rely on a fund's declared objectives when making asset allocation decisions, and to managers of 401(k) plans, in which individuals can't be expected to keep tabs on a fund's stylistic dalliances.

Putnam organizes its U.S. diversified equity funds into three groups. "Basic value" and "core growth" funds make extensive use of computers to winnow stocks from, say, thousands of potential picks to just a couple of hundred. Characteristics that historically have signaled superior performance—such as a low price-to-sales ratio for value stocks or a history of positive earnings surprises for growth stocks—help pinpoint potential winners. Only then do managers and analysts—typically working in teams on each fund—start their fundamental research. The third major group—"specialty growth"—uses fewer screens, since data for small-cap stocks are sparser and less reliable, and the impact of management is far greater. The results of Putnam's system? Its diversified equity funds win top honors among the ten largest fund groups for the one-, three-, and five-year periods.

IDS. An American Express subsidiary, IDS is a familiar name in the Midwest, where many investors swear by its parent company's financial planners. IDS equity funds haven't garnered much attention because they are sold mostly through those planners and typically don't aim to shoot out any lights. Each manager's results are measured against those of 20 rival funds with similar objectives, capitalization, and style. The manager's bonus kicks in when he or she outperforms ten of them—but tops out when he or she beats 15. Explains senior vice president Peter Anderson: "We want to incentivize managers, but we don't want them swinging for the fences, doing crazy things."

Weaknesses in IDS's lineup: Its international funds have been middling, and until recently small-company results have lagged. Anderson says additional research support and new management are helping IDS turn the corner in small-company funds.

DEAN WITTER. Like Merrill Lynch and IDS, Dean Witter benefits mightily from its own sales force—in this case, more than 8,800 stockbrokers. But Dean Witter long encouraged those brokers to steer customers to its own funds by paying them more to do so. Last year the Securities and Exchange Commission broadly criticized the practice, and soon thereafter Dean Witter said it would cease paying unequal commissions. Still, a recent visit by FORTUNE to a Dean Witter office found a broker hawking only Dean Witter funds. (By contrast, brokers at two Merrill Lynch offices didn't push any Merrill funds.)

Dean Witter declined FORTUNE's request to interview an official of its fund group. But a former executive says fund managers are given varying amounts of liberty: Some enjoy relatively free rein and others come under closer supervision of the chief investment officer (currently Joseph McAlinden). Says the former executive: "There's no across-the-firm discipline. It's quite eclectic."

Results are eclectic too. A new foreign-stock fund—International Small Cap—lifts Dean Witter to the No. 2 slot on our foreign list over one year. The growth funds have done poorly longer term, better recently. Past performance suggests investors should avoid its growth and income funds.

TWENTIETH CENTURY. Earnings attract investors. In 1971, following that simple idea, Chairman James E. Stowers Jr., a self-taught computer buff, programmed the office mainframe to identify companies with accelerating earnings growth. Still in use at headquarters in Kansas City, the program has been tweaked and improved over 25 years to factor in all sorts of ratios and signals that can portend an earnings acceleration: comparable store sales in the case of retailers, book-to-bill ratios for chip companies, car-loading data for railroads. As a company's earnings growth rate rises, Twentieth Century throws wads of money into the stock. When growth starts to fade—by as little as one percentage point in some cases—the funds may sell with a vengeance.

Seven teams of managers and analysts run the funds. When a team gets the computer's latest picks, it digs in, checking for glitches, calling companies to uncover seasonal distortions, quizzing management to ascertain the sustainability of each swing in earnings. "We are fundamental investors using quantitative tools," says chief investment officer Robert Puff. The company runs a technologically sophisticated trading desk. Its predilection for hot stocks and its zero cash policy make its funds among the most volatile.

FUND FAMILIES RANKED BY

U.S. DIVERSIFIED EQUITY FUNDS*			
		Average annual return	
	1 yr.	3 yr.	5 yr.
1 **Putnam**	31.5%	20.0%	19.6%
2 **T. Rowe Price**	27.5%	18.4%	17.3%
3 **Vanguard**	24.9%	16.8%	16.2%
4 **Fidelity**	21.3%	16.8%	17.6%
5 **Franklin**	21.8%	16.6%	12.9%
6 **Twentieth Century**	21.2%	16.0%	17.6%
7 **Dean Witter**	27.3%	15.5%	15.3%
8 **Merrill Lynch**	21.8%	14.9%	15.3%
9 **IDS**	23.3%	14.3%	15.0%
10 **American**	19.6%	14.2%	14.7%

*Listed by three-year performance through June 30.

FOREIGN FUNDS* **

		Average annual return		
		1 yr.	3 yr.	5 yr.
1	Putnam	19.8%	16.1%	13.3%
2	American	16.9%	15.4%	14.2%
3	Franklin	14.9%	15.1%	13.1%
4	Vanguard	15.0%	13.6%	11.0%
5	Twentieth Century	24.3%	12.9%	14.0%
6	T. Rowe Price	19.2%	12.8%	10.8%
7	IDS	19.3%	11.9%	10.1%
8	Fidelity	16.9%	9.6%	9.6%
9	Merrill Lynch	11.9%	6.8%	N.A.
10	Dean Witter	20.8%	N.A.	N.A.

*Listed by three-year performance through June 30. N.A. Not Applicable. **Non-U.S. multiregional.

GROWTH FUNDS*

		Average annual return		
		1 yr.	3 yr.	5 yr.
1	Franklin	25.0%	21.5%	12.8%
2	T. Rowe Price	28.0%	19.5%	17.4%
3	Putnam	30.4%	19.3%	18.2%
4	Vanguard	25.1%	18.9%	16.3%
5	IDS	26.5%	17.1%	16.8%
6	Fidelity	20.8%	16.8%	17.7%
7	Merrill Lynch	23.3%	16.1%	15.7%
8	Dean Witter	29.0%	14.0%	13.4%
9	American	15.9%	13.7%	15.1%
10	Twentieth Century	15.5%	11.6%	13.3%

*Listed by three-year performance through June 30.

GROWTH AND INCOME FUNDS*

		Average annual return		
		1 yr.	3 yr.	5 yr.
1	Fidelity	27.3%	17.8%	16.1%
2	Vanguard	24.4%	15.9%	15.7%
3	Putnam	25.1%	15.9%	15.6%
4	Twentieth Century	26.4%	15.8%	16.5%
5	T. Rowe Price	24.0%	15.4%	14.6%
6	American	22.9%	15.2%	15.0%
7	Merrill Lynch	19.2%	15.0%	15.5%
8	Dean Witter	20.9%	13.9%	14.3%
9	IDS	20.9%	13.2%	14.1%
10	Franklin	20.8%	11.6%	11.8%

*Listed by three-year performance through June 30.

EQUITY INCOME FUNDS*

		Average annual return		
		1 yr.	3 yr.	5 yr.
1	T. Rowe Price	24.9%	17.1%	16.2%
2	Fidelity	21.0%	16.0%	18.2%
3	Vanguard	25.9%	14.4%	14.9%
4	Merrill Lynch	22.8%	12.5%	12.2%
5	IDS	19.8%	12.1%	15.3%
6	American	17.9%	11.5%	12.7%
7	Putnam	17.6%	11.4%	12.1%
8	Franklin	11.2%	7.6%	11.3%
9	Twentieth Century	23.3%	N.A.	N.A.
10	Dean Witter	N.A.	N.A.	N.A.

*Listed by three-year performance through June 30. N.A. Not applicable.

AGGRESSIVE GROWTH FUNDS*

		Average annual return		
		1 yr.	3 yr.	5 yr.
1	Putnam	39.0%	24.7%	26.5%
2	IDS	33.6%	16.2%	14.5%
3	Fidelity	18.1%	15.7%	17.7%
4	Twentieth Century	24.2%	15.5%	20.2%

*Listed by three-year performance through June 30.

SMALL-COMPANY FUNDS*

		Average annual return		
		1 yr.	3 yr.	5 yr.
1	Putnam	54.6%	30.6%	27.5%
2	Twentieth Century	25.1%	25.3%	25.5%
3	Franklin	24.0%	23.3%	18.5%
4	Dean Witter	34.7%	21.9%	21.2%
5	T. Rowe Price	33.1%	21.1%	20.4%
6	Vanguard	25.9%	16.9%	17.7%
7	Fidelity	20.0%	15.8%	21.4%
8	Merrill Lynch	20.1%	14.1%	16.4%
9	IDS	23.6%	11.9%	14.0%

*Listed by three-year peformance through June 30.

THE 1996 FORTUNE 500 DIRECTORY

LIKE OLD MAN RIVER, corporate America's profits seem a force of nature by now—rolling along mightily from one year to the next. Earnings of companies in the FORTUNE 500 rose 13.4% in 1995, the fourth straight year of double-digit increases (excluding 1992–93 write-offs for retiree health benefits). The latest results are especially impressive because the U.S. economy grew only 2% last year, and inflation was just 2.8%. Also noteworthy: the broad swath of industries where profits surged, from heavy manufacturing to high tech to financial services. GM, No. 1 on the FORTUNE 500, saw earnings rise 40% last year, on top of a gangbusters 99% increase the year before.

The driving force of this five-year-old business expansion has been corporate restructuring. Will it continue? Most economists and stock market strategists think corporate managers have about run out of ways to make their organizations more efficient. Even so, NatWest Securities chief strategist Peter Canelo believes earnings will again grow at double-digit rates this year because the economy is picking up briskly, the consensus "worrywarts" notwithstanding. Rising domestic and foreign demand will benefit a broad array of industries, including cyclical groups such as metals and machinery producers, he says. **—Joe Spiers**

RANK 1995	COMPANY	REVENUES $ millions	PROFITS $ millions	Rank	ASSETS $ millions	Rank
1	**GENERAL MOTORS** Detroit	**168,828.6**	**6,880.7**	1	**217,123.4**	7
2	**FORD MOTOR** Dearborn, Mich.	**137,137.0**	**4,139.0**	6	**243,283.0**	3
3	**EXXON** Irving, Texas	**110,009.0**ᴱ	**6,470.0**	3	**91,296.0**	26
4	**WAL-MART STORES** Bentonville, Ark.[1]	**93,627.0**	**2,740.0**	1?	**37,871.0**	67
5	**AT&T** New York	**79,609.0**	**139.0**	345	**88,884.0**	28
6	**INTL. BUSINESS MACHINES** Armonk, N.Y.	**71,940.0**	**4,178.0**	5	**80,292.0**	33
7	**GENERAL ELECTRIC** Fairfield, Conn.	**70,028.0**	**6,573.0**	2	**228,035.0**	5
8	**MOBIL** Fairfax, Va.	**66,724.0**ᴱ	**2,376.0**	18	**42,138.0**	62
9	**CHRYSLER** Auburn Hills, Mich.	**53,195.0**	**2,025.0**	22	**53,756.0**	50
10	**PHILIP MORRIS** New York	**53,139.0**ᴱ	**5,450.0**	4	**53,811.0**	49
11	**PRUDENTIAL INS. CO. OF AMERICA** Newark, N.J.	**41,330.0**	**579.0**	130	**219,380.0**	6
12	**STATE FARM GROUP** Bloomington, Ill.	**40,809.9**	**1,271.2**	49	**85,262.3**	29
13	**E.I. DU PONT DE NEMOURS** Wilmington, Del.	**37,607.0**ᴱ	**3,293.0**	10	**37,312.0**	68
14	**TEXACO** White Plains, N.Y.	**36,787.0**ᴱ	**607.0**	125	**24,937.0**	98
15	**SEARS ROEBUCK** Hoffman Estates, Ill.[2]	**35,181.0**[3]	**1,801.0**	31	**33,130.0**	78
16	**KMART** Troy, Mich.[1]	**34,654.0**	**(571.0)**	487	**15,397.0**	146
17	**PROCTER & GAMBLE** Cincinnati[4]	**33,434.0**	**2,645.0**	14	**28,125.0**	88
18	**CHEVRON** San Francisco	**32,094.0**ᴱ	**930.0**	69	**34,330.0**	75
19	**CITICORP** New York	**31,690.0**	**3,464.0**	8	**256,853.0**	2
20	**HEWLETT-PACKARD** Palo Alto[5]	**31,519.0**	**2,433.0**	16	**24,427.0**	99
21	**PEPSICO** Purchase, N.Y.	**30,421.0**	**1,606.0**	36	**25,432.0**	94
22	**METROPOLITAN LIFE INSURANCE** New York	**27,977.0**	**(559.4)**	486	**158,800.0**	13
23	**AMOCO** Chicago	**27,665.0**ᴱ	**1,862.0**	26	**29,845.0**	84
24	**MOTOROLA** Schaumburg, Ill.	**27,037.0**	**1,781.0**	32	**22,801.0**	109
25	**AMERICAN INTERNATIONAL GROUP** New York	**25,874.0**	**2,510.4**	15	**134,136.4**	16

STOCKHOLDERS' EQUITY		MARKET VALUE 3/15/96		EARNINGS PER SHARE					TOTAL RETURN TO INVESTORS			
							1985–95 annual growth rate				1985–95 annual rate	
				1995	% change from				1995			
$ millions	Rank	$ millions	Rank	$	1994	%	Rank		%	Rank	%	Rank
23,345.5	5	39,308.8	23	7.21	40.0	1.6	234		28.5	255	9.2	299
24,547.0	4	34,907.9	27	3.58	(28.0)	4.7	202		8.1	370	16.9	103
40,436.0	1	98,092.6	4	5.18	27.3	4.8	200		38.1	192	16.7	107
14,762.0	14	54,495.4	11	1.19	1.7	23.4	25		5.3	380	19.3	64
17,274.0	11	98,121.7	3	0.09	(97.0)	(23.8)	316		32.1	231	13.8	192
22,423.0	6	68,256.8	7	7.23	44.0	(3.8)	286		25.7	278	(1.8)	366
29,609.0	2	126,523.3	1	3.90	40.8	11.8	111		45.3	142	18.2	80
17,951.0	10	44,191.5	17	5.87	128.4	8.7	149		37.5	200	19.6	62
10,959.0	28	23,313.6	45	5.30	(47.6)	(1.6)	272		16.5	326	14.5	168
13,985.0	16	79,612.9	5	6.48	18.9	17.3	57		64.8	58	28.2	15
11,410.0	26	N.A.		N.A.	—	—			—		—	
25,143.0	3	N.A.		N.A.	—	—			—		—	
8,436.0	42	45,120.0	16	5.61	40.3	13.8	86		28.4	257	16.1	125
9,519.0	35	21,888.1	48	2.10	(33.8)	(8.5)	301		37.3	204	17.7	86
4,385.0	119	19,571.2	56	4.50	23.0	2.5	228		30.7	241	11.3	261
5,280.0	88	4,708.5	237	(1.25)	(298.4)	—			(42.3)	444	(0.8)	364
10,589.0	30	57,058.2	10	3.71	20.1	14.6	79		36.7	208	20.0	54
14,355.0	15	35,791.3	25	1.43	(45.0)	(4.5)	290		22.0	299	15.9	131
19,581.0	9	33,221.7	31	7.21	2.6	7.3	169		66.1	53	15.1	150
11,839.0	22	50,931.8	12	4.63	50.8	17.1	62		69.4	44	17.4	95
7,313.0	50	49,146.8	13	2.00	(8.3)	12.0	108		56.9	81	23.5	31
6,600.0	60	N.A.		N.A.	—	—			—		—	
14,848.0	13	34,898.0	28	3.76	4.4	0.1	259		25.4	283	13.5	204
11,048.0	27	32,872.3	32	2.93	10.6	34.4	17		(1.1)	405	20.7	49
19,827.1	8	43,684.2	19	5.30	15.7	18.4	46		42.2	162	17.8	84

RANK 1995	COMPANY	REVENUES $ millions	PROFITS $ millions	Rank	ASSETS $ millions	Rank
26	**CONAGRA** Omaha[6]	24,108.9	495.6	151	10,801.0	190
27	**KROGER** Cincinnati	23,937.8	302.8	225	5,044.7	288
28	**DAYTON HUDSON** Minneapolis[1]	23,516.0	311.0	221	12,570.0	174
29	**LOCKHEED MARTIN** Bethesda, Md.[7]	22,853.0	682.0	114	17,648.0	131
30	**UNITED TECHNOLOGIES** Hartford	22,802.0	750.0	93	15,958.0	140
31	**ALLSTATE** Northbrook, Ill.	22,793.0	1,904.0	25	70,029.0	39
32	**FED. NATL. MORTGAGE ASSN.** Washington, D.C.	22,246.0	2,372.0	19	316,550.0	1
33	**MERRILL LYNCH** New York	21,513.0	1,114.0	57	176,857.0	12
34	**J.C. PENNEY** Plano, Texas[1]	21,419.0	838.0	78	17,102.0	135
35	**UNITED PARCEL SERVICE** Atlanta	21,045.0	1,043.0	61	12,645.0	173
36	**DOW CHEMICAL** Midland, Mich.	20,957.0	2,078.0	21	23,582.0	105
37	**BANKAMERICA CORP.** San Francisco	20,386.0	2,664.0	13	232,446.0	4
38	**GTE** Stamford, Conn.	19,957.0	(2,144.0)*	493	37,019.0	69
39	**INTERNATIONAL PAPER** Purchase, N.Y.	19,797.0	1,153.0	53	23,977.0	102
40	**BOEING** Seattle	19,515.0	393.0	188	22,098.0	114
41	**XEROX** Stamford, Conn.	18,963.0¶	(472.0)	484	25,969.0	92
42	**CIGNA** Philadelphia	18,955.0	211.0	299	95,903.0	24
43	**JOHNSON & JOHNSON** New Brunswick, N.J.	18,842.0	2,403.0	17	17,873.0	128
44	**LOEWS** New York	18,770.0	1,765.7	33	65,058.0	41
45	**AMERICAN STORES** Salt Lake City[1]	18,308.9	316.8	220	7,363.0	236
46	**PRICECOSTCO** Issaquah, Wash.[8]	18,247.3	133.9	349	4,437.4	305
47	**USX** Pittsburgh	18,214.0ᴱ	214.0	296	16,743.0	138
48	**COCA-COLA** Atlanta	18,018.0	2,986.0	11	15,041.0	148
49	**BELLSOUTH** Atlanta	17,886.0	(1,232.0)*	491	31,880.0	79
50	**SARA LEE** Chicago[4]	17,719.0	804.0	82	12,431.0	179

STOCKHOLDERS' EQUITY		MARKET VALUE 3/15/96		EARNINGS PER SHARE					TOTAL RETURN TO INVESTORS			
				1995 $	% change from 1994	1985–95 annual growth rate %	Rank		1995 %	Rank	1985–95 annual rate %	Rank
$ millions	Rank	$ millions	Rank									
2,495.4	206	10,417.3	110	2.06	13.8	13.3	92		35.2	217	18.4	77
(1,603.0)	493	4,515.5	246	2.52	18.3	2.1	231		54.9	89	26.5	21
3,403.0	160	6,048.7	193	4.03	(30.2)	3.3	218		8.6	366	7.4	320
6,433.0	63	15,135.6	73	3.28	(23.6)	(1.3)	270		81.4	23	14.1	184
4,021.0	136	13,542.9	84	5.70	29.5	10.4	130		54.8	91	11.7	250
12,680.0	18	18,515.3	58	4.24	—	—			77.3	29	—	
10,959.0	28	34,261.5	29	2.15	10.7	47.8	5		75.0	35	33.1	9
6,141.0	69	9,769.1	122	5.44	14.5	17.0	63		45.6	139	14.6	165
5,884.0	72	11,211.6	103	3.48	(18.9)	10.1	132		11.3	353	17.6	89
5,151.0	94	N.A.		1.83	12.3	8.1	155		—		—	
7,361.0	49	23,233.3	46	7.72	129.1	43.6	9		8.8	363	14.3	177
20,222.0	7	27,148.6	38	6.49	21.1	—			69.4	45	17.8	82
6,871.0	56	40,465.0	21	(2.21)	(186.7)	—			52.6	100	17.5	93
7,797.0	48	10,244.3	111	4.50	214.7	23.6	24		2.9	391	14.7	162
9,898.0	33	27,817.2	37	1.15	(54.2)	(3.6)	283		69.6	43	15.6	137
4,641.0	109	14,357.8	81	(4.69)	(169.7)	—			42.0	164	13.7	197
7,157.0	52	8,941.8	135	2.86	(62.7)	—			68.8	47	10.5	276
9,045.0	37	62,629.5	8	3.72	19.2	16.0	70		59.1	71	23.1	34
8,240.0	43	9,279.3	129	14.98	573.3	15.3	76		81.9	22	12.4	231
2,354.5	214	4,317.9	258	2.16	(10.7)	15.4	74		1.5	397	14.6	166
1,530.7	298	3,686.3	285	0.69	—	(3.8)	284		18.4	317	(7.6)	376
4,328.0	122	N.A.		N.A.	—	—			—		—	
5,392.0	85	101,279.7	2	2.37	19.7	17.8	49		46.1	133	29.3	12
11,825.0	23	36,029.0	24	(1.24)	(157.0)	—			67.7	50	16.1	126
4,273.0	126	15,973.6	68	1.62	337.8	13.6	88		29.9	250	20.6	50

RANK 1995	COMPANY	REVENUES $ millions	PROFITS $ millions	Rank	ASSETS $millions	Rank
51	**COLUMBIA/HCA HEALTHCARE** Nashville	17,695.0	961.1*	66	19,892.0	119
52	**FLEMING** Oklahoma City	17,501.6	42.0	422	4,296.7	316
53	**AMERICAN EXPRESS** New York	16,942.0	1,564.0	38	107,405.0	22
54	**AMR** Fort Worth	16,910.0	167.0*	323	19,556.0	122
55	**ATLANTIC RICHFIELD** Los Angeles	16,739.0ᴱ	1,376.0	43	23,999.0	101
56	**MERCK** Whitehouse Station, N.J.	16,681.1	3,335.2	9	23,831.8	104
57	**TRAVELERS GROUP** New York	16,583.0	1,834.0	28	114,500.0	21
58	**SUPERVALU** Eden Prairie, Minn.⁹	16,563.8	43.3	421	4,305.1	314
59	**SAFEWAY** Oakland	16,397.5	326.3*	215	5,194.3	282
60	**NATIONSBANK CORP.** Charlotte, N.C.	16,298.0	1,950.0	24	187,298.0	9
61	**INTEL** Santa Clara, Calif.	16,202.0	3,566.0	7	17,504.0	132
62	**NEW YORK LIFE INSURANCE** New York	16,201.7	625.2	119	74,280.6	36
63	**MINNESOTA MINING & MFG.** St. Paul	16,105.0	976.0	64	14,183.0	158
64	**CATERPILLAR** Peoria, Ill.	16,072.0	1,136.0	55	16,830.0	136
65	**RJR NABISCO HOLDINGS** New York	16,008.0	611.0	121	31,518.0	81
66	**HOME DEPOT** Atlanta[1]	15,470.4	731.5	102	7,354.0	237
67	**EASTMAN KODAK** Rochester, N.Y.	15,269.0	1,252.0	50	14,477.0	154
68	**MCI COMMUNICATIONS** Washington, D.C.	15,265.0	548.0	137	19,301.0	124
69	**FEDERATED DEPARTMENT STORES** Cincinnati[1]	15,048.5	74.6	398	14,295.1	156
70	**UAL** Elk Grove Township, Ill.	14,943.0	349.0	206	11,641.0	185
71	**CHEMICAL BANKING CORP.** New York[10]	14,884.0	1,805.0	30	182,926.0	11
72	**COMPAQ COMPUTER** Houston	14,755.0	789.0	88	7,818.0	228
73	**ALLIEDSIGNAL** Morristown, N.J.	14,346.0	875.0	75	12,465.0	177
74	**MCDONNELL DOUGLAS** Berkeley, Mo.	14,332.0	(416.0)	482	10,466.0	198
75	**GEORGIA-PACIFIC** Atlanta	14,292.0	1,018.0	63	12,335.0	180

STOCKHOLDERS' EQUITY		MARKET VALUE 3/15/96		EARNINGS PER SHARE				TOTAL RETURN TO INVESTORS			
				1995 $	% change from 1994	1985–95 annual growth rate %	Rank	1995 %	Rank	1985–95 annual rate %	Rank
$ millions	Rank	$ millions	Rank								
7,129.0	53	23,982.8	42	2.90	61.1	—		39.4	185	—	
1,083.3	356	635.5	443	1.12	(25.8)	(9.0)	302	(6.9)	413	(2.8)	368
8,220.0	44	23,433.1	44	3.11	13.1	5.8	190	43.7	153	9.2	300
3,720.0	146	6,938.5	171	2.11	(53.2)	(9.8)	305	39.4	184	6.0	330
6,758.0	57	18,093.5	59	8.42	49.6	—		14.3	343	11.1	264
11,735.7	24	76,495.6	6	2.70	13.4	20.4	38	76.8	31	27.1	19
11,700.0	25	19,692.2	55	5.51	42.7	10.7	128	97.6	11	—	
1,193.2	342	2,135.8	362	0.61	(76.4)	(8.3)	300	33.6	225	6.0	331
795.4	386	5,862.6	196	1.34	36.7	—		61.6	62	—	
12,801.0	17	20,295.9	54	7.13	16.5	12.0	106	59.7	70	16.0	127
12,159.0	19	48,348.2	14	4.03	53.8	117.9	1	78.2	28	28.0	16
3,756.4	143	N.A.		N.A.	—	—		—		—	
6,884.0	55	26,587.6	40	2.32	(25.9)	4.9	198	28.3	258	15.2	149
3,388.0	161	13,969.1	82	5.72	21.7	18.9	44	8.8	364	12.5	226
10,329.0	32	9,105.0	133	1.53	22.4	—		16.1	332	—	
4,987.8	100	23,602.5	43	1.54	16.7	47.0	6	4.3	384	44.5	1
5,121.0	95	25,293.1	41	3.67	121.1	14.2	82	44.4	149	13.6	201
9,602.0	34	19,160.9	57	0.80	(39.4)	12.8	99	42.5	158	16.8	105
4,273.7	125	6,660.3	180	0.39	(72.3)	—		41.6	166	—	
(239.0)	486	2,494.8	340	20.01	—	—		104.3	9	13.9	189
11,912.0	21	16,971.3	64	6.73	45.0	(0.9)	266	70.5	41	9.3	296
4,614.0	111	10,613.3	108	2.88	(10.8)	33.4	18	21.5	300	36.1	7
3,592.0	153	15,905.8	69	3.09	15.3	—		42.3	161	12.5	227
3,041.0	174	10,180.2	113	(3.66)	(172.5)	—		96.3	12	17.5	92
3,519.0	155	6,484.6	185	11.29	224.4	21.3	31	(1.7)	407	13.1	209

RANK 1995	COMPANY	REVENUES $ millions	PROFITS $ millions	Rank	ASSETS $ millions	Rank
76	**J.P. MORGAN & CO.** New York	13,838.0	1,296.0	47	184,879.0	10
77	**DIGITAL EQUIPMENT** Maynard, Mass.[4]	13,813.1	121.8	361	9,947.2	201
78	**KIMBERLY-CLARK** Irving, Texas	13,788.6	33.2	427	11,439.2	187
79	**BRISTOL-MYERS SQUIBB** New York	13,767.0	1,812.0	29	13,929.0	161
80	**SPRINT** Westward, Kans.	13,599.5	395.3*	186	15,195.9	147
81	**PHILLIPS PETROLEUM** Bartlesville, Okla.	13,521.0[E]	469.0	157	11,978.0	183
82	**LEHMAN BROTHERS HOLDINGS** New York[11]	13,476.0	242.0	270	115,303.0	20
83	**BELL ATLANTIC** Philadelphia	13,429.5	1,858.3	27	24,156.8	100
84	**AMERITECH** Chicago	13,427.8	2,007.6	23	22,011.2	115
85	**NYNEX** New York	13,406.9	(1,849.9)*	492	26,220.0	91
86	**AMERICAN HOME PRODUCTS** Madison, N.J.	13,376.1	1,680.4	35	21,362.9	118
87	**MCKESSON** San Francisco[12]	13,325.5	404.5	180	3,479.2	336
88	**GOODYEAR TIRE & RUBBER** Akron	13,165.9	611.0	121	9,789.6	204
89	**TEXAS INSTRUMENTS** Dallas	13,128.0	1,088.0	60	9,215.0	214
90	**ROCKWELL INTERNATIONAL** Seal Beach, Calif.[13]	13,009.0	742.0	95	12,505.0	175
91	**AETNA LIFE & CASUALTY** Hartford	12,978.0	251.7	260	84,323.7	31
92	**ARCHER DANIELS MIDLAND** Decatur, Ill.[4]	12,671.9	795.9	85	9,756.9	205
93	**SBC COMMUNICATIONS** San Antonio	12,669.7	(930.0)*	490	22,002.5	116
94	**IBP** Dakota City, Neb.	12,667.6	257.9	254	2,027.6	422
95	**ALCOA** Pittsburgh	12,654.9	790.5	87	13,643.4	165
96	**ALBERTSON'S** Boise[1]	12,585.0	465.0	159	4,135.9	319
97	**ANHEUSER-BUSCH** St. Louis	12,325.5[¶,E]	642.3	117	10,590.9	195
98	**DELTA AIR LINES** Atlanta[4]	12,194.0	408.0**	178	12,143.0	182
99	**MAY DEPARTMENT STORES** St. Louis[1]	12,187.0[¶]	752.0	91	10,122.0	199
100	**ITT HARTFORD GROUP** Hartford[14]	12,150.0	559.0	133	93,855.0	25

STOCKHOLDERS' EQUITY		MARKET VALUE 3/15/96		EARNINGS PER SHARE				TOTAL RETURN TO INVESTORS			
					% change	1985–95 annual				1985–95 annual	
				1995	from	growth rate		1995		rate	
$ millions	Rank	$ millions	Rank	$	1994	%	Rank	%	Rank	%	Rank
10,451.0	31	15,003.5	74	6.42	6.6	5.1	194	49.4	117	14.0	187
3,528.3	154	9,858.7	121	0.59	—	(16.8)	310	92.9	13	(0.3)	362
3,650.4	151	21,270.6	50	0.12	(96.4)	(22.1)	315	73.7	36	21.4	41
5,822.0	75	42,635.9	20	3.58	(1.1)	6.4	185	55.0	88	14.3	176
4,642.6	108	12,396.6	92	1.12	(56.1)	28.7	21	47.6	125	17.5	91
3,188.0	166	10,220.7	112	1.79	(3.2)	2.2	230	7.9	372	15.6	139
3,698.0	149	2,482.4	342	1.76	—	—		45.5	141	—	
6,683.6	58	26,894.3	39	4.24	—	4.5	206	41.1	169	15.6	138
7,014.5	54	30,117.1	36	3.63	—	7.1	175	52.1	102	18.8	71
6,079.2	70	21,080.4	52	(4.34)	(329.6)	—		55.4	86	14.8	160
5,543.0	80	30,841.1	35	5.42	9.1	8.7	148	60.7	66	16.6	112
1,013.5	365	2,450.2	343	N.A.	—	—		59.0	72	—	
3,281.7	162	7,868.1	154	4.02	7.2	7.7	162	38.1	191	14.5	170
4,095.0	133	9,942.9	118	5.63	54.9	—		39.0	188	13.2	208
3,782.0	141	12,410.2	91	3.42	19.2	5.5	192	51.5	106	14.8	158
7,272.8	51	8,658.3	139	2.21	(46.6)	(4.0)	289	53.7	97	8.3	311
5,854.2	74	9,695.8	123	1.47	65.4	17.4	55	(7.7)	415	14.8	159
6,255.8	68	31,153.5	34	(1.53)	(155.8)	—		46.8	130	20.7	46
1,022.9	364	2,286.4	351	2.67	40.9	—		67.8	49	—	
4,444.7	115	10,754.3	107	4.43	111.0	—		24.0	290	13.8	193
1,952.5	249	9,576.9	125	1.84	16.5	19.1	42	15.2	341	25.2	26
4,433.9	116	17,167.1	63	2.49	(36.3)	5.8	189	35.2	216	14.8	161
1,827.0	258	4,332.9	255	6.32	—	(0.3)	261	46.2	131	8.3	309
4,585.0	112	12,541.9	88	2.73	(10.8)	7.3	168	28.3	260	14.0	188
4,702.0	106	5,518.3	214	N.A.	—	—		—		—	

RANK 1995	COMPANY	REVENUES $ millions	PROFITS $ millions	Rank	ASSETS $ millions	Rank
101	SYSCO Houston[4]	12,118.0	251.8	259	3,094.7	357
102	WALT DISNEY Burbank, Calif.[13]	12,112.1	1,380.1	42	14,605.8	153
103	WINN-DIXIE STORES Jacksonville[4]	11,787.8	232.2	278	2,482.8	391
104	WEYERHAEUSER Federal Way, Wash.	11,787.7	798.9	84	13,253.0	168
105	VIACOM New York	11,780.2	222.5	287	29,026.0	87
106	US WEST Englewood, Colo.	11,746.0	1,317.0	46	25,071.0	97
107	RAYTHEON Lexington, Mass.	11,716.0	792.5	86	9,740.1	206
108	NATIONWIDE INS. ENTERPRISE Columbus, Ohio	11,702.4	182.7	312	60,664.0	44
109	TEACHERS INSURANCE & ANNUITY New York	11,646.2	752.0	92	79,794.6	34
110	MELVILLE Rye, N.Y.	11,516.4¶	(657.1)	489	3,961.6	322
111	NORTHWESTERN MUTUAL LIFE INS. Milwaukee	11,483.3	458.5	160	54,875.5	47
112	CHASE MANHATTAN CORP. New York[15]	11,336.0	1,165.0	52	121,173.0	19
113	ASHLAND Russell, Ky.[13]	11,251.1[E]	23.9	433	6,991.6	241
114	APPLE COMPUTER Cupertino, Calif.[13]	11,062.0	424.0	172	6,231.0	252
115	WMX TECHNOLOGIES Oak Brook, Ill.	10,979.3	603.9	126	18,695.3	126
116	MORGAN STANLEY GROUP New York[16]	10,949.0	720.0	106	143,753.0	14
117	FIRST CHICAGO NBD CORP. Chicago	10,681.0	1,150.0	54	122,002.0	18
118	FIRST UNION CORP. Charlotte, N.C.	10,582.9	1,430.2	40	131,879.9	17
119	PRINCIPAL MUTUAL LIFE INSURANCE Des Moines	10,561.0	554.0	135	56,947.0	46
120	CSX Richmond	10,504.0	618.0	120	14,282.0	157
121	OCCIDENTAL PETROLEUM Los Angeles	10,423.0[E]	511.0	148	17,815.0	129
122	WALGREEN Deerfield, Ill.[8]	10,395.1	320.8	218	3,252.6	347
123	DEERE Moline, Ill.[5]	10,290.5	706.1	110	13,847.4	164
124	COASTAL Houston	10,223.4[E]	270.4	246	10,658.8	192
125	TRW Cleveland	10,172.4	446.2	166	5,890.0	262

STOCKHOLDERS' EQUITY		MARKET VALUE 3/15/96		EARNINGS PER SHARE				TOTAL RETURN TO INVESTORS			
					% change from	1985–95 annual growth rate				1985–95 annual rate	
				1995				1995			
$ millions	Rank	$ millions	Rank	$	1994	%	Rank	%	Rank	%	Rank
1,403.6	317	6,052.4	192	1.38	16.9	16.7	65	28.2	264	20.4	51
6,650.8	59	47,107.1	15	2.60	27.5	23.2	27	28.8	252	24.4	29
1,241.2	332	5,324.4	221	3.11	7.2	8.9	146	48.0	123	18.2	78
4,486.0	114	9,093.7	134	3.93	37.4	16.1	69	19.3	314	11.9	244
12,091.6	20	14,603.2	78	0.43	514.3	—		16.3	330	—	
7,948.0	46	14,418.6	80	N.A.	—	—		—		—	
4,292.0	124	12,512.5	89	3.25	44.1	10.9	123	50.9	109	16.6	113
5,109.9	96	N.A.		N.A.	—	—		—		—	
4,056.2	134	N.A.		N.A.	—	—		—		—	
1,547.8	295	3,625.5	286	(6.41)	(333.1)	—		4.2	385	5.4	338
2,786.0	187	N.A.		N.A.	—	—		—		—	
9,134.0	36	12,616.4	86	5.76	(1.9)	(1.0)	268	82.4	21	11.9	243
1,655.4	281	2,424.7	345	0.08	(97.3)	(27.7)	317	5.1	381	9.8	287
2,901.0	184	3,199.6	304	3.45	32.2	21.4	30	(17.3)	429	12.3	233
4,942.3	101	14,901.1	75	1.24	(23.5)	11.2	119	16.4	328	14.4	173
5,174.0	92	7,527.4	160	N.A.	—	—		38.3	190	—	
8,450.0	41	12,351.1	94	3.45	3.0	9.3	139	50.0	114	17.0	100
9,043.1	38	16,815.0	66	5.04	1.2	8.8	147	39.9	181	14.4	172
4,018.0	137	N.A.		N.A.	—	—		—		—	
4,242.0	128	9,498.6	127	2.94	(5.6)	—		34.1	223	15.3	144
4,630.0	110	8,120.4	144	1.31	—	(11.7)	308	16.3	329	3.5	346
1,792.6	261	7,968.8	147	1.30	14.0	13.0	96	39.1	186	17.4	94
3,085.4	171	11,025.0	105	2.71	(61.3)	19.7	41	64.0	60	17.1	98
2,678.8	193	4,121.8	264	2.40	17.1	4.1	209	45.7	138	9.3	298
2,172.0	226	5,770.3	203	6.69	32.5	—		20.7	307	9.5	294

RANK 1995	COMPANY	REVENUES $ millions	PROFITS $ millions	Rank	ASSETS $ millions	Rank
126	**PFIZER** New York	10,021.4	1,572.9	37	12,729.3	172
127	**EMERSON ELECTRIC** St. Louis[13]	10,012.9	907.7	72	9,399.0	213
128	**ABBOTT LABORATORIES** Abbott Park, Ill.	10,012.2	1,688.7	34	9,412.6	212
129	**TEXTRON** Providence	9,973.0	479.0	154	23,172.0	107
130	**ALCO STANDARD** Wayne, Pa.[13]	9,891.8	202.7	303	4,737.6	296
131	**MCDONALD'S** Oak Brook, Ill.	9,794.5	1,427.3	41	15,414.6	145
132	**BAXTER INTERNATIONAL** Deerfield, Ill.	9,730.0¶	649.0	116	9,437.0	211
133	**PACIFIC GAS & ELECTRIC** San Francisco	9,621.8	1,338.9	44	26,850.3	89
134	**WESTINGHOUSE ELECTRIC** Pittsburgh	9,605.0	15.0	441	16,752.0	137
135	**FEDERAL HOME LOAN MORTGAGE** McLean, Va.	9,519.0	1,091.0	59	137,181.0	15
136	**PUBLIX SUPER MARKETS** Lakeland, Fla.	9,470.7	242.1	269	2,559.0	388
137	**TOYS "R" US** Paramus, N.J.[1]	9,426.9	148.1	336	6,735.4	243
138	**FEDERAL EXPRESS** Memphis[6]	9,392.1	297.6	228	6,433.4	246
139	**LIBERTY MUTUAL INSURANCE GROUP** Boston	9,308.0	410.0	176	36,587.0	70
140	**FLUOR** Irvine, Calif.[5]	9,301.4	231.8	279	3,228.9	349
141	**ENRON** Houston	9,189.0	519.7	145	13,238.9	169
142	**SOUTHERN** Atlanta	9,180.0	1,103.0	58	30,554.0	82
143	**NORTHWEST AIRLINES** St. Paul	9,084.9	392.0**	189	8,412.3	219
144	**PACIFIC TELESIS GROUP** San Francisco	9,042.0	(2,312.0)*	494	15,841.0	142
145	**BANC ONE CORP.** Columbus, Ohio	8,970.9	1,277.9	48	90,454.0	27
146	**MONSANTO** St. Louis	8,962.0	739.0	98	10,611.0	194
147	**MARRIOTT INTERNATIONAL** Washington, D.C.	8,960.7	246.9	266	4,018.0	321
148	**UNION PACIFIC** Bethlehem, Pa.	8,942.0¶	946.0	68	19,446.0	123
149	**SALOMON** New York	8,933.0	457.0	161	188,000.0	8
150	**TENNECO** Greenwich, Conn.	8,899.0	735.0	100	13,451.0	166

STOCKHOLDERS' EQUITY		MARKET VALUE 3/15/96		EARNINGS PER SHARE				TOTAL RETURN TO INVESTORS			
				1995 $	% change from 1994	1985–95 annual growth rate %	Rank	1995 %	Rank	1985–95 annual rate %	Rank
$ millions	Rank	$ millions	Rank								
5,506.6	81	39,998.2	22	2.50	19.3	11.3	117	66.6	52	20.7	47
4,870.8	102	17,895.0	60	4.06	15.3	8.4	151	34.5	220	15.1	151
4,396.8	117	32,279.6	33	2.12	13.4	15.9	72	30.4	244	19.7	59
3,412.0	159	6,700.9	179	5.51	14.8	5.0	195	37.5	199	—	
1,868.5	254	5,715.2	207	1.67	203.6	11.2	120	47.4	126	19.8	58
7,861.3	47	35,684.3	26	1.97	17.3	13.5	90	55.3	87	18.7	73
3,704.0	148	12,352.9	93	2.35	10.3	10.7	126	53.0	98	14.4	175
9,001.2	39	9,988.4	117	2.99	35.3	1.2	238	25.0	284	11.4	257
1,508.0	303	7,890.0	152	(0.05)	(171.4)	—		35.5	214	0.2	360
5,863.0	73	14,732.1	77	5.69	12.0	17.3	58	68.2	48	—	
1,614.7	286	N.A.		1.07	3.9	(3.1)	280	—		—	
3,433.3	158	7,441.6	162	0.53	(71.4)	2.6	226	(29.0)	438	7.6	316
2,245.6	222	3,968.2	272	5.27	44.4	12.6	101	22.6	297	2.0	352
4,660.0	107	N.A.		N.A.	—	—		—		—	
1,430.8	312	5,862.2	197	2.78	19.8	—		54.8	92	16.7	110
3,165.2	168	8,775.4	137	2.07	15.0	—		27.9	267	17.8	83
8,772.0	40	15,404.9	72	1.66	9.2	0.4	252	30.2	248	16.8	106
(818.0)	489	4,656.7	239	4.17	42.8	—		223.8	2	—	
2,190.0	224	11,300.0	102	(5.43)	(298.9)	—		26.4	276	14.5	171
8,197.5	45	14,807.4	76	2.91	32.3	11.3	116	54.9	90	15.2	148
3,732.0	145	17,703.3	61	6.36	19.5	—		78.7	27	21.9	39
1,053.6	360	6,212.4	187	1.87	23.8	—		37.1	206	—	
6,364.0	66	14,442.1	79	4.60	72.9	8.2	153	50.0	113	12.7	219
4,143.0	130	3,856.5	277	3.64	—	(0.4)	262	(4.0)	412	(0.1)	361
3,148.0	169	9,557.7	126	4.16	89.1	18.7	45	20.7	306	7.7	315

RANK 1995	COMPANY	REVENUES $ millions	PROFITS $ millions	Rank	ASSETS $ millions	Rank
151	ITT INDUSTRIES White Plains, N.Y.[14]	8,884.0[17]	708.0*	109	5,879.0	263
152	BANKERS TRUST NEW YORK CORP. New York	8,600.0	215.0	295	104,000.0	23
153	BERGEN BRUNSWIG Orange, Calif.[13]	8,447.6	63.9	408	2,405.5	396
154	CPC INTERNATIONAL Englewood Cliffs, N.J.	8,431.5	512.1	147	7,501.6	234
155	EDISON INTERNATIONAL Rosemead, Calif.[10]	8,405.0	739.0	97	23,946.0	103
156	GENERAL MILLS Minneapolis[6]	8,393.6¶	367.4	197	3,358.2	342
157	SUN Philadelphia	8,370.0[E]	140.0	343	5,184.0	283
158	COLGATE-PALMOLIVE New York	8,358.2	172.0	317	7,642.3	232
159	WHIRLPOOL Benton Harbor, Mich.	8,347.0	209.0	301	7,800.0	229
160	JOHNSON CONTROLS Milwaukee[13]	8,330.3	195.8	307	4,320.9	312
161	WOOLWORTH New York[1]	8,224.0	(164.0)	473	3,506.0	335
162	H.J. HEINZ Pittsburgh[19]	8,086.8	591.0	128	8,247.2	221
163	TIME WARNER New York	8,067.0	(166.0)*	474	22,132.0	113
164	COLLEGE RETIREMENT EQUITIES FUND New York	7,950.6	N.A.		80,789.7	32
165	DEAN WITTER DISCOVER New York	7,934.4	856.4	76	38,208.0	66
166	FLEET FINANCIAL GROUP Boston[20]	7,919.4	610.0	123	84,432.2	30
167	LIMITED Columbus, Ohio[1]	7,881.4	961.5	65	5,266.6	281
168	CARDINAL HEALTH Dublin, Ohio[4]	7,806.1	85.0	387	1,841.8	437
169	DANA Toledo	7,794.5	288.1	234	5,694.1	268
170	NORWEST CORP. Minneapolis	7,582.3	956.0	67	72,134.4	38
171	ELI LILLY Indianapolis	7,535.4¶	2,290.9	20	14,412.5	155
172	UNOCAL El Segundo, Calif.	7,527.0[E]	260.3	252	9,891.0	202
173	AMERADA HESS New York	7,524.8	(394.4)	481	7,756.4	230
174	USAIR GROUP Arlington, Va.	7,474.3	119.3	364	6,955.0	242
175	STONE CONTAINER Chicago	7,351.2	255.5*	256	6,398.9	247

STOCKHOLDERS' EQUITY		MARKET VALUE 3/15/96		EARNINGS PER SHARE				TOTAL RETURN TO INVESTORS			
					% change	1985–95 annual growth rate				1985–95 annual rate	
				1995	from			1995			
$ millions	Rank	$ millions	Rank	$	1994	%	Rank	%	Rank	%	Rank
627.0	415	2,971.4	316	N.A.	—	—		—		—	
5,000.0	99	5,252.4	224	2.03	(71.7)	(9.3)	304	28.3	259	11.5	256
519.3	434	979.1	428	1.61	11.2	7.6	164	27.7	270	8.1	313
1,987.3	243	10,075.0	116	3.43	52.4	16.7	64	32.0	232	21.7	40
6,360.0	67	7,402.9	163	1.66	9.2	0.2	257	27.9	268	10.1	284
141.0	476	9,188.4	131	2.33	(21.0)	—		23.7	291	19.7	60
1,699.0	269	2,155.5	361	1.29	53.6	(12.2)	309	(0.1)	403	5.5	335
1,679.8	272	11,519.3	99	1.04	(72.8)	4.1	208	13.7	346	19.0	67
1,877.0	253	4,320.2	257	2.80	33.3	1.2	241	8.6	365	11.4	258
1,340.2	323	2,910.4	321	4.53	19.2	6.6	183	44.4	150	14.7	163
1,229.0	337	2,112.1	365	(1.23)	(441.7)	—		(12.5)	423	1.8	354
2,472.9	208	12,614.7	87	2.38	1.3	9.4	137	40.0	178	15.2	147
3,667.0	150	16,854.8	65	(0.57)	—	—		8.8	362	10.8	268
N.A.		N.A.		N.A.	—	—		—		—	
4,833.7	103	9,120.4	132	4.88	12.2	—		40.7	173	—	
6,364.8	65	10,428.7	109	1.57	(58.1)	(3.9)	287	31.8	236	11.8	246
3,201.0	164	6,929.6	172	2.68	114.4	21.0	34	(3.5)	411	6.4	326
548.2	429	2,900.9	323	2.01	—	20.5	36	18.4	319	25.2	25
1,164.6	348	3,378.0	292	2.84	22.9	6.8	181	28.5	254	12.3	232
5,312.1	87	12,268.6	95	2.76	12.7	17.9	48	45.5	140	24.7	28
5,432.6	84	33,574.4	30	4.03	81.1	15.9	73	77.1	30	18.5	75
2,930.0	181	7,877.6	153	0.91	—	(2.6)	278	10.0	358	11.2	262
2,660.4	196	4,952.7	232	(4.24)	(636.7)	—		17.6	322	8.3	308
(835.8)	491	1,108.9	421	0.55	—	(18.1)	312	211.8	3	(8.9)	377
1,005.3	368	1,425.1	398	2.63	—	42.1	11	(15.8)	424	3.3	348

RANK 1995	COMPANY	REVENUES $ millions	PROFITS $ millions	Rank	ASSETS $ millions	Rank
176	**TOSCO** Stamford, Conn.	**7,284.1**	**77.1**	394	**2,003.2**	424
177	**CAMPBELL SOUP** Camden, N.J.[21]	**7,278.0**	**698.0**	111	**6,315.0**	249
178	**FARMLAND INDUSTRIES** Kansas City[8,22]	**7,256.9**	**N.A.**		**2,185.9**	410
179	**REYNOLDS METALS** Richmond	**7,252.0**	**389.0**	190	**7,740.0**	231
180	**RALSTON PURINA** St. Louis[13]	**7,210.3**	**296.4**	229	**4,567.2**	302
181	**GENERAL RE** Stamford, Conn.	**7,210.2**	**824.9**	80	**35,946.0**	72
182	**AFLAC** Columbus, Ga.	**7,190.6**	**349.1**	205	**25,338.0**	95
183	**PHARMACIA & UPJOHN** Wilmington, Del.[23]	**7,094.6**	**738.7**	99	**11,460.6**	186
184	**LOWE'S** North Wilkesboro, N.C.[1]	**7,075.4**	**226.0**	283	**3,556.4**	332
185	**PPG INDUSTRIES** Pittsburgh	**7,057.7**	**767.6**	90	**6,194.3**	256
186	**WARNER-LAMBERT** Morris Plains, N.J.	**7,039.8**	**739.5**	96	**6,101.0**	257
187	**KELLOGG** Battle Creek, Mich.	**7,003.7**	**490.3**	152	**4,414.6**	306
188	**CHAMPION INTERNATIONAL** Stamford, Conn.	**6,972.0**	**771.8**	89	**9,543.3**	208
189	**UNICOM** Chicago	**6,910.0**	**639.5**	118	**23,247.0**	106
190	**TELE-COMMUNICATIONS** Englewood, Colo.	**6,851.0**	**(171.0)**	475	**25,130.0**	96
191	**EATON** Cleveland	**6,821.7**	**398.8**	185	**5,052.6**	286
192	**NORTHROP GRUMMAN** Los Angeles	**6,818.0**	**252.0**	258	**5,455.0**	274
193	**MASS. MUTUAL LIFE INS.** Springfield, Mass.[24]	**6,804.1**	**229.4**	281	**39,339.4**	65
194	**JAMES RIVER CORP. OF VA.** Richmond	**6,799.5**	**126.4**	354	**7,258.9**	238
195	**GILLETTE** Boston	**6,794.7**	**823.5**	81	**6,340.3**	248
196	**COCA-COLA ENTERPRISES** Atlanta	**6,773.0**	**82.0**	389	**9,064.0**	215
197	**HONEYWELL** Minneapolis	**6,731.3**	**333.6**	213	**5,060.2**	285
198	**LEVI STRAUSS ASSOCIATES** San Francisco[11]	**6,707.6**	**734.7**	101	**4,709.2**	297
199	**LINCOLN NATIONAL** Fort Wayne	**6,633.3**	**482.2**	153	**63,257.7**	42
200	**UNITED SERVICES AUTOMOBILE ASSN.** San Antonio	**6,610.9**	**730.3**	103	**22,244.1**	111

STOCKHOLDERS' EQUITY		MARKET VALUE 3/15/96		EARNINGS PER SHARE				TOTAL RETURN TO INVESTORS			
				1995 $	% change from 1994	1985–95 annual growth rate %	Rank	1995 %	Rank	1985–95 annual rate %	Rank
$ millions	Rank	$ millions	Rank								
627.1	414	1,705.0	388	2.06	(9.3)	3.6	216	32.8	227	8.7	305
2,468.0	209	15,571.1	71	2.80	11.6	13.9	85	39.9	179	19.9	55
687.3	404	N.A.		N.A.	—	—		—		—	
2,617.0	199	3,712.5	283	5.35	276.8	—		18.5	316	14.4	174
494.2	438	7,125.5	168	2.72	33.3	—		42.9	156	—	
6,587.0	61	11,678.7	98	9.92	24.5	21.2	32	27.2	271	13.9	191
2,134.1	229	4,342.0	253	2.33	23.1	20.5	37	37.6	196	19.9	57
6,388.9	64	20,967.5	53	1.43	(48.2)	2.7	224	31.0	240	9.1	302
1,656.7	278	5,668.5	211	1.41	(2.1)	13.1	94	(3.0)	410	19.6	63
2,569.2	201	9,236.6	130	3.80	56.4	12.8	98	26.7	274	17.2	97
2,246.0	221	13,927.8	83	5.48	6.0	—		30.0	249	18.5	76
1,590.9	289	16,687.5	67	2.24	(28.9)	7.0	178	35.8	213	18.9	69
3,646.7	152	4,584.3	243	8.01	2,007.9	17.6	54	15.6	336	7.3	323
5,770.0	77	6,713.2	178	2.98	79.5	(3.9)	288	44.5	147	9.6	292
4,550.0	113	12,892.9	85	(0.11)	(222.2)	—		13.6	348	23.0	35
1,975.3	246	4,626.9	241	5.13	16.6	8.2	154	11.3	352	12.9	215
1,459.0	309	3,004.6	315	5.11	609.7	1.0	243	56.8	82	8.3	310
2,073.0	238	N.A.		N.A.	—	—		—		—	
2,254.2	220	2,385.2	347	0.81	—	(9.2)	303	22.1	298	1.4	356
2,513.3	205	23,075.4	47	1.85	17.8	19.0	43	41.1	171	31.2	10
1,435.0	311	3,728.0	282	0.62	19.2	—		49.6	116	—	
2,040.1	242	6,793.3	174	2.62	21.9	5.5	193	58.2	76	13.6	200
2,115.3	232	N.A.		N.A.	—	—		—		—	
4,378.1	120	5,274.4	223	4.60	36.5	6.5	184	60.2	69	13.0	213
5,215.0	91	N.A.		N.A.	—	—		—		—	

RANK 1995	COMPANY	REVENUES $ millions	PROFITS $ millions	Rank	ASSETS $ millions	Rank
201	R.R. DONNELLEY & SONS Chicago	6,511.8	298.8	227	5,384.8	277
202	AMERICAN GENERAL Houston	6,495.0	545.0	138	61,153.0	43
203	UNISYS Blue Bell, Pa.	6,460.4	(624.6)	488	7,113.2	240
204	CONSOLIDATED EDISON OF NEW YORK New York	6,401.5ᴱ	723.9	105	13,949.9	160
205	PNC BANK CORP. Pittsburgh²⁵	6,389.5	408.1	177	73,404.0	37
206	QUAKER OATS Chicago⁴	6,365.2	802.0	83	4,826.9	291
207	ITT New York²⁶	6,346.0	147.0	338	8,692.0	217
208	NAVISTAR INTERNATIONAL Chicago⁵	6,342.0	164.0	329	5,566.0	269
209	ENTERGY New Orleans	6,274.4	520.0	144	22,265.9	110
210	BURLINGTON NORTHERN SANTA FE Fort Worth²⁷	6,183.0	92.0	381	18,269.0	127
211	GUARDIAN LIFE INS. CO. OF AMERICA New York	6,172.3	125.0	356	15,811.0	143
212	PUBLIC SERVICE ENTERPRISE GROUP Newark, N.J.	6,164.2	662.3	115	17,171.4	134
213	TRANSAMERICA San Francisco	6,101.1	470.5	156	47,944.5	55
214	DILLARD DEPARTMENT STORES Little Rock¹	6,097.1	167.2	322	4,778.5	294
215	CHUBB Warren, N.J.	6,089.2	696.6	112	22,996.5	108
216	KEYCORP Cleveland	6,054.0	825.0	79	66,339.1	40
217	ASSOCIATED INSURANCE Indianapolis	6,037.5	(98.0)	469	5,345.7	280
218	HALLIBURTON Dallas	5,951.3	168.3	320	3,646.6	329
219	MICROSOFT Redmond, Wash.⁴	5,937.0	1,453.0	39	7,210.0	239
220	ARROW ELECTRONICS Melville, N.Y.	5,919.4	202.5	304	2,701.0	379
221	AMERICAN BRANDS Old Greenwich, Conn.	5,904.9ᴱ	540.4	140	8,021.2	225
222	SUN MICROSYSTEMS Mountain View, Calif.⁴	5,901.9	335.8	212	3,544.6	333
223	UNION CARBIDE Danbury, Conn.	5,888.0	925.0	70	6,256.0	251
224	JOHN HANCOCK MUTUAL LIFE INS. Boston	5,845.5	340.8	209	54,505.1	48
225	TANDY Fort Worth	5,839.1	212.0	298	2,722.1	378

STOCKHOLDERS' EQUITY		MARKET VALUE 3/15/96		EARNINGS PER SHARE					TOTAL RETURN TO INVESTORS			
							1985–95 annual growth rate					1985–95 annual rate
				1995 $	% change from 1994		%	Rank	1995 %	Rank	%	Rank
$ millions	Rank	$ millions	Rank									
2,173.2	225	5,677.0	210	1.95	11.4		7.2	170	35.9	211	11.7	247
5,801.0	76	7,295.7	166	2.64	7.8		4.1	210	28.1	265	11.9	241
1,860.2	256	1,114.3	420	(4.35)	—		—		(36.2)	442	(10.9)	378
6,062.7	71	7,312.8	165	2.93	(1.7)		3.2	219	32.2	230	12.2	235
5,768.0	78	9,938.2	119	1.19	(53.7)		(4.8)	291	61.4	63	11.5	255
1,147.6	350	4,616.9	242	5.97	255.4		20.3	39	16.0	333	12.9	216
2,936.0	180	7,099.2	169	N.A.	—		—		—		—	
870.0	381	802.3	438	1.83	154.2		—		(29.8)	439	(18.8)	380
6,471.7	62	6,184.5	189	2.28	53.0		1.3	237	43.8	152	15.1	152
5,037.0	97	12,435.9	90	0.67	(84.7)		(22.0)	314	65.4	55	18.5	74
1,115.0	353	N.A.		N.A.	—		—		—		—	
5,444.9	83	6,331.6	186	2.71	(2.5)		0.3	254	24.5	287	12.0	238
4,299.9	123	5,204.7	226	6.58	20.7		11.8	110	51.5	107	13.7	195
2,478.3	207	4,140.3	263	1.48	(33.6)		6.8	180	7.0	375	8.9	303
5,262.7	89	8,263.2	142	7.85	31.9		23.4	26	28.0	266	16.4	117
5,152.5	93	8,671.2	138	3.45	0.0		8.7	150	51.6	105	15.0	154
1,314.9	325	N.A.		N.A.	—		—		—		—	
1,749.8	265	6,610.9	181	1.47	(5.8)		—		56.6	83	9.7	291
5,333.0	86	60,811.2	9	2.32	23.4		—		43.6	154	—	
1,195.9	341	2,353.0	348	4.21	75.4		—		19.9	311	10.8	269
3,863.1	140	7,940.2	148	2.89	(20.4)		4.6	203	24.6	286	15.6	134
2,122.6	230	8,409.2	140	3.61	78.7		—		157.0	4	—	
2,045.0	241	6,537.1	183	6.44	163.9		—		30.6	242	18.7	72
2,533.5	203	N.A.		N.A.	—		—		—		—	
1,601.3	288	2,969.4	317	3.12	7.2		4.0	212	(15.8)	425	1.9	353

215

RANK 1995	COMPANY	REVENUES $ millions	PROFITS $ millions	Rank	ASSETS $ millions	Rank
226	CONTINENTAL AIRLINES Houston	5,825.0	224.0	286	4,821.0	292
227	MERISEL El Segundo, Calif.[28]	5,801.8	(9.2)	449	1,468.8	458
228	W.R. GRACE Boca Raton, Fla.	5,784.2¶	(325.9)	479	6,297.6	250
229	BROWNING-FERRIS INDUSTRIES Houston[13]	5,779.4	384.6	193	7,460.4	235
230	INGERSOLL-RAND Woodcliff Lake, N.J.[29]	5,729.0	270.3	247	5,563.3	270
231	AMERICAN ELECTRIC POWER Columbus, Ohio	5,670.3	529.9	142	15,902.3	141
232	UNITED HEALTHCARE Minnetonka, Minn.	5,670.0	286.0*	235	6,200.0	254
233	TEXAS UTILITIES Dallas	5,638.7	(138.6)	472	21,535.9	117
234	DRESSER INDUSTRIES Dallas[5]	5,628.7	197.1	306	4,707.4	298
235	ARAMARK Philadelphia[13]	5,600.6	93.5	377	2,599.7	386
236	FPL GROUP Juno Beach, Fla.	5,592.5	553.3	136	12,459.2	178
237	CIRCUIT CITY STORES Richmond[9]	5,582.9	167.9	321	2,004.1	423
238	BLACK & DECKER Towson, Md.	5,566.2¶	224.0*	284	5,545.3	271
239	TYSON FOODS Springdale, Ark.[13]	5,511.2	219.2	291	4,444.3	304
240	LORAL New York[12]	5,484.4	288.4	233	4,810.3	293
241	MANPOWER Milwaukee	5,484.2	128.0	352	1,517.8	454
242	DUN & BRADSTREET Wilton, Conn.	5,415.1	320.8	217	5,515.8	272
243	BANK OF BOSTON CORP. Boston	5,410.6	541.0	139	47,397.0	56
244	ST. PAUL COS. St. Paul	5,409.6	521.2	143	19,656.5	121
245	WELLS FARGO & CO. San Francisco[30]	5,409.0	1,032.0	62	50,316.0	53
246	CORNING Corning, N.Y.	5,346.1	(50.8)	462	5,987.1	260
247	BANK OF NEW YORK CO. New York	5,327.0	914.0	71	53,685.0	51
248	PAINE WEBBER GROUP New York	5,320.1	80.8	391	45,671.3	58
249	OFFICE DEPOT Delray Beach, Fla.	5,313.2	132.4	351	2,531.2	389
250	DELL COMPUTER Austin, Texas[1]	5,296.0	272.0	245	2,148.0	413

STOCKHOLDERS' EQUITY		MARKET VALUE 3/15/96		EARNINGS PER SHARE				TOTAL RETURN TO INVESTORS			
				1995 $	% change from 1994	1985–95 annual growth rate %	Rank	1995 %	Rank	1985–95 annual rate %	Rank
$ millions	Rank	$ millions	Rank								
305.0	457	1,130.3	417	7.20	—	—		353.3	1	—	
231.3	466	80.3	460	N.A.	—	—		(45.3)	446	—	
1,231.8	336	7,808.2	156	(3.40)	(486.4)	—		56.1	84	14.1	186
2,741.8	190	6,725.6	176	1.93	29.5	9.2	141	5.7	378	8.6	306
1,795.5	260	4,492.4	247	2.55	27.5	12.9	97	13.8	345	15.7	133
4,339.8	121	7,544.5	159	2.85	5.2	2.7	225	32.0	233	14.1	185
3,200.0	165	11,106.6	104	1.57	(83.5)	38.6	14	45.0	145	38.3	4
5,731.8	79	8,836.0	136	(0.61)	(125.4)	—		40.4	175	12.5	228
1,656.8	277	5,198.2	227	1.08	(45.5)	—		33.0	226	14.2	181
252.3	464	N.A.		1.88	11.2	—		—		—	
4,392.5	118	7,980.2	146	3.16	8.6	0.2	258	38.1	193	12.2	234
877.5	380	2,944.2	319	1.72	26.5	21.6	29	24.6	285	24.9	27
1,423.2	314	3,230.3	300	2.42	76.6	—		50.3	111	7.4	321
1,467.7	307	3,261.2	297	1.51	—	17.8	50	23.4	293	19.3	65
1,687.5	271	8,090.0	145	3.38	24.3	14.2	81	89.1	14	16.7	108
455.0	442	2,698.3	332	1.65	47.3	—		0.5	402	—	
1,182.5	345	10,118.5	114	1.89	(48.9)	(0.3)	260	23.3	294	8.5	307
3,751.0	144	5,310.1	222	4.55	22.0	4.9	196	84.7	19	12.6	225
3,719.2	147	4,564.7	244	5.99	17.0	17.7	51	28.2	262	15.0	153
4,055.0	135	11,342.5	101	20.37	37.8	17.2	60	52.8	99	25.7	23
2,103.0	233	7,928.1	149	(0.23)	(117.4)	—		9.5	359	10.1	282
5,223.0	90	10,101.5	115	4.57	16.6	7.9	158	69.9	42	16.4	116
1,552.3	294	2,058.4	368	0.54	31.7	(1.1)	269	37.1	207	7.5	318
1,003.0	369	3,163.3	306	0.85	23.2	—		(16.6)	427	—	
973.0	371	3,106.6	309	2.67	58.0	—		68.9	46	—	

RANK 1995	COMPANY	REVENUES $ millions	PROFITS $ millions	Rank	ASSETS $ millions	Rank
251	CONSOLIDATED FREIGHTWAYS Palo Alto	5,281.1	57.4	414	2,750.1	375
252	GENUINE PARTS Atlanta	5,261.9	309.2	222	2,274.1	406
253	CUMMINS ENGINE Columbus, Ind.	5,245.0	224.0	284	3,056.0	359
254	AMP Harrisburg, Pa.	5,227.2	427.3	170	4,518.0	303
255	AMERICAN STANDARD Piscataway, N.J.	5,221.5	111.7*	368	3,519.6	334
256	MEAD Dayton	5,179.4	350.0	204	4,372.8	309
257	FOXMEYER HEALTH Carrollton, Texas[12]	5,177.1	41.6	423	1,777.0	440
258	RYDER SYSTEM Miami	5,167.4	147.7	337	5,893.8	261
259	SCHERING-PLOUGH Madison, N.J.	5,150.6	886.6	73	4,664.6	299
260	HOUSEHOLD INTERNATIONAL Prospect Heights, Ill.	5,144.4	453.2	163	29,218.8	86
261	CASE Racine, Wis.	5,105.0	337.0	211	5,469.0	273
262	BEST BUY Eden Prairie, Minn.[9]	5,079.6	57.7	412	1,507.1	455
263	VONS Arcadia, Calif.	5,070.7	68.1	405	2,186.5	409
264	VF Wyomissing, Pa.	5,062.3	157.3	332	3,447.1	338
265	BOISE CASCADE Boise	5,057.7	351.9	202	4,656.2	300
266	CROWN CORK & SEAL Philadelphia	5,053.8	74.9	396	5,051.7	287
267	EASTMAN CHEMICAL Kingsport, Tenn.	5,040.0	559.0	134	4,854.0	289
268	ECKERD Largo, Fla.[1]	4,997.1	93.4	378	N.A.	
269	PANENERGY Houston[31]	4,967.5	303.6	223	7,627.3	233
270	LYONDELL PETROCHEMICAL Houston	4,936.0	389.0	190	2,606.0	385
271	COOPER INDUSTRIES Houston	4,885.9	94.0	376	6,063.9	258
272	BETHLEHEM STEEL Bethlehem, Pa.	4,867.5	179.6	315	5,700.3	267
273	PACCAR Bellevue, Wash.	4,848.2	252.8	257	4,390.5	308
274	FIRST INTERSTATE BANCORP Los Angeles[32]	4,827.5	885.1	74	58,071.0	45
275	INLAND STEEL INDUSTRIES Chicago	4,781.5	146.8	339	3,558.3	331

STOCKHOLDERS' EQUITY		MARKET VALUE 3/15/96		EARNINGS PER SHARE				TOTAL RETURN TO INVESTORS			
				1995 $	% change from 1994	1985–95 annual growth rate %	Rank	1995 %	Rank	1985–95 annual rate %	Rank
$ millions	Rank	$ millions	Rank								
722.4	401	1,170.0	413	1.10	14.6	(6.1)	295	20.5	309	1.7	355
1,650.9	283	5,450.8	216	2.52	8.2	9.3	140	17.6	323	12.7	220
1,183.0	344	1,663.3	389	5.52	(9.7)	7.7	161	(16.2)	426	2.9	350
2,768.0	189	9,348.2	128	1.96	11.4	14.6	78	7.6	373	10.5	277
(390.1)	487	2,192.7	354	1.50	—	—		—		—	
2,160.2	227	2,823.7	324	6.33	(43.5)	15.4	75	9.5	360	11.5	253
304.2	458	267.9	451	1.52	38.2	—		85.0	18	0.5	357
1,240.0	333	2,168.4	358	1.86	(4.6)	0.7	245	15.4	338	4.8	341
1,662.9	276	21,126.7	51	2.40	(0.4)	17.7	52	51.8	104	25.5	24
2,895.9	185	6,536.9	184	4.31	22.4	9.0	145	64.4	59	17.6	88
1,520.0	301	3,795.0	279	4.60	—	—		114.3	5	—	
376.1	452	779.1	440	1.33	166.0	35.4	16	(48.0)	448	17.6	90
623.3	419	1,355.9	402	1.55	154.1	—		56.9	80	—	
1,771.5	264	3,594.2	288	2.41	(42.6)	0.7	246	11.5	351	10.4	278
1,694.4	270	2,027.6	371	5.93	—	11.1	121	31.2	239	5.5	336
1,461.2	308	6,091.8	190	0.83	(43.5)	1.4	236	10.6	355	15.4	143
1,528.0	299	5,743.3	206	6.78	67.4	—		27.1	273	—	
N.A.		1,634.1	390	2.73	85.7	—		49.4	118	—	
2,227.3	223	4,391.2	252	2.03	34.4	(3.3)	281	46.2	132	9.4	295
380.0	451	2,520.0	339	4.86	74.8	—		(8.3)	416	—	
1,716.4	266	4,018.3	268	0.84	—	(4.9)	292	12.0	350	9.1	301
1,238.3	335	1,548.0	396	1.24	254.3	—		(22.9)	432	(0.5)	363
1,251.2	330	1,913.9	376	6.50	23.6	14.0	84	1.5	398	12.1	236
4,154.0	129	12,138.0	96	11.02	26.5	4.9	197	108.5	7	15.6	135
748.6	393	1,255.9	409	2.69	48.6	—		(28.1)	437	2.2	351

RANK 1995	COMPANY	REVENUES $ millions	PROFITS $ millions	Rank	ASSETS $ millions	Rank
276	**MASCO** Taylor, Mich.	**4,779.0**	**(441.7)**	483	**3,778.6**	327
277	**NIKE** Beaverton, Ore.[6]	**4,760.8**	**399.7**	183	**3,142.7**	353
278	**LEAR SEATING** Southfield, Mich.	**4,714.4**	**91.6**	382	**3,061.3**	358
279	**HUMANA** Louisville	**4,702.0**	**190.0**	309	**2,878.0**	366
280	**DUKE POWER** Charlotte, N.C.	**4,676.7**	**714.5**	107	**13,358.5**	167
281	**BINDLEY WESTERN** Indianapolis	**4,672.5**	**16.4**	440	**844.1**	482
282	**AMERISOURCE HEALTH** Malvern, Pa.[33]	**4,668.9**	**10.2***	442	**838.7**	483
283	**NORFOLK SOUTHERN** Norfolk, Va.	**4,668.0**	**712.7**	108	**10,904.8**	189
284	**THRIFTY PAYLESS HOLDINGS** Wilsonville, Ore.[13]	**4,658.8**	**(34.7)***	459	**2,094.0**	418
285	**DOMINION RESOURCES** Richmond	**4,651.7**	**425.0**	171	**13,903.3**	162
286	**AON** Chicago	**4,610.7¶**	**403.0**	181	**19,736.0**	120
287	**FMC** Chicago	**4,566.6**	**215.6**	294	**4,301.1**	315
288	**SEAGATE TECHNOLOGY** Scotts Valley, Calif.[4,34]	**4,539.6**	**260.1**	253	**3,361.3**	341
289	**TYCO INTERNATIONAL** Exeter, N.H.[4]	**4,534.7**	**214.0**	297	**3,381.5**	340
290	**RITE AID** Camp Hill, Pa.[9]	**4,533.9**	**141.3**	341	**2,472.6**	393
291	**MELLON BANK CORP.** Pittsburgh	**4,514.0**	**691.0**	113	**40,129.0**	64
292	**AVON PRODUCTS** New York	**4,492.1**	**256.5**	255	**2,052.8**	420
293	**BERKSHIRE HATHAWAY** Omaha[35]	**4,487.7**	**725.2**	104	**29,928.8**	83
294	**TJX** Framingham, Mass.[1]	**4,447.5**	**26.3***	431	**2,745.6**	376
295	**REVCO D.S.** Twinsburg, Ohio[6]	**4,431.9**	**58.3**	411	**2,157.0**	411
296	**H.F. AHMANSON** Irwindale, Calif.	**4,397.5**	**216.2**	293	**50,529.6**	52
297	**GAP** San Francisco[1]	**4,395.3**	**354.0**	200	**2,343.1**	399
298	**HOUSTON INDUSTRIES** Houston	**4,388.4**	**1,124.0**	56	**11,819.6**	184
299	**AVNET** Great Neck, N.Y.[4]	**4,300.0**	**140.3**	342	**2,125.6**	415
300	**LTV** Cleveland	**4,283.2**	**184.8**	311	**5,380.1**	278

STOCKHOLDERS' EQUITY		MARKET VALUE 3/15/96		EARNINGS PER SHARE				TOTAL RETURN TO INVESTORS			
				1995 $	% change from 1994	1985–95 annual growth rate %	Rank	1995 %	Rank	1985–95 annual rate %	Rank
$ millions	Rank	$ millions	Rank								
1,655.4	280	4,777.6	236	(2.77)	(327.0)	—		42.4	159	6.9	325
1,964.7	248	11,405.5	100	5.44	37.4	44.7	8	88.8	15	36.8	6
580.0	424	1,827.7	382	1.74	—	—		46.8	129	—	
1,287.0	327	3,885.3	274	1.17	6.4	(2.2)	276	21.0	301	10.8	270
5,469.2	82	9,884.4	120	3.25	12.8	5.7	191	30.3	245	16.3	120
200.8	469	187.9	454	1.42	6.0	6.0	187	10.2	357	6.3	328
(135.7)	484	698.4	442	0.56	—	—		—		—	
4,829.0	104	11,014.1	106	5.44	11.0	7.5	166	34.8	219	15.3	145
161.4	475	N.A.		N.A.	—	—		—		—	
4,742.0	105	6,717.3	177	2.45	(12.8)	0.2	256	22.6	296	13.1	210
2,674.0	195	5,617.5	212	3.48	10.8	6.7	182	61.4	64	15.8	132
653.4	408	2,706.3	330	5.72	22.7	(2.7)	279	17.1	324	18.2	79
1,541.8	296	5,888.1	195	3.52	14.3	67.7	3	97.9	10	20.7	48
1,634.7	285	5,452.1	215	2.83	4.8	11.7	112	51.1	108	20.7	45
1,011.8	366	2,722.1	328	1.67	1,418.2	7.0	176	50.4	110	13.0	214
4,106.0	132	7,476.7	161	4.50	86.0	(1.0)	267	83.8	20	9.6	293
192.7	470	5,895.9	194	3.76	35.7	—		30.2	247	16.0	130
17,217.1	12	43,879.5	18	611.00	45.5	4.9	199	57.4	78	29.4	11
764.6	389	1,892.2	378	0.23	(77.7)	(17.7)	311	25.9	277	3.4	347
773.1	388	1,867.2	380	0.91	18.2	—		19.6	313	—	
3,056.9	173	2,702.1	331	1.40	(11.9)	(6.1)	294	70.9	40	9.9	286
1,640.5	284	7,912.2	151	2.46	11.8	28.4	22	39.6	182	28.4	13
4,123.6	131	5,746.0	205	4.54	179.4	7.5	165	46.1	134	14.6	167
1,239.4	334	2,067.9	367	3.32	58.9	9.1	143	22.6	295	4.7	342
1,375.2	322	1,380.0	401	1.71	32.6	—		(16.7)	428	—	

RANK 1995	COMPANY	REVENUES $ millions	PROFITS $ millions	Rank	ASSETS $ millions	Rank
301	UNION CAMP Wayne, N.J.	4,211.7	451.1	165	4,838.3	290
302	PECO ENERGY Philadelphia	4,186.2	609.7	124	14,960.6	149
303	PHELPS DODGE Phoenix	4,185.4	746.6	94	4,645.9	301
304	SUPERMARKETS GENL. HOLDINGS Woodbridge, N.J.[1]	4,182.1	75.5	395	N.A.	
305	DOLE FOOD Westlake Village, Calif.	4,152.8	23.3	434	2,442.2	394
306	ILLINOIS TOOL WORKS Glenview, Ill.	4,152.2	387.6	192	3,613.1	330
307	MUTUAL OF OMAHA INSURANCE Omaha	4,134.3	70.7	401	10,663.4	191
308	UNUM Portland, Me.	4,122.9	281.1	238	14,787.8	151
309	STOP & SHOP Quincy, Mass.[1]	4,116.1	67.9*	406	N.A.	
310	NORDSTROM Seattle[1]	4,113.5	165.1	325	2,733.0	377
311	JEFFERSON SMURFIT St. Louis	4,093.0	243.1	268	2,783.3	371
312	FIRST DATA Hackensack, N.J.[36]	4,081.2	(84.2)	466	12,217.8	181
313	CHIQUITA BRANDS INTERNATIONAL Cincinnati	4,026.6	9.2*	443	2,623.5	383
314	SERVICE MERCHANDISE Brentwood, Tenn.	4,018.5	50.3	416	1,940.6	431
315	GANNETT Arlington, Va.	4,006.7	477.3	155	6,503.8	244
316	WABAN Natick, Mass.[1]	3,978.4	73.0	400	1,332.5	467
317	NIAGARA MOHAWK POWER Syracuse, N.Y.	3,917.3	248.0	263	9,477.9	210
318	STUDENT LOAN MARKETING ASSN. Washington, D.C.	3,916.6	496.4	150	48,920.5	54
319	FHP INTERNATIONAL Fountain Valley, Calif.[4]	3,909.4	37.3	424	2,315.8	401
320	AIR PRODUCTS & CHEMICALS Allentown, Pa.[13]	3,891.0	368.2	196	5,816.0	264
321	CMS ENERGY Dearborn, Mich.	3,890.0	204.0	302	8,143.0	224
322	ROHM & HAAS Philadelphia	3,884.0	292.0	231	3,916.0	323
323	WILLAMETTE INDUSTRIES Portland, Ore.	3,873.6	514.8	146	3,413.6	339
324	PITNEY BOWES Stamford, Conn.	3,861.2	583.1	129	7,844.6	227
325	GENERAL PUBLIC UTILITIES Parsippany, N.J.	3,804.7	440.1	168	9,869.7	203

STOCKHOLDERS' EQUITY		MARKET VALUE 3/15/96		EARNINGS PER SHARE				TOTAL RETURN TO INVESTORS			
				1995 $	% change from 1994	1985–95 annual growth rate %	Rank	1995 %	Rank	1985–95 annual rate %	Rank
$ millions	Rank	$ millions	Rank								
2,121.7	231	3,607.4	287	6.45	298.1	17.4	56	4.3	383	9.7	289
5,032.7	98	5,859.8	198	2.64	50.0	0.3	253	30.4	243	14.2	180
2,677.7	194	4,643.8	240	10.65	179.5	42.7	10	3.7	388	23.5	32
N.A.		N.A.		N.A.	—	—		—		—	
508.4	437	2,557.9	337	0.39	(65.8)	—		76.6	32	12.7	223
1,924.2	251	7,861.4	155	3.29	34.3	26.5	23	36.5	210	22.6	37
1,326.8	324	N.A.		N.A.	—	—		—		—	
2,302.9	216	4,266.7	259	3.87	85.2	—		49.0	119	—	
N.A.		1,329.8	404	1.30	(7.1)	—		(9.3)	419	—	
1,423.0	315	4,007.9	269	2.02	(18.2)	12.0	107	(2.4)	408	14.1	183
(487.2)	488	1,262.5	408	2.19	—	—		(44.1)	445	—	
3,145.1	170	15,742.7	70	(0.39)	(115.2)	—		63.3	61	27.5	18
672.2	406	833.5	436	0.02	—	(28.2)	318	2.4	393	5.8	334
386.7	450	560.7	446	0.50	(9.1)	16.0	71	2.6	392	7.5	317
2,145.6	228	9,604.1	124	3.41	5.6	8.0	157	18.2	320	10.1	283
555.1	427	857.5	435	2.20	12.8	—		4.9	382	—	
2,954.0	179	974.2	429	1.44	44.0	(6.7)	297	(27.2)	435	(1.7)	365
1,081.2	358	5,252.2	225	7.20	46.6	11.4	115	109.5	6	7.7	314
1,140.1	351	1,315.5	405	0.29	(83.0)	—		10.7	354	—	
2,398.0	211	6,988.8	170	3.29	50.9	10.7	125	20.6	308	15.2	146
1,469.0	306	2,597.2	334	2.27	8.6	—		35.4	215	16.7	111
1,781.0	263	4,676.9	238	4.22	11.3	7.7	160	15.7	335	12.8	218
1,846.9	257	3,258.2	298	9.34	189.2	22.9	28	20.8	303	16.7	109
2,071.1	239	7,390.3	164	3.83	120.1	15.0	77	52.5	101	17.2	96
2,974.6	177	3,799.5	278	3.79	166.9	17.3	59	37.7	195	20.3	52

RANK 1995	COMPANY	REVENUES $ millions	PROFITS $ millions	Rank	ASSETS $ millions	Rank
326	**MARSH & MCLENNAN** New York	3,770.3	402.9	182	4,329.5	310
327	**OWENS-ILLINOIS** Toledo	3,763.2	169.1	319	5,439.2	275
328	**WACHOVIA CORP.** Winston-Salem, N.C.	3,755.4	602.5	127	44,981.3	59
329	**BEAR STEARNS** New York[4]	3,753.6	240.6	271	74,597.2	35
330	**NORTHEAST UTILITIES** Berlin, Conn.	3,749.0	282.4	236	10,545.0	196
331	**DOVER** New York	3,745.9	278.3	241	2,666.7	382
332	**SUNTRUST BANKS** Atlanta	3,740.3	565.5	132	46,471.5	57
333	**CENTRAL & SOUTH WEST** Dallas	3,735.0	420.8	173	13,869.0	163
334	**PACIFICARE HEALTH SYSTEMS** Cypress, Calif.[13]	3,731.0	108.1	370	1,385.4	464
335	**SAFECO** Seattle	3,722.7	399.0	184	18,767.8	125
336	**GIANT FOOD** Landover, Md.[9]	3,695.6	94.2	375	1,416.7	461
337	**HERSHEY FOODS** Hershey, Pa.	3,690.7	281.9	237	2,830.6	369
338	**CONRAIL** Philadelphia	3,686.0	264.0	248	8,424.0	218
339	**BARNETT BANKS** Jacksonville	3,680.0	533.3	141	41,553.5	63
340	**GATEWAY 2000** North Sioux City, S.Dak.	3,676.3	173.0	316	1,124.0	471
341	**NGC** Houston	3,665.9	92.7	379	1,902.5	433
342	**WORLDCOM** Jackson, Miss.[37]	3,640.0	234.5	277	N.A.	
343	**MATTEL** El Segundo, Calif.	3,638.8	357.8	198	2,695.5	380
344	**DTE ENERGY** Detroit[38]	3,635.5	405.9	179	11,130.6	188
345	**AMERICAN FINANCIAL GROUP** Cincinnati[39]	3,629.6	191.2	308	14,953.9	150
346	**OWENS-CORNING** Toledo	3,612.0	231.0	280	3,261.0	345
347	**DIAL** Phoenix	3,575.1	(16.6)	451	4,225.2	318
348	**PREMARK INTERNATIONAL** Deerfield, Ill.	3,573.6	237.6	274	1,961.3	428
349	**CIRCLE K** Phoenix[19]	3,565.6	18.7*	438	1,019.0	474
350	**GREAT WESTERN FINANCIAL CORP.** Chatsworth, Calif.	3,556.4	261.0	251	44,586.8	60

STOCKHOLDERS' EQUITY		MARKET VALUE 3/15/96		EARNINGS PER SHARE					TOTAL RETURN TO INVESTORS			
						% change from 1994	1985–95 annual growth rate		1995		1985–95 annual rate	
				1995 $			%	Rank	%	Rank	%	Rank
$ millions	Rank	$ millions	Rank									
1,665.5	274	6,822.1	173	5.53	9.5	9.5	136		16.2	331	11.9	240
531.9	431	1,882.9	379	1.40	118.8	—			31.8	234	—	
3,773.8	142	7,623.6	157	3.50	11.8	9.1	142		46.9	128	16.4	119
2,352.5	215	2,781.9	326	1.70	(38.2)	—			39.9	180	13.1	211
2,423.6	210	2,626.5	333	2.24	(2.6)	(1.9)	275		21.0	302	12.1	237
1,227.7	338	5,395.0	218	2.45	38.4	13.2	93		45.2	144	16.4	118
4,269.6	127	7,922.5	150	4.94	13.0	11.5	113		46.9	127	17.0	101
3,470.0	156	5,553.2	213	2.10	1.0	1.5	235		31.8	237	14.7	164
732.0	399	3,038.0	313	3.62	12.4	21.2	33		31.8	234	26.0	22
3,982.6	138	4,408.9	251	3.17	27.1	10.3	131		37.5	201	15.4	141
755.5	392	1,893.7	377	1.59	(0.6)	7.6	163		48.6	122	11.7	249
1,083.0	357	5,699.6	208	3.40	60.4	11.0	122		37.6	198	17.0	99
2,977.0	176	6,072.4	191	3.19	(18.2)	—			42.3	160	—	
3,272.2	163	5,774.9	201	5.30	10.6	7.2	172		59.0	73	10.8	267
555.5	426	2,033.7	370	2.19	79.5	—			13.3	349	—	
552.4	428	1,205.9	410	0.82	—	—			—		—	
N.A.		8,159.7	143	1.30	—	—			81.4	24	—	
1,275.2	328	7,557.2	158	1.26	40.6	12.5	102		54.4	93	22.6	38
3,436.3	157	4,843.4	235	2.80	4.9	1.9	233		41.7	165	17.0	102
1,440.1	310	1,789.1	383	3.87	—	10.9	124		20.8	304	6.0	329
(212.0)	485	2,184.1	355	4.64	28.5	0.5	249		40.8	172	23.5	33
548.2	430	2,775.0	327	(0.20)	(112.4)	—			43.0	155	12.4	229
1,008.8	367	3,206.0	303	3.72	9.7	—			15.4	339	—	
262.8	463	725.9	441	0.97	—	—			—		—	
2,822.5	186	3,091.8	310	1.72	1.8	(1.5)	271		65.3	57	11.3	260

225

RANK 1995	COMPANY	REVENUES $ millions	PROFITS $ millions	Rank	ASSETS $ millions	Rank
351	**GENERAL DYNAMICS** Falls Church, Va.	**3,544.0**¶	**321.0**	216	**3,164.0**	352
352	**PENN TRAFFIC** Syracuse, N.Y.[1]	**3,536.6**	**(79.6)**	465	**N.A.**	
353	**U.S. HEALTHCARE** Blue Bell, Pa.	**3,517.8**	**380.7**	194	**1,667.1**	445
354	**FOOD 4 LESS HOLDINGS** La Habra, Calif.[28]	**3,494.0**	**(216.0)**	476	**3,107.0**	355
355	**TIMES MIRROR** Los Angeles	**3,491.0**	**1,226.8**	51	**3,817.2**	326
356	**REEBOK INTERNATIONAL** Stoughton, Mass.	**3,481.5**	**164.8**	327	**1,656.2**	448
357	**HARRIS** Melbourne, Fla.[4]	**3,480.9**	**154.5**	334	**2,836.0**	368
358	**INTELLIGENT ELECTRONICS** Exton, Pa.[41,42]	**3,474.6**	**(19.0)**	453	**894.2**	478
359	**NUCOR** Charlotte, N.C.	**3,462.0**	**274.5**	244	**2,296.1**	404
360	**TEMPLE-INLAND** Diboll, Texas	**3,460.0**	**281.0**	239	**12,764.0**	171
361	**USF&G** Baltimore	**3,458.8**	**209.4**	300	**14,650.9**	152
362	**NATIONAL CITY CORP.** Cleveland	**3,449.9**	**465.1**	158	**36,199.0**	71
363	**TURNER BROADCASTING** Atlanta	**3,437.0**	**103.0**	373	**4,395.4**	307
364	**FRED MEYER** Portland, Ore.[1]	**3,428.7**	**30.3**	429	**1,671.6**	443
365	**PACIFICORP** Portland, Ore.	**3,400.9**	**505.0**	149	**14,015.2**	159
366	**PROVIDIAN** Louisville	**3,388.0**	**345.0**	208	**26,839.0**	90
367	**COMPUTER SCIENCES** El Segundo, Calif.[12]	**3,372.5**	**110.7**	369	**2,333.7**	400
368	**QUANTUM** Milpitas, Calif.[12]	**3,368.0**	**81.6**	390	**1,481.0**	457
369	**COMCAST** Philadelphia[43]	**3,362.9**	**(43.9)***	461	**9,580.3**	207
370	**MORTON INTERNATIONAL** Chicago[4]	**3,354.9**	**294.1**	230	**2,756.0**	374
371	**FIRST BANK SYSTEM** Minneapolis	**3,328.3**	**568.1**	131	**33,874.0**	76
372	**LITTON INDUSTRIES** Woodland Hills, Calif.[21]	**3,319.7**	**135.0**	347	**2,559.6**	387
373	**TENET HEALTHCARE** Santa Monica, Calif.[6,44]	**3,318.0**	**165.0**	326	**7,918.0**	226
374	**TRANS WORLD AIRLINES** St. Louis	**3,316.8**	**(227.5)****	477	**N.A.**	
375	**MAPCO** Tulsa	**3,310.0**	**74.7**	397	**2,293.3**	405

STOCKHOLDERS' EQUITY		MARKET VALUE 3/15/96		EARNINGS PER SHARE				TOTAL RETURN TO INVESTORS			
					% change from 1994	1985–95 annual growth rate				1985–95 annual rate	
				1995 $		%	Rank	1995 %	Rank	%	Rank
$ millions	Rank	$ millions	Rank								
1,567.0	293	3,731.6	281	5.10	36.0	1.2	240	40.1	177	13.4	206
N.A.		169.4	456	(7.32)	(720.3)	—		(60.5)	451	—	
964.1	372	7,177.6	167	2.42	0.0	32.0	20	15.8	334	28.3	14
(73.1)	482	N.A.		N.A.	—	—		—		—	
1,806.2	259	4,003.3	270	10.02	—	—		—		—	
895.3	379	2,182.3	356	2.07	(31.5)	16.4	67	(27.9)	436	21.2	42
1,248.8	331	2,578.0	336	3.95	40.1	7.0	177	31.7	238	10.6	273
183.3	471	215.9	453	N.A.	—	—		(21.6)	430	—	
1,382.1	320	5,390.5	219	3.14	20.8	16.4	66	3.7	386	21.1	43
1,975.0	247	2,545.4	338	5.01	113.2	13.6	89	(0.4)	404	11.8	245
1,716.1	267	1,741.5	386	1.63	(23.8)	—		25.4	282	(3.1)	370
2,921.0	183	4,912.2	233	3.03	12.2	7.2	173	33.9	224	16.9	104
437.7	443	5,828.3	199	0.36	350.0	36.0	15	58.5	75	23.6	30
571.2	425	794.4	439	1.07	328.0	—		(26.8)	434	—	
3,944.6	139	5,756.6	204	1.64	8.6	(0.5)	264	23.4	292	10.2	281
2,961.0	178	4,141.7	262	3.60	19.2	10.6	129	35.1	218	13.5	203
1,148.6	349	3,976.5	271	2.09	12.4	12.0	105	37.7	194	20.2	53
509.5	436	1,027.0	427	1.72	2,766.7	13.5	91	6.6	376	10.5	275
(827.7)	490	4,340.1	254	(0.18)	—	—		16.5	325	—	
1,663.5	275	5,680.2	209	1.96	289.4	—		27.8	269	—	
2,725.0	191	8,304.0	141	4.19	17.4	4.0	214	54.3	94	14.3	179
758.1	390	2,260.1	352	2.84	—	(2.4)	277	20.3	310	5.3	339
1,986.0	244	4,260.1	260	0.93	—	(0.6)	265	46.0	135	9.3	297
N.A.		N.A.		(1.05)	—	—		—		—	
642.3	409	1,629.8	391	2.41	(8.7)	3.0	221	8.5	367	13.3	207

RANK 1995	COMPANY	REVENUES $ millions	PROFITS $ millions	Rank	ASSETS $ millions	Rank
376	CONSOLIDATED NATURAL GAS Pittsburgh	3,307.3	21.3	437	5,418.3	276
377	WESTVACO New York[5]	3,302.7	280.8	240	4,252.7	317
378	TURNER CORP. New York	3,281.5	1.3	444	792.9	487
379	UNIVERSAL Richmond[4]	3,280.9	25.6	432	1,808.0	438
380	CENTEX Dallas[12]	3,277.5	92.2	380	2,049.7	421
381	W.W. GRAINGER Skokie, Ill.	3,276.9	186.7	310	1,662.7	447
382	SHERWIN-WILLIAMS Cleveland	3,273.8	200.7	305	2,141.1	414
383	HARCOURT GENERAL Chestnut Hill, Mass.[5]	3,241.9	165.9	324	2,884.3	365
384	ALLMERICA FINANCIAL Worcester, Mass.	3,238.9	133.9	348	17,757.7	130
385	BEVERLY ENTERPRISES Fort Smith, Ark.	3,228.6	(8.1)	448	2,506.5	390
386	PARKER HANNIFIN Cleveland[4]	3,214.4	218.2	292	2,302.2	402
387	CYPRUS AMAX MINERALS Englewood, Colo.	3,207.0	124.0	357	6,196.0	255
388	SERVICEMASTER Downers Grove, Ill.	3,202.5	105.9[45]	371	1,649.9	449
389	ASARCO New York	3,197.8	169.2	318	4,326.7	311
390	PACIFIC MUTUAL LIFE INS. Newport Beach, Calif.	3,160.5	85.1	386	22,221.6	112
391	SOUTHERN PACIFIC RAIL San Francisco	3,151.3	(3.4)	446	4,749.4	295
392	OLIN Norwalk, Conn.	3,149.5	139.9	344	2,272.0	407
393	PRAXAIR Danbury, Conn.[46]	3,146.0	262.0	250	4,134.0	320
394	AVERY DENNISON Pasadena	3,113.9	143.7	340	1,963.6	427
395	COMERICA Detroit	3,112.6	413.4	175	35,469.9	73
396	ALLTEL Little Rock	3,109.7	354.6	199	5,073.1	284
397	WELLPOINT HEALTH NETWKS. Woodland Hills, Calif.	3,107.1	180.0	314	2,679.3	381
398	TECH DATA Clearwater, Fla.	3,086.6	21.5	436	1,043.9	472
399	SMITH'S FOOD & DRUG CENTERS Salt Lake City	3,083.7¶	(40.5)	460	1,686.2	442
400	FOSTER WHEELER Clinton, N.J.	3,081.9	28.5	430	2,775.8	372

STOCKHOLDERS' EQUITY		MARKET VALUE 3/15/96		EARNINGS PER SHARE				TOTAL RETURN TO INVESTORS			
					% change	1985–95 annual growth rate				1985–95 annual rate	
				1995	from			1995			
$ millions	Rank	$ millions	Rank	$	1994	%	Rank	%	Rank	%	Rank
2,045.8	240	4,026.8	267	0.23	(88.3)	(21.5)	313	34.4	221	10.7	272
2,080.6	236	3,144.2	308	2.78	169.0	9.9	134	9.0	361	11.6	252
61.3	480	47.6	463	(0.11)	(131.4)	—		1.5	396	(7.3)	375
390.0	449	950.5	430	0.73	180.8	(5.9)	293	28.4	256	12.0	239
668.2	407	817.1	437	3.04	16.9	10.7	127	53.9	95	11.6	251
1,179.1	347	3,496.4	289	3.64	45.6	11.4	114	16.4	327	14.8	157
1,212.1	339	3,709.6	284	2.34	8.8	11.3	118	24.2	289	16.0	128
941.1	375	3,351.2	293	2.16	(2.7)	6.4	186	20.8	305	10.9	266
1,574.2	292	1,272.2	406	N.A.	—	—		—		—	
820.3	384	1,119.9	419	(0.16)	(121.1)	—		(26.1)	433	(4.9)	371
1,191.5	343	2,790.4	325	2.96	353.1	8.1	156	15.4	337	10.2	280
2,365.0	213	2,590.9	335	1.13	(33.1)	—		3.0	390	11.5	254
746.7	394	3,017.2	314	2.17	19.9	17.2	61	28.8	253	18.1	81
1,707.5	268	1,423.6	399	4.00	161.4	—		14.8	342	8.9	304
723.3	400	N.A.		N.A.	—	—		—		—	
1,060.9	359	3,864.4	276	(0.02)	(101.3)	—		32.4	229	—	
841.0	382	2,158.9	360	5.50	50.7	—		50.1	112	11.7	248
1,121.0	352	5,420.0	217	1.82	25.5	—		66.1	54	—	
815.8	385	2,925.3	320	2.70	37.1	8.3	152	45.0	146	13.6	202
2,607.7	200	4,537.0	245	3.54	7.9	12.6	100	71.7	39	19.9	56
1,935.6	250	5,774.9	202	1.86	30.1	9.8	135	1.3	399	21.0	44
1,670.2	273	3,345.7	295	1.81	(15.4)	—		10.3	356	—	
285.7	461	573.3	445	0.56	(38.5)	—		(11.8)	422	—	
416.7	446	608.0	444	(1.62)	(193.6)	—		3.3	389	—	
625.9	416	1,838.1	381	0.79	(56.8)	0.4	250	45.9	136	15.5	140

RANK 1995	COMPANY	REVENUES $ millions	PROFITS $ millions	Rank	ASSETS $ millions	Rank
401	**BRUNSWICK** Lake Forest, Ill.	3,076.5	127.2	353	2,360.5	398
402	**LONG ISLAND LIGHTING** Hicksville, N.Y.	3,075.1	303.3	224	12,484.4	176
403	**READER'S DIGEST ASSOCIATION** Pleasantville, N.Y.[4]	3,068.5	264.0	249	1,958.7	430
404	**STAPLES** Framingham, Mass.[1]	3,068.1	73.7	399	1,406.2	462
405	**APPLIED MATERIALS** Santa Clara, Calif.[5]	3,061.9	454.1	162	2,965.4	363
406	**YELLOW** Overland Park, Kans.	3,056.6	(30.1)	456	1,434.9	459
407	**FLORIDA PROGRESS** St. Petersburg	3,055.6	238.9	273	5,791.1	266
408	**GEICO** Washington, D.C.[47]	3,054.0	247.6	264	5,795.5	265
409	**HORMEL FOODS** Austin, Minn.[5]	3,046.2	120.4	363	1,223.9	468
410	**MAYTAG** Newton, Iowa	3,039.5	(20.5)*	454	2,125.1	416
411	**CINERGY** Cincinnati	3,031.4	347.2	207	8,220.1	223
412	**VALERO ENERGY** San Antonio	3,019.8	59.8	409	2,876.7	367
413	**PROGRESSIVE** Mayfield Village, Ohio	3,011.9	250.5	262	5,352.5	279
414	**CAROLINA POWER & LIGHT** Raleigh	3,006.6	372.6	195	8,227.2	222
415	**BOATMEN'S BANCSHARES** St. Louis	2,996.1	418.8	174	33,703.8	77
416	**OWENS & MINOR** Richmond	2,976.5	(11.3)	450	857.8	480
417	**ORACLE** Redwood City, Calif.[6]	2,966.9	441.5	167	2,424.5	395
418	**DIAMOND SHAMROCK** San Antonio	2,956.7	47.3	418	2,245.4	408
419	**MICRON TECHNOLOGY** Boise[8]	2,952.7	844.1	77	2,774.9	373
420	**WHITMAN** Rolling Meadows, Ill.	2,946.5	133.5	350	2,363.3	397
421	**MERCANTILE STORES** Fairfield, Ohio[1]	2,944.3	123.2	360	2,075.0	419
422	**MICROAGE** Tempe, Ariz.[5]	2,941.1	0.2	445	572.6	491
423	**MCGRAW-HILL** New York	2,935.3	227.1	282	3,104.4	356
424	**BALTIMORE GAS & ELECTRIC** Baltimore	2,934.8	338.0	210	8,316.7	220
425	**YORK INTERNATIONAL** York, Pa.	2,929.9	(96.1)	468	1,927.0	432

STOCKHOLDERS' EQUITY		MARKET VALUE 3/15/96		EARNINGS PER SHARE				TOTAL RETURN TO INVESTORS			
				1995	% change from 1994	1985–95 annual growth rate		1995		1985–95 annual rate	
$ millions	Rank	$ millions	Rank	$		%	Rank	%	Rank	%	Rank
1,043.1	361	2,206.8	353	1.32	(2.2)	1.2	239	30.3	246	11.0	265
2,516.9	204	2,039.0	369	2.10	(2.3)	(6.2)	296	19.2	315	12.6	224
640.8	410	4,976.6	231	2.35	11.4	—		8.1	369	—	
611.4	420	3,043.0	312	0.70	64.1	—		47.7	124	—	
1,783.5	262	6,207.5	188	2.56	96.9	40.1	12	86.4	17	40.7	3
422.7	445	316.2	450	(1.07)	—	—		(46.9)	447	(5.5)	372
2,078.1	237	3,172.9	305	2.50	9.6	0.6	248	25.6	279	12.8	217
1,868.4	255	N.A.		3.66	23.2	7.1	174	45.2	143	16.5	115
732.0	398	1,956.3	375	1.57	1.9	12.1	104	1.8	394	16.5	114
637.4	411	2,160.8	359	(0.19)	(113.7)	—		39.0	189	4.3	345
2,548.8	202	4,480.5	248	2.22	70.8	60.2	4	39.1	187	16.0	129
1,033.8	363	1,082.7	423	1.10	175.0	0.4	251	48.8	121	7.3	322
1,475.8	305	3,215.9	302	3.26	(9.2)	20.1	40	40.4	176	22.7	36
2,718.5	192	5,118.1	229	2.48	22.2	2.5	227	37.4	202	16.2	123
2,928.1	182	4,997.0	230	3.25	(4.4)	4.0	213	57.3	79	13.9	190
235.3	465	350.6	449	(0.53)	(453.3)	—		(9.3)	418	15.4	142
1,211.4	340	21,275.5	49	1.00	56.3	—		44.1	151	—	
624.7	418	903.6	434	1.48	(39.6)	—		1.6	395	—	
1,896.2	252	6,753.5	175	3.95	106.3	113.6	2	80.3	25	37.2	5
627.8	413	2,418.5	346	1.26	29.9	(1.9)	274	37.3	203	14.5	169
1,485.0	304	2,127.7	364	3.35	19.2	(7.0)	298	19.8	312	(2.9)	369
168.4	474	134.6	459	0.02	(98.4)	—		(30.9)	440	—	
1,035.1	362	4,433.5	250	2.28	11.2	4.6	204	34.3	222	9.7	290
3,081.9	172	3,909.5	273	2.02	4.7	0.8	244	37.2	205	12.4	230
624.8	417	2,017.4	372	(2.36)	(198.3)	—		28.2	263	—	

RANK 1995	COMPANY	REVENUES $ millions	PROFITS $ millions	Rank	ASSETS $ millions	Rank
426	**KERR-MCGEE** Oklahoma City	2,928.0	(31.2)	457	3,232.0	348
427	**ALUMAX** Norcross, Ga.	2,926.1	237.4	275	3,135.0	354
428	**PITTSTON** Stamford, Conn.	2,926.1	98.0	374	1,807.0	439
429	**U.S. INDUSTRIES** Iselin, N.J.[13]	2,908.4¶	(89.3)	467	1,900.0	434
430	**RELIANCE GROUP HOLDINGS** New York	2,906.0	88.1	385	9,988.2	200
431	**PETER KIEWIT SONS'** Omaha[28]	2,902.0	244.0	267	3,463.0	337
432	**ESTÉE LAUDER** New York[4]	2,899.1	121.2	362	1,721.7	441
433	**U.S. BANCORP** Portland, Ore.	2,897.3	329.0	214	31,794.3	80
434	**AMERICAN PRESIDENT** Oakland	2,896.0	30.3	428	1,878.8	436
435	**FLAGSTAR** Spartanburg, S.C.	2,893.8¶	(55.2)	464	1,500.9	456
436	**AUTOMATIC DATA PROCESSING** Roseland, N.J.[4]	2,893.7	394.8	187	3,201.1	350
437	**NASH FINCH** Minneapolis	2,888.8	17.4	439	514.3	492
438	**SOUTHWEST AIRLINES** Dallas	2,872.8	182.6	313	3,256.1	346
439	**SHAW INDUSTRIES** Dalton, Ga.	2,869.8	52.3	415	1,665.2	446
440	**BRUNO'S** Birmingham, Ala.[4]	2,869.6	33.3	426	895.6	477
441	**CORESTATES FINANCIAL CORP.** Philadelphia	2,868.0	452.2	164	29,620.6	85
442	**TRIBUNE** Chicago	2,863.6	278.2	242	3,288.3	343
443	**NORAM ENERGY** Houston	2,862.1ᴱ	65.5	407	3,666.0	328
444	**CONSECO** Carmel, Ind.	2,860.7	220.4	290	17,297.5	133
445	**REPUBLIC NEW YORK CORP.** New York	2,859.6	288.6	232	43,881.6	61
446	**HASBRO** Pawtucket, R.I.	2,858.2	155.6	333	2,616.4	384
447	**WILLIAMS** Tulsa[48]	2,855.7	1,318.2	45	10,494.8	197
448	**FLEETWOOD ENTERPRISES** Riverside, Calif.	2,855.7	84.6	388	1,345.1	465
449	**LOUISIANA-PACIFIC** Portland, Ore.	2,843.2	(51.7)	463	2,805.4	370
450	**ENGELHARD** Iselin, N.J.	2,840.1	137.5	346	1,645.6	450

STOCKHOLDERS' EQUITY		MARKET VALUE 3/15/96		EARNINGS PER SHARE				TOTAL RETURN TO INVESTORS			
				1995 $	% change from 1994	1985–95 annual growth rate %	Rank	1995 %	Rank	1985–95 annual rate %	Rank
$ millions	Rank	$ millions	Rank								
1,416.0	316	3,244.4	299	(0.60)	(134.5)	—		41.4	167	9.9	285
1,399.3	318	1,561.7	395	5.05	501.2	—		7.9	371	—	
522.0	433	N.A.		N.A.	—	—		—		—	
412.1	447	1,107.0	422	N.A.	—	—		—		—	
678.3	405	920.6	432	0.73	92.1	—		75.3	34	—	
1,607.0	287	N.A.		N.A.	—	—		—		—	
335.1	454	4,090.8	266	N.A.	—	—		—		—	
2,617.0	198	4,865.1	234	2.09	49.3	7.4	167	66.8	51	17.7	87
469.2	441	548.6	447	0.95	(60.1)	0.2	255	(7.5)	414	11.3	259
(1,131.0)	492	143.2	458	(1.64)	(122.9)	—		(55.4)	450	—	
2,096.6	235	11,691.3	97	2.77	18.4	16.2	68	28.2	261	18.8	70
215.3	468	176.7	455	1.60	12.7	3.1	220	15.3	340	5.1	340
1,427.3	313	4,479.9	249	1.23	0.8	13.6	87	37.6	197	14.9	156
710.2	402	1,579.8	393	0.38	(57.3)	7.2	171	1.1	400	26.9	20
429.8	444	N.A.		0.43	(10.4)	2.2	229	42.0	163	4.5	344
2,379.4	212	5,788.0	200	3.22	86.1	0.6	247	52.0	103	13.7	198
1,379.9	321	4,206.7	261	4.00	20.5	10.1	133	13.7	347	10.4	279
637.3	412	1,120.8	418	0.47	42.4	(10.2)	306	71.9	38	(1.9)	367
1,111.7	354	1,401.4	400	9.39	87.8	46.8	7	45.8	137	42.6	2
3,007.8	175	3,218.0	301	4.66	(19.5)	5.8	188	41.1	170	13.5	205
1,525.6	300	3,090.5	311	1.76	(10.2)	4.0	211	7.5	374	11.2	263
3,187.1	167	5,136.4	228	12.77	450.4	39.4	13	79.9	26	16.2	124
608.1	421	1,145.7	415	1.82	27.3	4.7	201	41.2	168	10.6	274
1,656.0	279	2,710.7	329	(0.48)	(115.2)	—		(9.1)	417	16.3	122
737.7	395	2,953.0	318	0.96	17.1	11.9	109	49.7	115	19.0	66

RANK 1995	COMPANY	REVENUES $ millions	PROFITS $ millions	Rank	ASSETS $ millions	Rank
451	**COMPUSA** Dallas[4]	**2,813.1**	**23.0**	435	**610.5**	490
452	**UTILICORP UNITED** Kansas City	**2,798.5**	**79.8**	393	**3,885.9**	324
453	**AID ASSOCIATION FOR LUTHERANS** Appleton, Wis.	**2,795.8**	**114.5**	367	**15,442.5**	144
454	**GRAYBAR ELECTRIC** St. Louis	**2,774.4**	**36.7**	425	**823.3**	484
455	**CALDOR** Norwalk, Conn.[42]	**2,764.5**	**(4.6)***	447	**1,417.9**	460
456	**KNIGHT-RIDDER** Miami	**2,751.8**	**160.1**	331	**3,005.7**	361
457	**SCHULLER** Denver[49]	**2,733.8¶**	**116.0**	365	**2,474.1**	392
458	**HEALTH SYSTEMS INTL.** Woodland Hills, Calif.	**2,732.1**	**89.6**	384	**1,213.6**	469
459	**ECHLIN** Branford, Conn.[8]	**2,717.9**	**154.4**	335	**1,961.0**	429
460	**ULTRAMAR** Greenwich, Conn.	**2,714.4**	**69.6**	403	**1,971.3**	425
461	**BECTON DICKINSON** Franklin Lakes, N.J.[13]	**2,712.5**	**251.7**	261	**2,999.5**	362
462	**SONOCO PRODUCTS** Hartsville, S.C.	**2,706.2**	**164.5**	328	**2,115.4**	417
463	**KELLY SERVICES** Troy, Mich.	**2,689.8**	**69.5**	404	**718.7**	489
464	**PAYLESS CASHWAYS** Kansas City[11]	**2,685.7**	**(128.5)**	471	**1,344.4**	466
465	**SCI SYSTEMS** Huntsville, Ala.[4]	**2,673.8**	**45.2**	420	**981.3**	475
466	**PP&L RESOURCES** Allentown, Pa.[50]	**2,650.0**[E]	**350.4**	203	**9,491.7**	209
467	**ALLEGHENY POWER SYSTEM** New York	**2,647.8**	**239.7**	272	**6,447.3**	245
468	**LONGS DRUG STORES** Walnut Creek, Calif.[1]	**2,644.4**	**46.2**	419	**853.6**	481
469	**BAKER HUGHES** Houston[13]	**2,637.5**	**105.4**	372	**3,166.6**	351
470	**COLUMBIA GAS SYSTEM** Wilmington, Del.	**2,635.2**	**(360.7)****	480	**6,057.0**	259
471	**ARMSTRONG WORLD INDUSTRIES** Lancaster, Pa.	**2,635.1**	**123.3**	359	**2,149.8**	412
472	**DEAN FOODS** Franklin Park, Ill.[6]	**2,630.2**	**80.1**	392	**1,202.4**	470
473	**STANLEY WORKS** New Britain, Conn.	**2,624.3**	**59.1**	410	**1,670.0**	444
474	**COMPUTER ASSOCIATES INTL.** Islandia, N.Y.[12]	**2,623.0**	**431.9**	169	**3,269.4**	344
475	**BALL** Muncie, Ind.	**2,591.7**	**(18.6)**	452	**1,612.5**	451

STOCKHOLDERS' EQUITY		MARKET VALUE 3/15/96		EARNINGS PER SHARE				TOTAL RETURN TO INVESTORS			
				1995 $	% change from 1994	1985–95 annual growth rate %	Rank	1995 %	Rank	1985–95 annual rate %	Rank
$ millions	Rank	$ millions	Rank								
171.0	473	1,034.1	426	1.21	—	—		107.5	8	—	
946.3	373	1,333.0	403	1.72	(17.3)	(0.4)	263	17.8	321	15.0	155
942.7	374	N.A.		N.A.	—	—		—		—	
174.2	472	N.A.		8.11	101.2	—		—		—	
294.3	459	72.1	461	N.A.	—	—		(85.4)	453	—	
1,111.0	355	3,347.5	294	3.19	1.3	3.8	215	27.1	272	7.2	324
1,180.5	346	1,568.3	394	0.73	630.0	—		44.4	148	10.7	271
285.9	460	1,786.8	384	1.83	3.4	—		5.8	377	—	
909.3	378	2,179.2	357	2.60	23.8	9.0	144	24.4	288	13.8	194
703.4	403	1,265.2	407	1.73	10.9	—		5.4	379	—	
1,398.4	319	5,328.4	220	3.59	17.7	13.1	95	58.6	74	19.0	68
918.7	376	2,493.8	341	1.72	29.0	12.3	103	28.9	251	16.3	121
476.1	439	1,140.4	416	1.83	13.7	7.9	159	3.7	387	5.4	337
308.2	455	159.7	457	(3.36)	(439.4)	—		(54.1)	449	—	
349.8	453	1,047.4	424	1.63	114.5	9.4	138	72.2	37	11.9	242
2,768.5	188	3,757.8	280	2.05	45.4	4.3	207	42.8	157	13.7	196
2,300.0	217	3,424.9	290	2.00	(10.3)	1.1	242	40.6	174	13.6	199
522.8	432	929.5	431	2.29	(2.6)	2.8	223	55.6	85	7.5	319
1,513.6	302	4,116.2	265	0.57	159.1	(7.6)	299	36.5	209	5.8	333
1,539.9	297	2,134.4	363	(7.15)	(250.2)	—		86.7	16	4.5	343
775.0	387	2,325.5	349	2.90	(44.4)	3.3	217	65.3	56	14.2	182
584.5	422	1,038.5	425	2.01	11.0	6.9	179	(2.8)	409	6.0	332
734.6	397	2,438.3	344	1.33	(52.5)	(3.5)	282	48.9	120	12.7	221
1,578.1	291	17,570.2	62	2.57	9.8	32.7	19	76.5	33	35.1	8
582.7	423	914.0	433	(0.72)	(130.6)	—		(10.2)	420	3.2	349

RANK 1995	COMPANY	REVENUES $ millions	PROFITS $ millions	Rank	ASSETS $millions	Rank
476	NORTHERN STATES POWER Minneapolis	2,568.6	275.8	243	6,228.6	253
477	HANNAFORD BROS. Scarborough, Me.	2,568.1	70.2	402	961.8	476
478	TELEDYNE Los Angeles	2,567.8	162.0	330	1,606.2	452
479	MBNA Newark, Del.	2,565.4	353.1	201	13,228.9	170
480	MAXXAM Houston	2,565.2	57.5	413	3,832.3	325
481	PROVIDENT COS. Chattanooga[51]	2,555.3	115.6	366	16,301.3	139
482	CALIBER SYSTEM Akron[52]	2,547.6[53]	(27.2)	455	1,389.3	463
483	OFFICEMAX Shaker Heights, Ohio[1]	2,542.5	125.8	355	1,587.9	453
484	MORRISON KNUDSEN Boise[28]	2,530.9	(484.0)	485	808.3	486
485	OLSTEN Melville, N.Y.	2,518.9	90.5	383	891.9	479
486	CENTERIOR ENERGY Independence, Ohio	2,515.5	220.5	289	10,643.1	193
487	SPARTAN STORES Grand Rapids[12,22]	2,512.4	N.A.		386.1	494
488	NEWELL Freeport, Ill.	2,498.4	222.5	288	2,931.2	364
489	PENNZOIL Houston	2,490.0	(305.1)	478	4,307.8	313
490	ROUNDY'S Pewaukee, Wis.[22]	2,488.2	N.A.		407.3	493
491	GOLDEN WEST FINANCIAL CORP. Oakland	2,470.0	234.5	276	35,118.2	74
492	AST RESEARCH Irvine, Calif.	2,467.8	(99.3)	470	1,021.5	473
493	OHIO EDISON Akron	2,465.8	317.2	219	8,823.9	216
494	FOUNDATION HEALTH Rancho Cordova, Calif.[4]	2,459.9	49.4	417	1,964.2	426
495	STATE STREET BOSTON CORP. Boston	2,445.7	247.1	265	25,785.2	93
496	USG Chicago	2,444.0	(32.0)	458	1,890.0	435
497	COTTER Chicago[22]	2,437.0	N.A.		819.6	485
498	ACE HARDWARE Oak Brook, Ill.[22]	2,436.0	N.A.		759.1	488
499	GENERAL INSTRUMENT Chicago	2,432.0	123.8	358	2,300.8	403
500	ADVANCED MICRO DEVICES Sunnyvale, Calif.	2,429.7	300.5	226	3,031.3	360
	TOTALS	4,691,173.5	244,007.5		10,491,239.5	

STOCKHOLDERS' EQUITY		MARKET VALUE 3/15/96		EARNINGS PER SHARE				TOTAL RETURN TO INVESTORS			
				1995 $	% change from 1994	1985–95 annual growth rate %	Rank	1995 %	Rank	1985–95 annual rate %	Rank
$ millions	Rank	$ millions	Rank								
2,267.9	219	3,268.8	296	3.91	13.0	2.8	222	18.4	318	13.1	212
518.7	435	1,151.6	414	1.67	11.3	14.4	80	(1.4)	406	15.6	136
395.6	448	1,618.4	392	2.88	—	(11.1)	307	32.8	228	0.4	358
1,265.1	329	6,543.3	182	1.54	30.5	—		60.7	65	—	
(83.8)	483	381.0	448	6.08	—	17.6	53	14.2	344	9.8	288
1,652.3	282	1,497.9	397	2.27	(16.2)	(3.8)	285	60.2	68	8.2	312
736.3	396	1,713.4	387	(0.69)	(238.0)	—		(11.3)	421	6.4	327
990.9	370	2,006.1	373	1.56	—	—		26.7	275	—	
99.8	479	49.6	462	N.A.	—	—		(64.2)	452	(12.5)	379
472.0	440	1,994.4	374	1.39	24.9	20.6	35	25.6	280	19.6	61
1,983.6	245	1,184.3	411	1.49	8.0	—		8.5	368	—	
125.8	477	N.A.		N.A.	—	—		—		—	
1,300.1	326	4,320.6	256	1.41	13.7	18.4	47	25.5	281	27.6	17
836.2	383	1,750.9	385	(6.60)	—	—		1.0	401	0.3	359
100.0	478	N.A.		N.A.	—	—		—		—	
2,278.4	218	2,902.7	322	4.00	7.8	4.5	205	57.9	77	14.3	178
263.2	462	262.5	452	(3.07)	(419.8)	—		(41.9)	443	(5.8)	374
2,619.7	197	3,394.7	291	2.05	4.1	(1.8)	273	35.9	212	12.7	222
756.9	391	2,094.0	366	0.90	(68.3)	—		39.5	183	—	
1,587.5	290	3,879.4	275	2.98	10.4	14.1	83	60.2	67	17.8	85
(37.0)	481	1,180.1	412	(0.71)	—	—		53.8	96	—	
306.5	456	N.A.		N.A.	—	—		—		—	
217.2	467	N.A.		N.A.	—	—		—		—	
915.3	377	3,161.5	307	1.00	(50.0)	—		(22.1)	431	—	
2,100.1	234	2,322.9	350	2.85	(5.6)	2.1	232	(33.6)	441	(5.5)	373
1,669,117.2		4,507,985.6									

N.A. Not available.

ᴱ Excise taxes have been deducted.

* Reflects an extraordinary charge of at least 10%.

** Reflects an extraordinary credit of at least 10%.

¶ Includes revenues of discontinued operations of at least 10%.

1–9

[1] Figures are for fiscal year ended Jan. 31, 1996.

[2] Figures do not include spinoff of Allstate (1995 rank: 31), June 30, 1995.

[3] Figure does not include discontinued operations of Allstate (1995 rank: 31).

[4] Figures are for fiscal year ended June 30, 1995.

[5] Figures are for fiscal year ended Oct. 31, 1995.

[6] Figures are for fiscal year ended May 31, 1995.

[7] Company formed by the combination of Lockheed (1994 rank: 261) and Martin Marietta (1994 rank: 391), March 15, 1995.

[8] Figures are for fiscal year ended August 31, 1995.

[9] Figures are for fiscal year ended Feb. 28, 1995.

10–19

[10] Figures do not include the acquisition of Chase Manhattan Corp. (1995 rank: 381), March 31, 1996.

[11] Figures are for fiscal year ended Nov. 30, 1995.

[12] Figures are for fiscal year ended March 31, 1995.

[13] Figures are for fiscal year ended Sept. 30, 1995.

[14] One of three companies resulting from the breakup of ITT (1994 rank: 102), Dec. 19, 1995.

[15] Acquired by Chemical Banking Corp. (1995 rank: 254), March 31, 1996.

[16] Fiscal year-end changed from Jan. 31 to Nov. 30, 1995. Figures are for ten months.

[17] Revenues from discontinued operations are not included.

[18] Name changed from SCEcorp, Jan. 26, 1996.

[19] Figures are for fiscal year ended April 30, 1995.

20–29

[20] Acquired Shawmut National Corp. (1994 rank: 479), Nov. 30, 1995.

[21] Figures are for fiscal year ended July 31, 1995.

[22] Cooperatives provide only net margin figures, which are not comparable with the profit figures on the list.

[23] Company formed by the merger of Pharmacia and Upjohn (1994 rank: 319), Nov. 2, 1995.

[24] Figures do not reflect acquistion of Connecticut Mutual Life Insurance (1995 rank: 567), March 1, 1996.

[25] Acquired Midlantic Corp. (1994 rank: 811), Dec. 31, 1995.

[26] One of three companies resulting from the breakup of ITT (1994 rank: 23), Dec. 19, 1995.

[27] Acquired Santa Fe Pacific (1994 rank: 386), Sept. 22, 1995.

[28] Figures are for four quarters ended Sept. 30, 1995.

[29] Acquired Clark Equipment (1994 rank: 880), May 31, 1995.

30–39

[30] Figures do not reflect acquisition of First Interstate Bancorp (1995 rank: 274), April 1, 1996.

[31] Name changed from Panhandle Eastern, Jan. 2, 1996.

[32] Acquired by Wells Fargo & Co. (1995 rank: 245), April 1, 1996.

[33] Name changed from AmeriSource Distribution, March 30, 1995.

[34] Acquired Conner Peripherals (1994 rank: 474), Feb. 2, 1996.

[35] Acquired Geico (1995 rank: 408), Jan. 2, 1996.

[36] Name changed from First Financial Management (1994 rank: 499). Acquired First Data (1994 rank: 609), Oct. 27, 1995.

[37] Name changed from LDDS Communications, May 25, 1995.

[38] Name changed from Detroit Edison, Jan. 1, 1996.

[39] American Premier Underwriters (1994 rank: 587) formed a holding company, April 3, 1995, and changed its name.

40–49

[40] Estimate.

[41] Acquired Future Now (1994 rank: 986), August 17, 1995.

[42] Figures are for four quarters ended Oct. 31, 1995.

[43] Acquired QVC (1994 rank: 687), Feb. 15, 1995.

[44] Name changed from National Medical Enterprises; acquired American Medical Holdings (1994 rank: 469), March 1, 1995.

[45] Limited partnership; profits after tax estimated at corporate rate.

[46] Figures do not reflect acquisition of CBI Industries (1995 rank: 607), March 13, 1996.

[47] Acquired by Berkshire Hathaway (1995 rank: 292), Jan. 2, 1996.

[48] Acquired Transco Energy (1994 rank: 401), May 1, 1995.

[49] Name changed from Manville, April 1, 1996.

50–53

[50] Name changed from Pennsylvania Power & Light (1994 rank: 417), April 27, 1995.

[51] Name changed from Provident Life & Accident Insurance, Dec. 27, 1995.

[52] Name changed from Roadway Services. Figures do not include Roadway Express (1995 rank: 521), spun off Jan. 2, 1996.

[53] Figure does not include discontinued operations of Roadway Express (1995 rank: 521).

THE 1996 FORTUNE 500 INDEX

A

ABBOTT LABORATORIES 128
ACE HARDWARE 498
ADVANCED MICRO DEVICES 500
AETNA LIFE & CASUALTY 91
AFLAC 182
AHMANSON (H.F.) 296
AID ASSOCIATION
    FOR LUTHERANS 453
AIR PRODUCTS & CHEM. 320
ALBERTSON'S 96
ALCOA 95
ALCO STANDARD 130
ALLEGHENY POWER SYSTEM 467
ALLIEDSIGNAL 73
ALLMERICA FINANCIAL 384
ALLSTATE 31
ALLTEL 396
ALUMAX 427
AMERADA HESS 173
AMERICAN BRANDS 221
AMERICAN
    ELECTRIC POWER 231
AMERICAN EXPRESS 53
AMERICAN
    FINANCIAL GROUP 345
AMERICAN GENERAL 202
AMERICAN
    HOME PRODUCTS 86
AMERICAN
    INTERNATIONAL GROUP 25
AMERICAN PRESIDENT 434
AMERICAN STANDARD 255
AMERICAN STORES 45
AMERISOURCE HEALTH 282
AMERITECH 84
AMOCO 23
AMP 254
AMR 54
ANHEUSER-BUSCH 97
AON 286
APPLE COMPUTER 114
APPLIED MATERIALS 405
ARAMARK 235
ARCHER DANIELS MIDLAND 92
ARMSTRONG
    WORLD INDUSTRIES 471

ARROW ELECTRONICS 220
ASARCO 389
ASHLAND 113
ASSOCIATED INSURANCE 217
AST RESEARCH 492
ATLANTIC RICHFIELD 55
AT&T 5
AUTOMATIC DATA PROC. 436
AVERY DENNISON 394
AVNET 299
AVON PRODUCTS 292

B

BAKER HUGHES 469
BALL 475
BALTIMORE
    GAS & ELECTRIC 424
BANC ONE CORP. 145
BANKAMERICA CORP. 37
BANKERS TRUST
    NEW YORK CORP. 152
BANK OF BOSTON CORP. 243
BANK OF NEW YORK CO. 247
BARNETT BANKS 339
BAXTER INTERNATIONAL 132
BEAR STEARNS 329
BECTON DICKINSON 461
BELL ATLANTIC 83
BELLSOUTH 49
BERGEN BRUNSWIG 153
BERKSHIRE HATHAWAY 293
BEST BUY 262
BETHLEHEM STEEL 272
BEVERLY ENTERPRISES 385
BINDLEY WESTERN 281
BLACK & DECKER 238
BOATMEN'S BANCSHARES 415
BOEING 40
BOISE CASCADE 265
BRISTOL-MYERS SQUIBB 79
BROWNING-FERRIS
    INDUSTRIES 229
BRUNO'S 440
BRUNSWICK 401
BURLINGTON
    NORTHERN SANTA FE 210

C

CALDOR 455
CALIBER SYSTEM 482
CAMPBELL SOUP 177
CARDINAL HEALTH 168
CAROLINA POWER & LIGHT 414
CASE 261
CATERPILLAR 64
CENTERIOR ENERGY 486
CENTEX 380
CENTRAL & SOUTH WEST 333
CHAMPION INTERNATIONAL 188
CHASE MANHATTAN CORP. 112
CHEMICAL BANKING CORP. 71
CHEVRON 18
CHIQUITA BRANDS
    INTERNATIONAL 313
CHRYSLER 9
CHUBB 215
CIGNA 42
CINERGY 411
CIRCLE K 349
CIRCUIT CITY STORES 237
CITICORP 19
CMS ENERGY 321
COASTAL 124
COCA-COLA 48
COCA-COLA ENTERPRISES 196
COLGATE-PALMOLIVE 158
COLLEGE RETIREMENT
    EQUITIES FUND 164
COLUMBIA GAS SYSTEM 470
COLUMBIA/HCA HEALTHCARE 51
COMCAST 369
COMERICA 395
COMPAQ COMPUTER 72
COMPUSA 451
COMPUTER ASSOCIATES
    INTERNATIONAL 474
COMPUTER SCIENCES 367
CONAGRA 26
CONRAIL 338
CONSECO 444
CONSOLIDATED EDISON
    OF NEW YORK 204
CONSOLIDATED
    FREIGHTWAYS 251

CONSOL. NATURAL GAS 376
CONTINENTAL AIRLINES 226
COOPER INDUSTRIES 271
CORESTATES FINAN. CORP. 441
CORNING 246
COTTER 497
CPC INTERNATIONAL 154
CROWN CORK & SEAL 266
CSX 120
CUMMINS ENGINE 253
CYPRUS AMAX MINERALS 387

D

DANA...169
DAYTON HUDSON 28
DEAN FOODS 472
DEAN WITTER DISCOVER 165
DEERE 123
DELL COMPUTER 250
DELTA AIR LINES 98
DIAL 347
DIAMOND SHAMROCK 418
DIGITAL EQUIPMENT 77
DILLARD DEPT. STORES 214
DISNEY (WALT) 102
DOLE FOOD 305
DOMINION RESOURCES 285
DONNELLEY (R.R.) & SONS 201
DOVER 331
DOW CHEMICAL 36
DRESSER INDUSTRIES 234
DTE ENERGY 344
DUKE POWER 280
DUN & BRADSTREET 242
DU PONT DE NEMOURS (E.I.) 13

E

EASTMAN CHEMICAL 267
EASTMAN KODAK 67
EATON 191
ECHLIN 459
ECKERD 268
EDISON INTERNATIONAL 155
EMERSON ELECTRIC 127
ENGELHARD 450
ENRON 141
ENTERGY 209
EXXON 3

F

FARMLAND INDUSTRIES 178

FEDERAL EXPRESS 138
FEDERAL HOME
  LOAN MORTGAGE 135
FEDERAL NATIONAL
  MORTGAGE ASSOCIATION 32
FEDERATED
  DEPARTMENT STORES 69
FHP INTERNATIONAL 319
FIRST BANK SYSTEM 371
FIRST CHICAGO NBD CORP. 117
FIRST DATA 312
FIRST INTERSTATE BANCORP ...274
FIRST UNION CORP. 118
FLAGSTAR 435
FLEET FINANCIAL GROUP 166
FLEETWOOD ENTERPRISES 448
FLEMING 52
FLORIDA PROGRESS 407
FLUOR 140
FMC 287
FOOD 4 LESS HOLDINGS 354
FORD MOTOR 2
FOSTER WHEELER 400
FOUNDATION HEALTH 494
FOXMEYER HEALTH 257
FPL GROUP 236

G

GANNETT 315
GAP 297
GATEWAY 2000 340
GEICO 408
GENERAL DYNAMICS 351
GENERAL ELECTRIC 7
GENERAL INSTRUMENT 499
GENERAL MILLS 156
GENERAL MOTORS 1
GENERAL PUBLIC UTILITIES 325
GENERAL RE 181
GENUINE PARTS 252
GEORGIA-PACIFIC 75
GIANT FOOD 336
GILLETTE 195
GOLDEN WEST
  FINANCIAL CORP. 491
GOODYEAR TIRE & RUBBER 88
GRACE (W.R.) 228
GRAINGER (W.W.) 381
GRAYBAR ELECTRIC 454
GREAT WESTERN
  FINANCIAL CORP. 350
GTE 38
GUARDIAN LIFE OF AMERICA 211

H

HALLIBURTON 218
HANNAFORD BROS. 477
HARCOURT GENERAL 383
HARRIS 357
HASBRO 446
HEALTH SYSTEMS
  INTERNATIONAL......................458
HEINZ (H.J.) 162
HERSHEY FOODS 337
HEWLETT-PACKARD 20
HOME DEPOT 66
HONEYWELL 197
HORMEL FOODS 409
HOUSEHOLD INTERNATIONAL ...260
HOUSTON INDUSTRIES 298
HUMANA 279

I

IBP...94
ILLINOIS TOOL WORKS 306
INGERSOLL-RAND 230
INLAND STEEL INDUSTRIES 275
INTEL 61
INTELLIGENT ELECTRONICS 358
INTERNATIONAL
  BUSINESS MACHINES 6
INTERNATIONAL PAPER 39
ITT 207
ITT HARTFORD GROUP 100
ITT INDUSTRIES 151

J

JAMES RIVER CORP.
  OF VIRGINA 194
JEFFERSON SMURFIT 311
JOHN HANCOCK
  MUTUAL LIFE 224
JOHNSON CONTROLS 160
JOHNSON & JOHNSON 43

K

KELLOGG 187
KELLY SERVICES 463
KERR-MCGEE 426
KEYCORP 216
KIEWIT (PETER) SONS' 431
KIMBERLY-CLARK 78
KMART 16
KNIGHT-RIDDER 456
KROGER 27

L

LAUDER (ESTÉE) 432
LEAR SEATING 278
LEHMAN BROTHERS HOLDINGS ..82
LIBERTY MUTUAL
    INSURANCE GROUP 139
LILLY (ELI) 171
LIMITED 167
LINCOLN NATIONAL 199
LITTON INDUSTRIES 372
LOCKHEED MARTIN 29
LOEWS 44
LONG ISLAND LIGHTING 402
LONGS DRUG STORES 468
LORAL 240
LOUISIANA-PACIFIC 449
LOWE'S 184
LTV 300
LYONDELL PETROCHEMICAL 270

M

MANPOWER 241
MAPCO 375
MARRIOTT INTERNATIONAL 147
MARSH & MCLENNAN 326
MASCO 276
MASS. MUTUAL
    LIFE INSURANCE 193
MATTEL 343
MAXXAM 480
MAY DEPARTMENT STORES 99
MAYTAG 410
MBNA 479
MCDONALD'S 131
MCDONNELL DOUGLAS 74
MCGRAW-HILL 423
MCI COMMUNICATIONS 68
MCKESSON 87
MEAD 256
MELLON BANK CORP. 291
MELVILLE 110
MERCANTILE STORES 421
MERCK 56
MERISEL 227
MERRILL LYNCH 33
METROPOLITAN
    LIFE INSURANCE 22
MEYER (FRED) 364
MICROAGE 422
MICRON TECHNOLOGY 419
MICROSOFT 219
MINNESOTA MINING &
    MANUFACTURING 63

MOBIL 8
MONSANTO 146
MORGAN (J.P.) & CO. 76
MORGAN STANLEY GROUP 116
MORRISON KNUDSEN 484
MORTON INTERNATIONAL 370
MOTOROLA 24
MUTUAL OF OMAHA
    INSURANCE 307

N

NASH FINCH 437
NATIONAL CITY CORP. 362
NATIONSBANK CORP. 60
NATIONWIDE
    INSURANCE ENTERPRISE 108
NAVISTAR INTERNATIONAL 208
NEWELL 488
NEW YORK LIFE INSURANCE 62
NGC 341
NIAGARA MOHAWK POWER 317
NIKE 277
NORAM ENERGY 443
NORDSTROM 310
NORFOLK SOUTHERN 283
NORTHEAST UTILITIES 330
NORTHERN STATES POWER 476
NORTHROP GRUMMAN 192
NORTHWEST AIRLINES 143
NORTHWESTERN
    MUTUAL LIFE 111
NORWEST CORP. 170
NUCOR 359
NYNEX 85

O

OCCIDENTAL PETROLEUM 121
OFFICE DEPOT 249
OFFICEMAX 483
OHIO EDISON 493
OLIN 392
OLSTEN 485
ORACLE 417
OWENS-CORNING 346
OWENS-ILLINOIS 327
OWENS & MINOR 416

P

PACCAR......................................273
PACIFICARE
    HEALTH SYSTEMS 334

PACIFIC GAS & ELECTRIC 133
PACIFIC MUTUAL
    LIFE INSURANCE 390
PACIFICORP 365
PACIFIC TELESIS GROUP 144
PAINE WEBBER GROUP 248
PANENERGY 269
PARKER HANNIFIN 386
PAYLESS CASHWAYS 464
PECO ENERGY 302
PENNEY (J.C.) 34
PENN TRAFFIC 352
PENNZOIL 489
PEPSICO 21
PFIZER 126
PHARMACIA & UPJOHN 183
PHELPS DODGE 303
PHILIP MORRIS 10
PHILLIPS PETROLEUM 81
PITNEY BOWES 324
PITTSTON 428
PNC BANK CORP. 205
PPG INDUSTRIES 185
PP&L RESOURCES 466
PRAXAIR 393
PREMARK INTERNATIONAL 348
PRICECOSTCO 46
PRINCIPAL MUTUAL LIFE 119
PROCTER & GAMBLE 17
PROGRESSIVE 413
PROVIDENT COS. 481
PROVIDIAN 366
PRUDENTIAL INSURANCE
    OF AMERICA 11
PUBLIC SERVICE
    ENTERPRISE GROUP 212
PUBLIX SUPER MARKETS 136

Q

QUAKER OATS 206
QUANTUM 368

R

RALSTON PURINA 180
RAYTHEON 107
READER'S DIGEST ASSN. 403
REEBOK INTERNATIONAL 356
RELIANCE GRP. HOLDINGS 430
REPUBLIC N.Y. CORP. 445
REVCO D.S. 295
REYNOLDS METALS 179
RITE AID 290

241

RJR NABISCO HOLDINGS 65
ROCKWELL INTERNATIONAL 90
ROHM & HAAS 322
ROUNDY'S 490
RYDER SYSTEM 258

S

SAFECO.................................335
SAFEWAY 59
SALOMON 149
SARA LEE 50
SBC COMMUNICATIONS 93
SCHERING-PLOUGH 259
SCHULLER 457
SCI SYSTEMS 465
SEAGATE TECHNOLOGY 288
SEARS ROEBUCK 15
SERVICEMASTER 388
SERVICE MERCHANDISE 314
SHAW INDUSTRIES 439
SHERWIN-WILLIAMS 382
SMITH'S FOOD & DRUG 399
SONOCO PRODUCTS 462
SOUTHERN 142
SOUTHERN PACIFIC RAIL 391
SOUTHWEST AIRLINES 438
SPARTAN STORES 487
SPRINT 80
ST. PAUL COS. 244
STANLEY WORKS 473
STAPLES 404
STATE FARM GROUP 12
STATE ST. BOSTON CORP. 495
STONE CONTAINER 175
STOP & SHOP 309
STRAUSS (LEVI) ASSOCIATES 198
STUDENT LOAN
    MARKETING ASSOCIATION 318
SUN 157
SUN MICROSYSTEMS 222
SUNTRUST BANKS 332
SUPERMARKETS
    GENERAL HOLDINGS 304
SUPERVALU 58
SYSCO 101

T

TANDY 225
TEACHERS
    INSURANCE & ANNUITY 109
TECH DATA 398
TELE-COMMUNICATIONS 190

TELEDYNE 478
TEMPLE-INLAND 360
TENET HEALTHCARE 373
TENNECO 150
TEXACO 14
TEXAS INSTRUMENTS 89
TEXAS UTILITIES 233
TEXTRON 129
THRIFTY PAYLESS HOLDINGS 284
TIMES MIRROR 355
TIME WARNER 163
TJX 294
TOSCO 176
TOYS "R" US 137
TRANS WORLD AIRLINES 374
TRANSAMERICA 213
TRAVELERS GROUP 57
TRIBUNE 442
TRW 125
TURNER BROADCASTING 363
TURNER CORP. 378
TYCO INTERNATIONAL...............289
TYSON FOODS 239

U

UAL 70
ULTRAMAR 460
UNICOM 189
UNION CAMP 301
UNION CARBIDE 223
UNION PACIFIC 148
UNISYS 203
UNITED HEALTHCARE 232
UNITED PARCEL SERVICE 35
UNITED TECHNOLOGIES 30
UNIVERSAL 379
UNOCAL 172
UNUM 308
U.S. BANCORP 433
USAA 200
USAIR GROUP 174
USF&G 361
USG 496
U.S. HEALTHCARE 353
U.S. INDUSTRIES 429
US WEST 106
USX 47
UTILICORP UNITED 452

V

VALERO ENERGY 412
VF 264

VIACOM 105
VONS 263

W

WABAN...................................316
WACHOVIA CORP. 328
WALGREEN 122
WAL-MART STORES 4
WARNER-LAMBERT 186
WELLPOINT
    HEALTH NETWORKS 397
WELLS FARGO & CO. 245
WESTINGHOUSE ELECTRIC 134
WESTVACO 377
WEYERHAEUSER 104
WHIRLPOOL 159
WHITMAN 420
WILLAMETTE INDUSTRIES 323
WILLIAMS 447
WINN-DIXIE STORES 103
WMX TECHNOLOGIES 115
WOOLWORTH 161
WORLDCOM 342

X

XEROX.......................................41

Y

YELLOW...................................406
YORK INTERNATIONAL 425

AMERICA'S MOST ADMIRED CORPORATIONS, 1996

T HE 417 CORPORATIONS included in the 14th annual Corporate Reputations survey are drawn from the new universe of companies that was created when the FORTUNE 500 industrial and service directories were merged last year. Seventy new names and five new industry groups make this the most comprehensive survey yet.

To determine the rankings, FORTUNE asked more than 11,000 executives, outside directors, and financial analysts to rate the ten largest companies by revenues (if there were that many—our minimum was five) in their industry by eight criteria: quality of management, quality of products or services, ability to attract, develop, and keep talented people, value as a long-term investment, use of corporate assets, financial soundness, innovativeness, and community and environmental responsibility. Companies were assigned to an industry group according to the business that contributed the most to their revenues.

BROKERAGE

Rank	LAST YEAR	Company	Score
1	3	Merrill Lynch	7.45
2	•	Charles Schwab	7.38
3	•	Bear Stearns	6.53
4	•	Lehman Brothers Holdings	5.17
5	•	Paine Webber Group	4.81
6	6	Salomon	4.34

COMMERCIAL BANKS

Rank	LAST YEAR	Company	Score
1	1	J.P. Morgan	7.65
2	•	Norwest	7.44
3	8	Citicorp	7.15
4	2	Banc One	7.09
5	4	NationsBank	6.96
6	6	BankAmerica	6.80
7	5	First Union	6.69
8	9	Chemical Banking	6.46
9	10	Chase Manhattan	5.96
10	3	Bankers Trust N.Y.	5.87

INSURANCE

Rank	LAST YEAR	Company	Score
1	1	American Intl. Group	7.15
2	•	State Farm Group	6.63
3	2	New York Life	6.37
4	4	Teachers Ins. & Annuity	6.33
5	7	Travelers Inc.	6.03
6	•	Nationwide Ins. Enterprise	5.81
7	7	Metropolitan Life	5.72
8	9	Cigna	5.35
9	10	Aetna Life & Casualty	5.17
10	9	Prudential Ins. of America	5.09

SAVINGS INSTITUTIONS

Rank	LAST YEAR	Company	Score
1	1	Golden West Financial	6.71
2	2	Washington Mutual Sav. Bank	6.54
3	5	Great Western Financial	5.95
4	3	H.F. Ahmanson	5.88
5	4	Standard Federal Bank	5.86
6	9	Glendale Federal Bank	4.77
7	10	California Federal Bank	4.45

DIVERSIFIED FINANCIAL

Rank	LAST YEAR	Company	Score
1	2	Berkshire Hathaway	7.97
2	4	Federal Natl. Mortgage Assn.	6.93
3	2	Morgan Stanley Group	6.71
4	5	Fed. Home Loan Mtg. Assn.	6.55
5	•	Household International	6.45
6	7	American Express	6.40
7	•	Dean Witter Discover	6.32
8	•	American General	6.13
9	•	Loews	6.00
10	•	ITT	5.71

AEROSPACE

Rank	LAST YEAR	Company	Score
1	1	Boeing	7.81
2	2	AlliedSignal	7.28
3	3	Martin Marietta	7.09
4	4	Lockheed	7.00
5	7	General Dynamics	6.54
6	5	United Technologies	6.52
7	8	McDonnell Douglas	6.37
8	6	Textron	6.24
9	9	Northrop Grumman	6.18
10	10	GenCorp	5.81

AIRLINES

Rank	LAST YEAR	Company	Score
1	1	Southwest Airlines	7.39
2	3	AMR	6.73
3	6	UAL	6.64
4	7	Northwest Airlines	6.24
5	5	Delta Air Lines	6.06
6	•	Alaska Air Group	5.90
7	•	America West Airlines	5.31
8	8	Continental Airlines	4.27
9	9	USAir Group	3.77
10	10	TWA	3.05

RAILROADS

Rank	LAST YEAR	Company	Score
1	2	Norfolk Southern	7.26
2	1	Union Pacific	7.10
3	3	CSX	6.86
4	4	Santa Fe Pacific	6.45
5	5	Conrail	6.23
6	8	Burlington Northern	6.18
7	7	Kansas City So. Industries	5.29
8	9	Chicago & NW Trans.	5.13
9	10	Southern Pacific Rail	4.57

PACKAGE & FREIGHT DELIVERY

Rank	LAST YEAR	Company	Score
1	1	United Parcel Service	7.71
2	2	Federal Express	7.02
3	•	Air Express International	5.92
4	•	Pittston	5.48
5	4	Airborne Freight	5.42

TRUCKING

Rank	LAST YEAR	Company	Score
1	3	Penske Truck Leasing	6.92
2	2	Roadway Services	6.59
3	4	Ryder System	6.51
4	6	Consolidated Freightways	6.46
5	•	Landstar System	6.03
6	5	J.B. Hunt Transport	5.95
7	8	TNT Freightways	5.86
8	7	Arkansas Best	5.45
9	9	Yellow	4.87
10	•	Amerco	4.29

INDUSTRIAL & FARM EQUIPMENT

Rank	LAST YEAR	Company	Score
1	1	Deere	7.23
2	2	Caterpillar	7.16
3	6	Dover	6.49
4	7	Black & Decker	6.44
5	4	Cummins Engine	6.41
6	3	Ingersoll-Rand	6.40
7	5	Parker Hannifin	6.25
8	7	Tenneco	6.16
9	4	American Standard	6.05
10	9	Dresser Industries	5.83

MOTOR VEHICLES & PARTS

Rank	LAST YEAR	Company	Score
1	1	Ford Motor	7.04
2	2	Chrysler	6.85
3	4	Dana	6.69
4	3	Eaton	6.65
5	3	Johnson Controls	6.62
6	•	Daimler-Benz	6.51
7	4	TRW	6.50
8	6	Paccar	6.28
9	8	General Motors	6.00
10	10	Navistar International	5.25

APPAREL

Rank	LAST YEAR	Company	Score
1	1	Levi Strauss Associates	7.99
2	3	VF	6.88
3	4	Russell	6.54
4	6	Liz Claiborne	6.53
5	5	Warnaco Group	6.46
6	7	Kellwood	5.27
7	7	Fruit of the Loom	5.24

WHOLESALERS

Rank	LAST YEAR	Company	Score
1	2	Sysco	7.34
2	•	Cardinal Health	7.20
3	3	McKesson	6.91
4	5	Genuine Parts	6.78
5	7	Alco Standard	6.67
6	4	Supervalu	6.54
7	6	Bergen Brunswig	6.16
8	8	Fleming	6.04
9	•	Merisel	5.37
10	9	FoxMeyer Health	5.23

FURNITURE

Rank	LAST YEAR	Company	Score
1	2	Leggett & Platt	7.10
2	1	Herman Miller	6.83
3	3	HON Industries	6.80
4	4	La-Z-Boy Chair	6.19
5	5	Kimball International	5.89
6	7	Interco	5.58

FOOD & DRUG STORES

Rank	LAST YEAR	Company	Score
1	1	Albertson's	7.77
2	2	Publix Super Markets	7.61
3	3	Walgreen	7.02
4	5	Safeway	6.88
5	6	Winn-Dixie Stores	6.64
6	4	Kroger	6.63
7	7	American Stores	6.04
8	8	Food Lion	5.32
9	9	Southland	4.66
10	10	A&P	4.25

SPECIALIST RETAILERS

Rank	LAST YEAR	Company	Score
1	1	Home Depot	7.91
2	•	Office Depot	6.81
3	•	Circuit City Stores	6.75
4	2	Toys "R" Us	6.64
5	3	Lowe's	6.56
6	5	Tandy	6.19
7	4	Limited	6.09
8	6	PriceCostco	5.79
9	8	Melville	5.08
10	10	Woolworth	4.40

GENERAL MERCHANDISE

Rank	LAST YEAR	Company	Score
1	1	Wal-Mart Stores	7.25
2	2	Nordstrom	7.10
3	3	J.C. Penney	6.81
4	5	May Department Stores	6.69
5	4	Dayton Hudson	6.46
6	7	Sears Roebuck	6.33
7	8	Federated Department Stores	6.11
8	•	Harcourt General	6.09
9	6	Dillard Department Stores	6.05
10	10	Kmart	3.36

FOOD SERVICES

Rank	LAST YEAR	Company	Score
1	•	McDonald's	8.05
2	2	PepsiCo	7.74
3	•	Wendy's International	7.06
4	•	Brinker International	6.71
5	•	Aramark	5.97
6	•	Morrison Restaurants	5.89
7	•	Shoney's	5.05
8	•	Flagstar	4.62
9	•	Family Restaurants	4.57
10	•	Foodmaker	4.52

HEALTH CARE

Rank	LAST YEAR	Company	Score
1	1	United HealthCare	7.65
2	3	Columbia/HCA Healthcare	7.37
3	10	Tenet HealthCare**	7.07
4	2	U.S. Healthcare	6.88
5	5	Humana	6.19
6	7	HealthTrust	5.96
7	6	FHP International	5.51
8	4	PacifiCare Health Systems	5.30
9	•	Caremark International	5.11
10	9	Beverly Enterprises	4.66

SOAPS, COSMETICS

Rank	LAST YEAR	Company	Score
1	1	Procter & Gamble	8.55
2	2	Intl. Flavors & Fragrances	7.64
3	4	Clorox	7.19
4	3	Colgate-Palmolive	6.94
5	5	Avon Products	6.59
6	•	Dial	5.89
7	8	Safety-Kleen	5.67
8	10	Alberto-Culver	5.64
9	6	Helene Curtis Industries	5.56

FOOD

Rank	LAST YEAR	Company	Score
1	1	General Mills	7.15
1	2	Sara Lee	7.15
3	3	ConAgra	6.87
4	4	CPC International	6.80
4	5	H.J. Heinz	6.80
6	•	Unilever U.S.	6.55
7	7	Philip Morris	6.53
8	8	Ralston Purina	6.07
9	9	IBP	6.06
10	6	Archer Daniels Midland	5.25

BEVERAGES

Rank	LAST YEAR	Company	Score
1	1	Coca-Cola	8.70
2	3	Anheuser-Busch	7.02
3	6	Coca-Cola Enterprises	6.87
4	4	Adolph Coors	6.01
5	8	Brown-Forman	5.51
6	7	J.E. Seagram	5.40
7	10	Whitman	5.07

TOBACCO

Rank	LAST YEAR	Company	Score
1	2	American Brands	6.65
2	1	UST	6.11
3	3	Universal	5.47
4	5	RJR Nabisco Holdings	5.45
5	4	Dibrell Brothers	5.21
6	6	Standard Commercial	4.44

ELECTRIC & GAS UTILITIES

Rank	LAST YEAR	Company	Score
1	1	Southern	7.08
2	•	FPL Group	6.95
3	2	Pacific Gas & Electric	6.54
4	4	American Electric Power	6.30
5	7	SCEcorp	6.12
6	8	Texas Utilities	6.09
7	3	Entergy	5.89
8	6	Public Svc. Enterprise Group	5.84
9	9	Consolidated Edison of N.Y.	5.53
10	10	Unicom	5.33

PIPELINES

Rank	LAST YEAR	Company	Score
1	1	Enron	7.78
2	2	Williams	7.06
3	3	Panhandle Eastern	6.80
4	•	Sonat	6.60
5	6	Tejas Gas	6.51
6	•	Equitable Resources	6.26
7	9	Enserch	5.65
8	10	Transco Energy	5.04
9	•	NorAm Energy	4.97

MINING, CRUDE OIL

Rank	LAST YEAR	Company	Score
1	1	Burlington Resources	6.39
1	5	Hanson Industries N.A.	6.39
3	3	Freeport-McMoRan	6.37
4	•	Cyprus Amax Minerals	6.12
5	6	Vulcan Materials	6.05
6	2	Mitchell Energy & Devel.	6.04
7	•	Zeigler Coal Holding	5.97
8	4	Louisiana Land & Exploration	5.79
9	8	Asarco	5.46
10	9	Oryx Energy	5.23

PETROLEUM REFINING

Rank	LAST YEAR	Company	Score
1	1	Shell Oil	7.46
2	4	Exxon	7.36
3	3	Mobil	7.28
4	2	Amoco	7.12
5	5	Chevron	6.77
6	6	Texaco	6.43
7	7	Arco	6.38
8	8	Phillips Petroleum	6.34
9	9	USX	5.46
10	10	Coastal	4.95

ENGINEERING, CONSTRUCTION

Rank	LAST YEAR	Company	Score
1	1	Fluor	7.18
2	2	Centex	6.83
3	3	Foster Wheeler	6.64
4	5	Pulte	6.49
5	6	Halliburton	6.19
6	•	Peter Kiewit Sons'	6.14
7	7	Turner Corp.	5.75
8	•	Emcor Group	5.47
9	•	Ryland Group	5.42
10	8	Morrison Knudsen	3.12

BUILDING MATERIALS, GLASS

Rank	LAST YEAR	Company	Score
1	1	Corning	7.68
2	2	Armstrong World Industries	7.05
3	3	Owens-Corning Fiberglas	6.53
4	6	Owens-Illinois	6.10
5	8	USG	5.95

METALS

Rank	LAST YEAR	Company	Score
1	2	Alcoa	7.28
2	1	Nucor	7.18
3	3	Phelps Dodge	6.91
4	4	Reynolds Metals	6.71
5	5	Alumax	6.24
6	6	Inland Steel Industries	5.39
7	8	LTV	5.30
8	9	Maxxam	5.11
9	10	National Steel	5.02
10	7	Bethlehem Steel	4.83

METAL PRODUCTS

Rank	LAST YEAR	Company	Score
1	1	Gillette	8.00
2	2	Illinois Tool Works	7.36
3	4	Newell	6.59
4	7	Crown Cork & Seal	6.46
5	3	Stanley Works	6.43
6	•	Hillenbrand Industries	6.33
7	5	Tyco International	6.25
8	6	Masco	6.07
9	9	Ball	6.02
10	9	MascoTech	5.87

PHARMACEUTICALS

Rank	LAST YEAR	Company	Score
1	1	Johnson & Johnson	8.32
2	3	Merck	8.26
3	2	Pfizer	8.06
4	4	Abbott Laboratories	7.22
5	6	Eli Lilly	7.11
6	5	Schering-Plough	7.08
7	7	Bristol-Myers Squibb	6.64
8	8	American Home Products	6.61
9	•	Rhône-Poulenc Rorer	5.98
10	9	Warner-Lambert	5.88

TEXTILES

Rank	LAST YEAR	Company	Score
1	2	Unifi	7.00
2	1	Shaw Industries	6.93
3	3	Springs Industries	6.90
4	5	WestPoint Stevens	6.26
5	6	Burlington Industries	5.98
6	7	Fieldcrest Cannon	5.86
7	8	Collins & Aikman	5.75
8	•	Mohawk Industries	5.66
9	9	Triarc	5.12
10	10	JPS Textile Group	4.50

RUBBER & PLASTIC PRODUCTS

Rank	LAST YEAR	Company	Score
1	1	Rubbermaid	8.35
2	2	Goodyear Tire & Rubber	7.51
3	3	M.A. Hanna	6.98
4	6	Premark International	6.71
5	4	Cooper Tire & Rubber	6.69
6	8	Mark IV Industries	6.16
7	7	Standard Products	6.06
8	•	Bridgestone/Firestone	6.03
9	•	Raychem	5.88
10	10	Foamex	5.06

CHEMICALS

Rank	LAST YEAR	Company	Score
1	1	Du Pont	7.71
2	2	Dow Chemical	7.19
3	3	Monsanto	6.83
4	4	PPG Industries	6.76
5	6	Bayer	6.60
6	8	Union Carbide	6.39
7	5	Hoechst Celanese	6.35
8	6	BASF	6.32
9	9	Occidental Petroleum	5.51
10	10	W.R. Grace	4.98

FOREST & PAPER PRODUCTS

Rank	LAST YEAR	Company	Score
1	1	Kimberly-Clark	7.40
2	2	International Paper	6.94
3	3	Weyerhaeuser	6.69
4	4	Mead	6.55
5	5	Georgia-Pacific	6.50
6	7	Champion International	5.71
7	6	Scott Paper	5.39
8	10	Boise Cascade	5.04
9	9	Stone Container	4.84
10	8	James River Corp. of Va.	4.80

ADVERTISING, MARKETING

Rank	LAST YEAR	Company	Score
1	•	CUC International	7.21
2	•	Interpublic Group	6.76
3	•	Omnicom Group	6.57
4	•	ADVO	6.26
5	•	QVC	6.10

ENTERTAINMENT

Rank	LAST YEAR	Company	Score
1	1	Walt Disney	8.05
2	2	Capital Cities/ABC	7.43
3	3	Viacom	7.16
4	5	Turner Broadcasting System	7.11
5	4	Time Warner	6.18
6	6	CBS*	4.58

HOTELS, CASINOS, RESORTS

Rank	LAST YEAR	Company	Score
1	•	Mirage Resorts	8.23
2	•	Promus	7.91
3	•	Marriott International	7.79
4	•	Host Marriott	7.17
5	•	Circus Circus Enterprises	6.86
6	•	MGM Grand	6.24
7	•	Caesars World	6.10
8	•	Hilton Hotels	6.06
9	•	Gillett Holdings	5.59
10	•	Bally Entertainment	5.28

PUBLISHING, PRINTING

Rank	LAST YEAR	Company	Score
1	1	Dow Jones	7.19
2	5	R.R. Donnelley & Sons	7.10
3	4	Tribune	7.08
4	1	Reader's Digest Association	6.98
5	3	Gannett	6.95
6	6	Knight-Ridder	6.67
7	8	New York Times	6.45
8	7	American Greetings	6.25
9	9	McGraw-Hill	6.23
10	10	Times Mirror	5.67

COMPUTER & DATA SERVICES

Rank	LAST YEAR	Company	Score
1	1	Microsoft	8.23
2	2	Oracle Systems	7.15
3	4	Automatic Data Processing	6.68
4	8	Computer Associates Intl.	6.59
5	6	First Data	6.53
6	7	Computer Sciences	6.18
6	5	First Financial Management‡	6.18
8	•	Novell	6.02
9	10	Comdisco	5.63
10	9	Dun & Bradstreet	5.44

COMPUTERS, OFFICE EQUIPMENT

Rank	LAST YEAR	Company	Score
1	1	Hewlett-Packard	8.19
2	2	Compaq Computer	7.04
3	3	Sun Microsystems	6.99
4	5	Intl. Business Machines	6.58
5	•	Dell Computer	6.30
6	7	Seagate Technology	6.22
7	6	Pitney Bowes	5.86
8	4	Apple Computer	5.85
9	10	Digital Equipment	5.61
10	9	Unisys	4.77

ELECTRONICS, ELECTRICAL EQUIPMENT

Rank	LAST YEAR	Company	Score
1	2	Intel	8.30
2	1	Motorola	8.19
3	3	General Electric	7.63
4	4	Emerson Electric	7.22
5	5	Texas Instruments	7.03
6	•	Siemens	6.36
7	8	Rockwell International	6.32
8	7	Raytheon	6.31
9	6	Whirlpool	6.28
10	10	Westinghouse Electric	4.77

TELECOMMUNICATIONS

Rank	LAST YEAR	Company	Score
1	2	SBC Communications	7.36
2	1	AT&T	7.35
3	4	BellSouth	6.88
4	6	Ameritech	6.68
5	5	Bell Atlantic	6.52
6	3	MCI Communications	6.27
7	9	GTE	6.12
8	8	Sprint	6.02
9	•	US West	5.98
10	10	Nynex	5.62

SCIENTIFIC, PHOTOGRAPHIC & CONTROL EQUIPMENT

Rank	LAST YEAR	Company	Score
1	1	Minnesota Mining & Mfg.	8.08
2	2	Xerox	7.12
3	6	Honeywell	6.67
4	•	Thermo Electron	6.64
5	7	Eastman Kodak	6.59
6	5	Becton Dickinson	6.19
7	10	EG&G	6.08
8	8	Baxter International	5.94
9	9	Polaroid	5.93
10	3	Bausch & Lomb	5.92